Societal Spectra

by

Virendra K. Goswami

Former Vice Chancellor: Sangam University & Sunrise University,
Founder President: 'Environment & Peace Foundation'
F-82, Sector-41, Noida – 201 303

2019

Studium Press (India) Pvt. Ltd.

Societal Spectra

ISBN: 978-93-85046-30-8

Published by:

Studium Press (India) Pvt. Ltd.
4735/22, 2nd Floor, Prakash Deep Building
(Near Delhi Medical Association),
Ansari Road, Darya Ganj, New Delhi-110 002
Tel.: + 91-11-43240200-15 (15 lines); Fax: 91-11-43240215
E-mail: pubdir@studiumpress.in

Printed in India

About the Author

Dr. V. K. Goswami, Ph.D. Indian Institute of Technology (IIT), Kharagpur, MS from the University of Wisconsin, USA. Post Doctorate Fellow (PDF) at the University of Illinois, Chicago, USA. 'Visiting Scientist' to United Nations Industrial Development Organization (UNIDO), ICTP, Italy. Expert Panelist International Civil Aviation Organization (ICAO), Canada and United Nations as well Wing Commander in the Indian Air Force (IAF).

Dr. Virendra Goswami worked at Space Science Engineering Centre, NASA NOAA (National Oceanic Atmospheric Administration) at University of Wisconsin, USA.

Founder Vice Chancellor: Sangam University & Vice Chancellor: Sunrise University. Had been, Director General of Management Institutes. & Director of Engineering Institutes as well as Vice-President Havells India Ltd. Founder President 'Environment & Peace Foundation (EPF)'. Prof. Emeritus & got awarded for Human Value Education at RVIT by His Excellency Ram Nayak, Governor, U.P on 05 Jun'17. Ph.D & M. Tech Examiner at Centre of Energy Studies at IIT Delhi. Expert panelist of Association of Indian Universities (AIU), a National level Accreditation body. Associated with SAARC Disaster Management Center (SDMC), Govt. of India .

Presented Papers in the field of Chemical Technology, Atmospheric Sciences, Space Sciences, Satellite Application, Control of Global Warming & Quality Higher Education at International and National Conferences held in India, USA, UK Latin America, South Africa, Canada and Europe (more than 31 countries of all the Continents). More than 44 years of teaching, research and administrative experience at Home and Abroad.

Special Invitee by the World Meteorological Organization (WMO) of United Nations, Geneva in 2001. Special Invitee in 'Next Practices Workshop (NPW)': Conducting Field Operations in a Changing World, April 21-23, 2015, New Orleans, Louisiana, USA under the aegis of National Center of Atmospheric Research (NCAR). Invited Speaker to the Coupled Data Assimilation Workshop, sponsored by Météo-France, the World Meteorological Organization, the European Union, MAPP Program and US CLIVAR, Toulouse, France October 2016, IV Family Child

Conference, Nigeria in Nov'16, 6th ICHVHE, IIT Kanpur, Feb'17 & by Angila Ruskin Univ. Cambridge in Apr'17. Lately, Invited Speaker at Lomonosov Moscow State University, Sep'17 & Univ. Of California, Berkley in Apr'18.

Honorary Director Of Asian Film & Television (AAFT): International Film Television Research Center (IFRTC) & International Chamber of Media & Entertainment Industry (ICMEI). Member: AGU (American Geophysical Union), AMS & IMS (American & Indian Meteorological Societies). Editor in Chief: Journal of Advanced Research in Alternative Energy, Environment and Ecology. Reviewer: US-Journal of Shipping and Ocean Engineering & Int. Natl. Journal of Climate Change: Impact & Responses. Member Editor: J. Mechanical Engg. & Automation (JMEA). An Advocate: Supreme Court of India amalgamated with more than 17 years legal experience in Civil & Military Courts (IAF).

Chaired Sessions in Int. Natl. Conf. Metering, Brazil-2003, Invitee in Emergency Higher Education Conf. 2005, FEMA, Emmitsburg, MD, USA.. Besides, headed various delegations at National & International Levels & Chaired session SSC-2006 (Int. Natl. Conf. on Solid State Chemistry), Pardubice, Czech Republic. Had been to Univ. of Limerick, Ireland in 2008. Presented Research Paper on Control of Global Warming at ESF Conference, 6-11 Jun'09, Innsbruck, Austria & France 2010. I was invited by Cambridge University, UK to present research paper on Control of Global Warming during 13-17 Dec'10. Also, invited in the Int. Natl. Conf. on Higher Education; held at Johannesburg (South Africa, during 3-4 May'13 .

I was Guest Speaker at ASSOCHAM-BIOTECHNOLOGY-13; held on 30 jul'13 in New Delhi. Chaired Sessions at'AISSQ-14 Science & Spirituality at IITBHU, Panelist at 3rd ICHVHE-14 at PTU Jalandhar , Transforming India Conclave (TIC-14), Key Note Speaker at CEED: ECONS-2014 & Natl. Conf. on Innovation, Barha Univ. Shimla on 30 May'14 & an Invitee in Cambridge English Summit-1 on 18 Sep'14.

Also, Special Guest Speaker at SAARC: INDIA Water Week, New Delhi on 16 Jan'2015 GWP-South Asia, Special Invitee at QS in conversation - India 02-04 Feb'15 & 08 Jul'15. State Guest Speaker in the International Seminar on 'Value Based Life' April 17-19, 2015, Bhopal, Government of M.P. India. Also, Chaired a Session in the 4th National Conf. on Climate Change held in New Delhi, on 18 Jun'15 & Solar Energy, 2017 & 2018, under the aegis of ASSOCHAM & Dept. of Science & Technology (DST), Govt. of India. Invited Speaker at'AISSQ-15 Science & Spirituality at IIT Kharagpur 01Nov'15.

Guest at Global Freedom Network (Australia)'s Conference: 'Joint Declaration Against Modern Slavery' held on 03 Dec'15 at India Habitat Center, New Delhi. & Special invitee at Observer Research Foundation (ORF) Kalpana Chawla Annual Space Dialogue, US-India Business Council (USIBC) 24-26 Feb'16 at India Habitat Center, New Delhi, India as well as 'Educon-Sakal', New Delhi on 10 Mar'2016. Invited as State Guest Speaker in the International Seminar on 'Simhastha' May 12-14, 2016, Ujjain, Government of M.P. India.

Preface

The book entitled 'Societal Spectra' is nothing but, a kind of 'Spectra' i.e range of opinions, values, situations, extremes of a group of people who live together in a particular social system i.e Society .

From the day one the mankind was persistently hunting towards inventions, innovations and improvements through its creativity, positive thinking, 'CAN make' attitude, aspirations, clarity, unconditional love, zeal, persistent hard work with firm determination to achieve only one thing *i.e* comforts and peace for all the humanity.

The achievements achieved through its traits were also sustained with the sincerity, truthfulness and honesty. They were methodological, systematic, logical, practical with passion to answer these 3 questions i.e. What is this? Why is it? and How is it?. The answers of these three questions as regards the necessities of the people not only created the Scientific attitude in the people in general but, created a Societal Spectra alike Solar Spectra having Visible, Infrared and Ultraviolet regions. The Society with a panorama of Scientists, Innovators, Researchers, Professionals and all human being; kept on enhancing the chain of this Spectra with the different spokes of different fields devised out of the single human mind and soul blessed by Great Almighty; only to mankind.

The present' Societal Spectra' is a flowery panorama of different colors of the Society picked up from the different gardens by the different Gardeners of different geographical regions exhibiting the beautiful innovative flowers of Science - Spirituality-Peace, Defense ,Space crafts, Railway, Agriculture, Metaphysics, Physical needs of men in the Visible Region (VR); expanding to BOKOHARAM, Religious Intellectuals into the Infra Red IR) & "Fallen Woman", Languages, Fight are covering the Ultra Violet (UV) region of the envisaged 'Societal Spectra' of our colorful Society.

The Gateway to the Garden of 'Societal Spectra' is the "Synchronization of Science, Spirituality and Peace" exploring the Synergy between Science ,Spirituality & Peace (Tranquility) and developing the two models viz. 'VG: Hub & Spoke Model' & the other 'VG: Life (L) Circle Model' as an humble endeavor of Dr. Virendra Goswami Also, based on Spirituality (Science of Soul) & the axiom i.e. "Peace is inversely proportional to Entropy i.e. Disorderliness", Peace Equation has been developed explaining that how the spirituality leads to Peace.

The modern era is inflicted with a 'Terrorism" virus and the defence personnel and Defence installations are most vulnerable. Its an imperative to defend the hacking of Computerized data related to the national internal and external security for the peace loving society. Dr Minish Bhatia paints the idea of analyzation of people and their social activities over suspicion scale by computing Susceptibility Index (SI) and developing a tow level decision model, designed for identification of possible terrorists by incorporating various data analytics techniques through "Smart Defence Solution for Defence Personnel"

After the defence of strategic Defense Data; the exploration of Space has been revealed by our Overseas friend Dr. LemiTürker in form of short review of electric propulsion (EP) technologies for satellites and spacecraft with brief past history and novel developments in main types of electric thrusters in the article entitled as "Electric Propulsion for Spacecrafts"

Railways are the dominant source of transportation for the modern Society. Although, German, French, AREMA methods-includes various methods for a realistic estimation of loads on track superstructure and the reactions/actions on the sleepers, through semi-analytic mathematical formulas but, it does not justify the systematic appearance of cracks at 60% of the concrete sleepers/ ties in the Railway network. Dr. Konstantinos Giannakos describes a sensitivity analysis for the influence of the stiffness (mainly fastening stiffness) on the estimation on Acting and Design Loads on Railway Infrastructure &Measurements on Ballasted and Slab Track in the fourth panorama of the 'Societal Spectra'.

Society is admixture of the poor and the rich. The country like India which is a second populous country of the World and most of the Indian live in rural belt and are dependent on agriculture and Dairy Entrepreneurship for their livelihood. This has been well represented by Dr. Majumdar through the case study of 24 Parganas District of West Bengal, India.

The sixth colour ofthe 'Societal Spectra' gets coloured with "Substance in Plato's Metaphysics" by Dr. Felix AgboOkwa by discussing Plato's theory of forms/ideas. Plato bifurcated the world into two- universals and Particulars. He accepts the reality of permanence which he asserts are substances/ideas that exists in the world of forms; they are immutable and eternal. At the same time, he asserts that particulars do exist in the world of appearance; they are mutable, susceptible to change and a pure imitation of the substances in the world of ideas.

Dr. Ismael TabuñarFortunadopicks up the red flower of the 'Societal Spectra' to take an Overview to the Physical Needs of Man, the Universe and Its Twelve Categories based on the theories postulated by Abraham Maslow& Peter Holy.

Dr. Okafor Samuel, O. steps out the visible region of the 'Societal Spectra'and narrates the social aspect of the society by unraveling of the susceptibility of religion to individual and group ideology (using Boko Haram as a case study) and the unseen roles of this to underdevelopment and neocolonialism.

BokoHaram (Jama'atu Ahles-Sunnah Lidda' AwatiWal Jihad) is one of the many sub groups who have appeared under the umbrella of religion to pursue unjust cause and perpetuate mayhem against the modern society thereby creating an orbit for the setting in of underdevelopment and cultural cum political imperialism in Nigeria.

Again ,in the invisible Ultraviolet Region of the 'Societal Spectra' reveals the approach of Religious Intellectuals Regarding to Religion Function before an after Islamic Revolution in Iran by Dr.Hamid Sarmadi in term of revival, reform, pluralism, hermeneutic and western received concepts that Iranian intellectuals sue adaptation with doctrines of traditional religion.

DrMajid Salem Mgamis enters into InfraRed region of the 'Societal Spectra' and investigates the image of the fallen woman in Victorian literature; with an aims to prove that the fallen women, though socially repulsed, proved to be a woman who strongly seeks the freedom out of the shackles of a patriarchal society, by highlighting her struggle.

In the same region of the 'Societal Spectra' the eleventh Gardener Dr. Felix AgboOkwa picks up the flower from the 'Societal Garden' acronym Carnap's pragmatic verification principle that for any statement to be meaningful, it must either be analytic or synthetic. Propositions outside the analytic/synthetic framework are considered pseudo-statements. Such as the statements and propositions found in Metaphysics.

The exit gate of the 'Societal Spectra' remains open with flagrance and discusses "The Fight" to overcome failure and fear by the group of Social Scientists named Ousman,PaModu,Cansu and Momodou. They have propounded that fights in life are enormous and infinite & we strive to be the best we can and wanting to see the best others can see in us.

"There is no point in failing instead the conflict of interest that we occasionally try to escape. The survival of the fittest is real and we should be ready to face it. There is no accuracy without trying and the failing should be challenges since the downfall of a man is not the end of the life. We are stronger than before if we allow experience to lead our ways. Failing once; earn hints for the preceding battle. Sometimes the success is delayed and only through the comeback that we can realize that it was the through time, effort, hardworking and dedication that shall swim us to the sea of victory.

Dear Erudite Readers I'm sure that you must have enjoyed the viewing this beautiful spectra of yours own life in shape of the 'Societal Spectra'; covering the few aspects of your life and would definitely help you to pick up the few beautiful flowers from the garden of Life with the below caption of Life *i.e.*

> "Life thy name is Struggle
>
> Struggle thy name is Life
>
> And where it ends,
>
> There strikes the arrow of Death."

Dr. V. K. Goswami
13 Aug'18
Editor

Table of Contents

1

Synchronization of Science, Sprituality and Peace

VIRENDRA GOSWAMI[1]*

ABSTRACT

Efforts have been made to synchronize Science, Spirituality and Peace with an aim to correlate all the three in order to find out the ways and means to establish Peace. Though all these three are different in characteristics but, are same in so many ways and are important for humanity. Science is logical, analytical, systematic knowledge of global phenomena backed with experimental proof. Spirituality is Science of Soul. Its intrinsic and transcendental of the five senses. PEACE is paramount for the prosperity of People and Planet. "Peace would prevail with every body's be well being, everywhere Happiness, Harmony in everybody and no misery be ever." Based on Spirituality and the axiom i.e. "Peace is inversely proportional to Entropy i.e. Disorderliness", Peace Equation has been developed explaining that how the spirituality leads to Peace. Next, the correlation of Peace and Success, Scientist and Spiritualists have been discussed with the theme that Spirituality and Science are two opposite sides of the same coin. The alum of Science and Spirituality together mint a coin of Peace. Lastly, based

[1] Former Vice Chancellor and Founder President: 'Environment and Peace Foundation'

**Corresponding E-mail*: vk_goswami1@rediffmail.com

on the above correlations and Synergy between Science, Spirituality and Peace (Tranquility), the two models viz. 'VG: Hub and Spoke Model' and the other 'VG: Life (L) Circle Model' have been developed.

Key words: *'VG: Hub and Spoke Model', 'VG: Life(L) Circle Model', VG: Peace Equation, Synchronization, Science, Spirituality, Entropy, Success, Transcendental, Secular, Soul, Synergy, Religion, Conscious, Meditation.*

1. INTRODUCTION

"I believe that a simple and unassuming manner of life is best for every one, best both for the body and for the mind."

— Albert Einstein Nobel Laureate in Physics.

"To know about Life. Matter and Their interaction is called Knowledge"

@Science is commonly defined as the systemic Knowledge. It can be elaborated as logical, analytical, systematic knowledge of global phenomena backed with experimental proof. Science is search of proven truth. Science is a beautiful garland of experimentally proven facts and phenomena perceivable through the five senses gifted by the great Almighty to His finest creation human beings along with the platform of beautiful nature amalgamated with peaceful environment. Science does not believe in absence of proof. Science does dream innovation inform of hypothesis, proves it theoretically first, followed by experimentation and resulting scientific laws. When the scientific dreams are out of creativity, then there is a birth of inventions. Scientific inventions are original in nature and further adorned with improvements and innovations. When these three Is (Improvement, Innovation and invention) are made use by the God's creation (humans and non-humans), its termed as applied sciences or engineering dealing with materials and hence, materialistic in nature, implicitly extrinsic amalgamated with objectivity and subjectivity. I think that: Science is an axiomatic presentation of Matter/Materialistic, Physical-Chemical-Biological Knowledge on Earthly life and beyond scientific laws.

@**Spirituality** has been nicely defined by Swami Vivekananda as "***Science of Conscious***". In other words the spirituality is Science of Soul *i.e.* Search for the eternal Truth. Hence, its intrinsic and transcendental of the five senses. If that is so, then this can only be realized, believed and may not be proved. Although, spirituality is a systematic, logical knowledge of Conscious/soul, so its subjective in nature and differs from individual to individual but, its an eternal, immortal, indestructible by any kind of weapons, fire, omnipresent and omniscience gift of God given to His creations.

> *"Nainam Chhindanti Shatrani, Nainam Dahti Pawka,*
> *Na Chainum klandeyetu, na shoshyati Maruta"*

—The GEETA (Chap. 1.23)

> *i.e.* the Self (Soul/Conscious) can not be wounded by weapons, burned by fire, moistened by water, or blown by wind."

—The GEETA (Chap. 1.23)

@ Spirituality is an axiomatic presentation of Vedic Knowledge on life.

Further, Science and Spirituality/religion are binding forces of humanity in the search for the ultimate meaning of life and the universe. Can we synchronize these two forces and if so then can be these tools to establish peace. These are the few questions are to be answered for the peaceful co-existence of humanity.

2. TO CONCEPTUALIZE SPIRITUALITY

In my view the practicing of spirituality leads to a religious soul. 20th century author Henry Nouwen asked three Basic Questions

... Who Am I ?

... How Do I Make a Difference ?

... Is there something More ?

These questions are applicable to everybody of us, so are the movements that help us to answer these questions. Still, each one of us shall have answers based on our conscious and our cultural, religious and philosophical background.

@ ln my view. SPIRITULITY is an orientation of ACTION. THOUGHT and MIND (ATM) as per VEDAS *i.e.* Word of GOD and Songs of Divine: The GEETA

The VEDAS belong to Humanity and do not propagate any Faith (Religion) in particular, except narrate the way of righteous living.

As the VEDAS first evolved from trans-Indus River (Sindhu) region; known as INDIA hence gets correlated with 'Hinduism' which is not a faith in particular but, the well illustrated 'Way of Life' for all the children of God living in one Global Family of the Great Almighty.

In other words, Spirituality is GOD's ATM which blesses only when one inserts the card of KARMA (Righteous Action).

 # HENCE, Do Your DUTY (ACTION) honestly, sincerely. Smilingly with priority as it leads to Spirituality and Mental Peace.

"niytam kuru krma twam karma Jayayo hyakarmanah Srirtryapi ca te Na prasidheykarmana"

"Its better to do your Duty than to remain without doing anything. Action is important because we cannot even maintain our own body without it."

—The GEETA (Chap. 3.8)

@. How SPIRITUALITY Leads to Mental Peace

Help the distress, down trodden

—Mother Teresa.

"Na Tavahm Kamay Rajyam na swargamna apunbhr-vam, kamay dukhtaptanam praninamartinashnam"

—Pt. Madan Mohan Malviya

i.e. "I do n't desire kingdom, neither heaven nor supreme attire (*Moksha*). I only wish that may I be helpful to the distress in getting rid of misery."

—Pt. Madan Mohan Malviya

 # Be Fearless, Stress free and free of worries.

There is an old couplet of village folks

"Chinta chita se badkar haijo ghun saman lug jaati hai. Murde ko chita jalati hai aur jinda ko chinta khati hai."

i.e. "Stress and Worries are worst than pyre as pyre burns the Dead-body, while the worries eats up the living ones disturbing the Peace."

 # *Know Self*

 # *Win over three A's: and SENSES.*

—ANXIETY

—*ANGER*

—ANGER

If, one does not control these three A's then it leads to Loss of Wisdom leading to loss of Peace of mind.

"Dhyayto visyanpumsa, Sangetesupjayte, Sangat sanjay tekamah, Kamakrodho bhijayte"

—The GEETA (Chap 3.62)

"Krodhati Bhavti Sammoha, Sammoha Smiriti Vibhrama, Smiriti Bhransad Budhinaso Budhinashat pranashyati"

—The GEETA (Chap 3.63)

i.e. "Thinking about sense objects brings an Attachment towards them. Attachment breeds desire, and desire leads to frustration, which in turn leads to Delusions."

—The GEETA (Chap 3.62)

When you are deluded, you loose your Memory, And with the loss of Memory, the power of discrimination is destroyed; With the destruction of discrimination, yourself itself is lost.

—The GEETA (Chap 3.63)

 # Keep on WATCH

Watch WORDS, ACTION, THOUGHT, CHARACTER and HEALTH

WORDS
ACTION
THOUGHT
CHARACTER
HEALTH

It's old saying that:

> *"Wealth is loss, nothing is lost. Health is lost, something is lost. When CHARACTER (ethics, action) is lost everything is lost",*

 # RESPECT all the FAITHS (Religion) and Believe in GOD

 # Do to others as you wish to get from them.

 # SERVE With LOVE: GIVE.GIVE.GIVE.....More you give-more you get Remember

> God has given us two hands. One to receive with it and one to give with it.
>
> *"An Equation means nothing to me, Unless it expresses a thought of GOD"*

—Srinivas Ramanujam

@. MEDITATION Leads to Spirituality and Mental Peace.

 # Practice Transcendental Meditation (TM) i.e. Meditation based on Human Conscious.

Organize Collective Program of Transcendental Meditation (TM) i.e. 'TM- Sidhi' in order to achieve Community Peace.

Create Coherent National Conscious through Technologies of Consciousness *i.e.* 'Maharishi Effect'; innovated by Maharishi Mahesh Yogi in beginning of 20th century.

Expand 'TM' over the Globe to optimize World Peace through spiritual development.

Apply PEACE BASED Technologies of Defense *i.e.* 'Invincible Defense'

3. PEACE

Peace is not only paramount for the development of any Nation but, a foundation for its sustenance *Peace and Development* encompasses: *Purpose, Principles, Philanthropy, Peaceful Interaction amalgamated with value based Knowledge*. In my view, "*Peace is inversely proportional to Entropy i.e. Disorderliness*"

Mathematically,

> Peace (P) = K< 1/Entropy (E) >, Where K = Karma (Action) is Constant.......<VG:PE>. Eqn(1) say

PEACE is paramount for the prosperity of People and Planet. "Peace would prevail with every body's be well being, everywhere Happiness, Harmony in everybody and no misery be ever." *i.e.*

> "*Sarve Bhavantu Sukhina, Sarve Santu Niramava, Sarve Bhadrani Pashvanti, Ma Kaschit Dukh Bhaa Bhavet*"

@ This WORLD 'Il Be In PEACE when

— Mental Peace exists

— Materialistic Peace exists

— Demographic Peace exists and

— Environmental Peace exits.

Through KNOWLEDGE (*i.e.* Quality Human Valued Education).

@ PEACE THROUGH SPIRITUALITY

Principle of spiritual unity is basis to establish Peace through Spirituality. The spiritual unity means respect to all religions, religious diversity and mankind must not be divided by Prophets and Holy Scriptures. Right from the day one God has created Diversity and there is a manifestation of unity through it in humanity.

The division and hatred in the society are due to:

— economic and political reasons,

— language, sectarianism, regionalism, food habits

— disregard for the moral values and teachings of the spiritual Masters.

— and rivalry among nations for domination.

@ Peace is Manifestation of 'Om', 'Amin', Ami (Secularisms of Vasudev Ktumbhkam)

i.e. WORLD FAMILY UNDER ONE GOD'. In other words we are children of the one God so we're 'Global Human[1] *vis-a-vis* 'Global Citizen[1]. Or

"ONE FAMILY, ONE GOD" GOD is omnipresent and omnipotent.

There are many religion in the World and all the Religions (Faiths) pray for the Peace.

In our country (India), there is an agglomeration of all the World's Religions *(Faiths), Cultures,* terrains, *seasons and languages. Our Country is Secular and* perhaps a Pilot Plant of the Great Almighty when HE created this World's Civilization.

@ PEACE and SUCCESS

In my view,

 # "Peace (P) is directly proportional to Success (S)"

i.e. <P = AS>, Eqn. (2) say <VG-PS> Eqn. Where, A (Action) is constant.

Peace (P) linear relationship with Success (S)

@. Success is achieved by

> "Only the Person having firm conviction and Iron volition can attain strength and Energy. At no stage of karma does he ever hesitate."

—Rigveda

**Hard work, persistence, perservence and Never QUIT

**Target Oriented approach with PASSION is the must to achieve the goals.

$ 'Success Mantra' i.e The elements of success are:

• *WATCH*	*Clear purpose*	*Team attribute*
• *Strong relationship*	*Communication*	*Trust and Confidence*
• *Accountability*	*Leadership*	

$. Einstein Success Equation

<S = X + Y + Z>

S–Success, X–Think (Dream), Y–Hardwork and Z–Rest(Quiet)

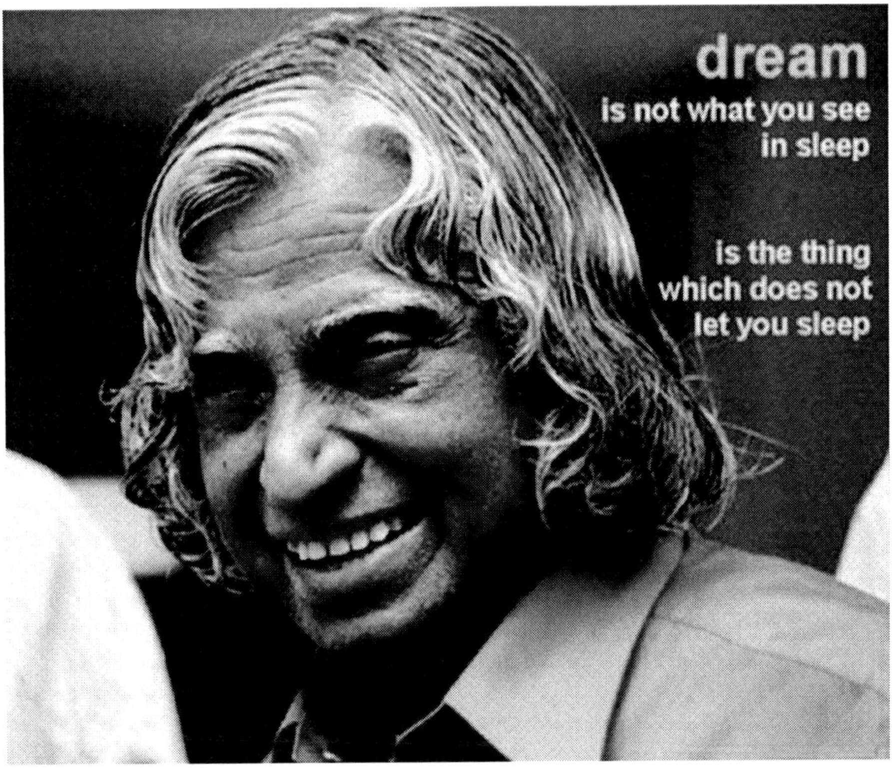

@ In my view SUCCESS *vis-a-vis* PEACE is embedded with (5 Cs)

- Character Conviction
- Commitment Courtesy Courage

Peace (P) is f (5 Cs) and Success (S) is f (5 Cs)

Peace (P) = f (S) = f (5Cs)..................(4) Ean.<VG : PS Eqn.>

Optimization of Peace is Dependent on 5 Cs and Has Linear Relationship with Peace and Success.

4. SCIENCE AND SPIRITUALITY

"The idea that' religion is faith; science is knowledge, ' I think is quite wrong. It misses the actual basis of science, which is faith.

—Charles Townes
Nobel laureate, Physics

Spirituality and Science are two opposite sides of the same coin. The alum of Science and Spirituality together mint a coin of Peace. Both are the creation of creative human mind. Both try to realize Self. Science relates to empirical, philosophical speculation processes and as spirituality deals with the soul, so it comprises the process of devotional service leading to religious paths. Though the processes may be different but, Scientist and Spiritualist have one common thing *i.e.* to know thyself, knowledge of Self, improvement of Self, pursuit of Truth either rationally or devotionally to serve the humanity.

Twice Nobel Laureate Winner Madam Curie said:

One cannot hope to build a better world without improving the individual. Toward this end, each of us must work toward his own highest development, accepting at the same time his share of responsibility for all humanity.

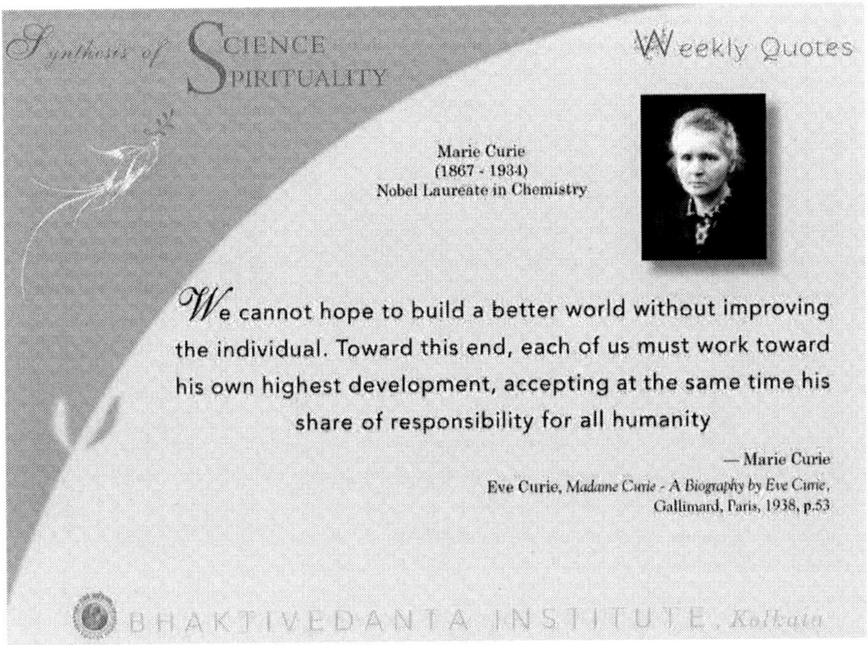

As a matter of fact, both Scientists and Spiritualists or religionists are engaged in search for the ultimate meaning of life and the universe. The difference is that a Scientist tries to explain the nature of reality within rationality, whereas the Spiritualists does so within and beyond rationality with a common factor of 'faith." To elaborate further, Scientist always plans an experiment, first in his mind with all the pros and cons of the methods are to be employed and selects the best one wherein; he has got faith to prove the theoretical facts/ideas/hypothesis through practical and tackle the problem before him. On the other hand Spiritualists would correspond to the faith that such an idea or vision has come to mind by the grace of God.

Max Planck, father of quantum physics stated, "...science demands also the believing spirit Anybody who has been seriously engaged in scientific work of any kind realizes that over the entrance of the gates to the temple of science are written words"

They must have faith. It is a quality which scientists cannot dispense with... This imaginative vision and faith in the ultimate success are indispensable. The pure rationalist has noplace here."

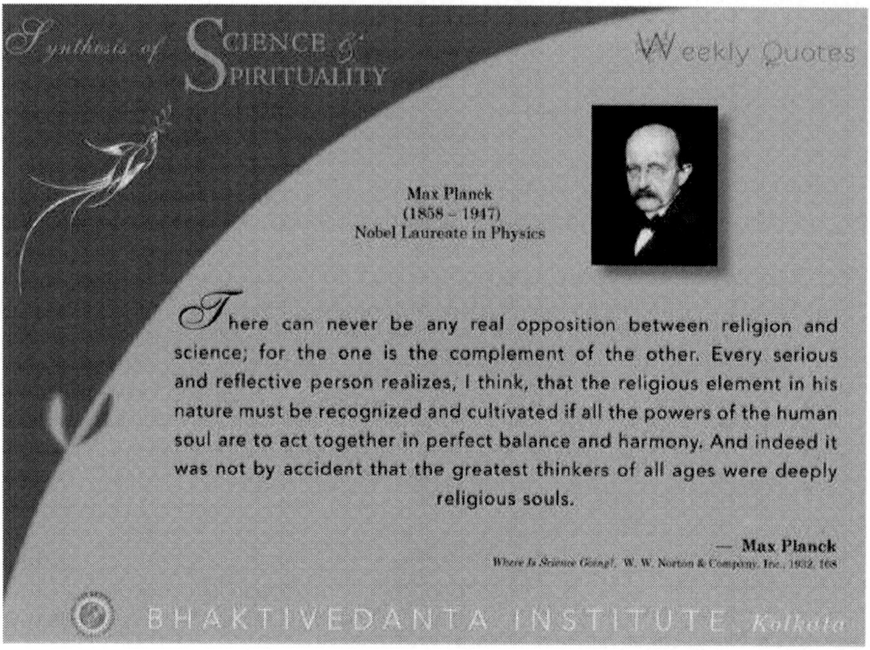

Srila Prabhupada in his purport of 'the Bhagavadgita (2.41) defined Faith as "unflinching trust in something sublime. "In other words, the source in which I put my faith must be convincing to me and it should be authorized.

In my view, every Scientist is a Spiritualist/ Religionists and follower of one or other faith/religion and so the Spiritualist but, every Spiritualist is not a Scientist.

In order to attain specialized knowledge of a particular field, be it scientific or spiritual, one has to put trust in the authenticity of the source. There are two technologies to put and verify the Trust/ Faith *viz*. Scientific and Spiritual. The Scientific Technology is based on Sanskrit dictum, "**phalena pariceycite**, " which means, literally, that we can test the nature of a tree by seeing what type of fruit it produced. It means Scientific verification is based on objectivity and the results produced experimentally. Getting the desired result in a practical reality through the devotional path with faith in God is the bases of Spiritual Technology. Therefore, genuine faith is a covalent bond between Science and Spirituality/Religion.

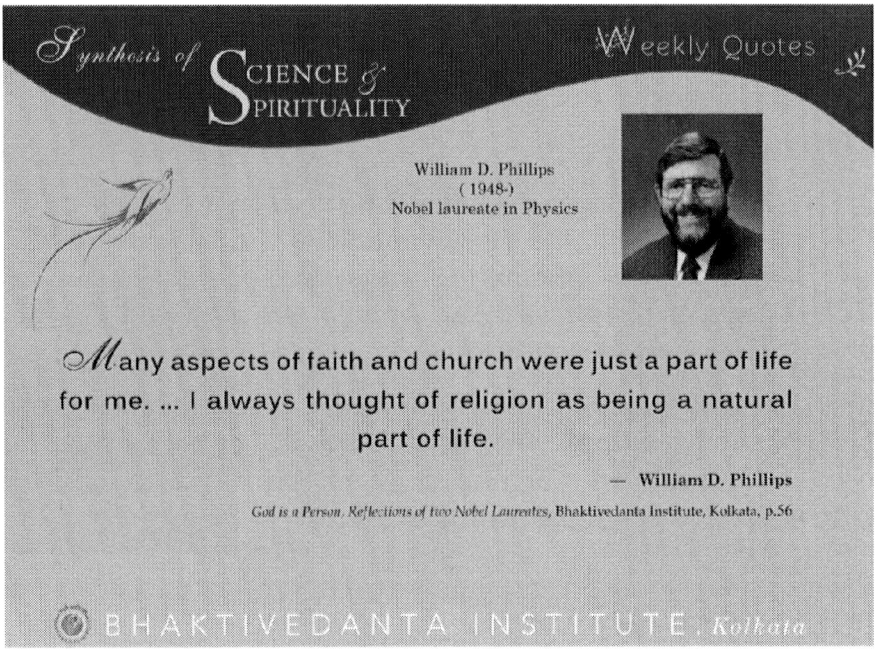

Both Scientists and Spiritualists believes in physical laws but, with a difference that a Spiritualist puts a suffix or a prefix of "By Grace Of God" *i.e.* he believes that Physical laws are created by the Supreme Being while a Scientist tend to dismiss religious things as being merely unverifiable "faith" or "belief" without realizing that such things *e.g.* mathematical axioms and physical theories also exist in scientific studies. *As a matter of fact both Scientists and Spiritualists are basically Scientists and be categorized as Physical Scientist and Spiritual Scientist, one follows rational process and the other devotional respectively with the sole aim of searching truth to serve the humanity. The earlier one believes more in Karma (Action) and the other on Luck (Dharma) with one common factor of Faith in the Supreme Lord of the Universe. Thus, both are Improver, Innovators and Inventors in their own way.*

@ Beliefs and Nature of Scientists and Spiritualists

Both believe in 3-Is (Improvements, Innovations and Inventions).

Inventors and Innovators are often famous for:

* their confidence,
* their perseverance and
* their passion.
* An open and curious mind allows an *Inventor / Innovator* to see beyond what is known/and what can be known. While seeing a new possibility, connection, or relationship can spark an *Invention*: the *Innovation* may add the new processes of its applications.

Next, Scientists and Spiritualists both are believer of some or other Religions/Faith with the few dictums below:

@ Religion is a spectrum of our life.

Religion shapes us and encompasses almost every part of our life. Religion is 'Dharma' ('Dharan') *i.e.* Adoption or Righteous Duty and just a Faith.

Its seven colors are: *viz.* culture, language and literature, history or civilization, social behavior or understanding of the humanity.

> *"In my view, Religion is just a faith amalgamated with the righteous path to serve the humanity and to achieve the eternal happiness under the feet of omnipotent, omniscience, Supreme Power the great Almighty God."*

> *"Majhab Nahin Sikhata Aapas Mein Vair Rakhna,*
> *Hindi, Hindu Vatan Hai Hindustan Hamara"*

— Iqbal

i.e. "No religion teaches hatred and enmity between the people"

@ Religions are the synergy of different paths

Religions are the synergy of different paths to reach one and only one destination *i.e.* serve the humanity with love with the flowers of diversity. Right from the day one God created the Universe with diversity but, without any tag of Religion *vis-a-vis* Faith. The newly born infant does not get birth with any tag of Religion *e.g.* Hindu, Muslim, Christian etc. but, only adopts the ways and means of the society, family, faith, religion wherein he gets birth and hence known by the socio-geo-political community. Anatomically we all are same with the same color of blood and the great Almighty never discriminated ad created bad or good human; its our deeds which makes us good and bad.

@ "*Ekam Sat Viyra Bahudha Vadanti*" (God is one and the

"*Ekam Sat Viyra Bahudha Vadanti*" (God is one and the wise call it by many names) is the message from from Rig Veda, which mentions the word "Buddha", *i.e.* "pluralism" in English is a solution to resolve conflicts.

> *"Mazil Ek par Rahen Alag Alag" i.e. "Destination is one but, paths are different"*

@ Be SECULAR and Keep one thing in mind

TEMPLE' is a 6 letter word.

'CHURCH' is a 6 letter word

'MOSQUE' is also a 6 letter word.

Also, 'GEETA' is a 5 letter word.

'BIBLE' is a 5 letter word.

'QURAN' also a 5 letter word.

These words have different Spelling. But the Thing they express the same. So Religion (Faith) does not a matter. The only thing is we are all 'INDIANS' /NATIVES, HUMANS and siblings of one GOD residing in one family of the WORLD.

@ Finally, both Scientist and Spiritualists are Leaders and ambassador of Peace with a strong conviction of

"I always Create, never Destroy

I always Believe, never Doubt

I am a Successful person, not a Victim

I have the Capacity and Knowledge to help People

I am a Leader"

5. Synergy between Science. Spirituality and Peace (Tranquility)

There seems to great Synergy between Science Spirituality and Peace (Tranquility) by way of its genesis and originality. The Synchronization of these three acronym SSP generates two models *viz.* 'VG: Hub and Spoke Model' and the other 'VG: Life (L) Circle Model'.

The first get envisaged by considering Peace (P) as a Hub and Science (Sc.) and Spirituality (Sp) as Spokes. The other give a model of Life (L) Circle assuming Sc; Sp; and P the three points of the acronym Life Circle.

Both these Models conclude that to establish Peace the synergy of Sc. and Sp is must *i.e.* 'VG: Hub and Spoke Model' and the other one *i.e.* 'VG: Life(L) Circle Model', narrates that the Life is a Synchronization of Sc; Sp; and P.

In addition to these three Sc; Sp andP the establishment of peace necessities clean environment, non-proliferation of weapons and understanding with positive attitude and passion to establish Peace, through lately established Environment and Peace Foundation[1] Founded By Dr. Virendra Goswami (2015) with a Mission:

----------- Stop the Nuclear Wars and Stop rise of WMD (Weapons of Mass Destruction)

----------- Adopt Safe, Scientific proven Technologies for National Security and Global Peace.

----------- To innovate the Scientific Techniques to Control Global Warming, Natural and Man-made Disasters and save the environment on Mother Earth

And Global Union of Scientist for Peace (GUSP) founded in 2005 by Maharishi Mahesh Yogi and re acronym by Dr. Virendra Goswami as 'Maharishi Mahesh Yogi Council of Scientist for Peace (MCSP) on 12 Jan'15 (97th Birthday).

Finally, let the echo of the composed song VG: 'PEACE Song' be echoed:

"Life thy name is PEACE,

_PEACE thy name is Life.

Where it ends, there strikes

The arrow of Death"

Dr. Virendra Goswami

2

Smart Defense Solution for Defense Personnel

MUNISH BHATIA[1]* AND SANDEEP K SOOD[1]

ABSTRACT

Smart Data analytics have been effectively used around the world for analysing the massive amount of data generated by modern day applications. Moreover, with the boost felt in Information and Communication Technology (ICT) sector, many multinational companies, like IBM, Amazon, Apple, and Microsoft are indulging smart data analytics for realizing optimal results. The work presented in this paper is focused on utilizing these powerful analyzation concepts in the field of National Defence. Specifically, a framework is proposed to identify possible terrorists or internal extremists of an attack or incident in the country by analysing different activity records. Though identification of internal extremists and terrorists remained a major concern for every defence agency, still recent terrorist attacks in various countries have discovered the inability to successfully eliminate such people. The proposed work is aimed at analyzation of people and their social activities over suspicion scale. Moreover, Suspectibility Index (SI) is defined for every person on the basis of their activity records

[1] Department of Computer Science and Engineering, Guru Nanak Dev University, Regional Campus, Gurdaspur, Punjab, India.

**Corresponding E-mail*: munishbhatia90@gmail.com

that can be suspicious with respect to the attack. Furthermore, a two level decision model is designed for identification of possible terrorists by incorporating various data analytics techniques. In order to validate the system, a synthetic data is generated by using Internet of Things (IoT) Technology for monitoring 20 students during their college stay. Results obtained shows that the system is highly accurate and effective in analyzing data for various activities.

Key words: Smart data analytics, Spatial mining, Temporal mining, Co-location mining, Terrorists.

I. INTRODUCTION

Innovative developments in Information and Communication Technology (ICT) has to led to generation of massive amount of data from everyday lives[1][2]. Social Computing[3], E-Healthcare[4], and E-Commerce[5] are some of the industrial areas where voluminous data are being produced regularly[6][7]. In such global sectors, smart data analytics have emerged as a group of vital techniques for not only managing data efficiently but to provide accurate results in time sensitive manner[8][9]. Numerous researchers around the world have put forth valid arguments regarding the potential benefits of information analyzation from various data repositories[10]. In fact, these benefits are quiet valuable if considered for other national sectors like defence, energy, and transportation[11]. In the field of defence, data analyzation has been necessary for every government in terms of weapons management, personnel management, and geographical tracking, thereby providing an effective defence service environment. However, major terrorist attacks in Paris[12], India[13], and USA[14] have questioned the entire world for its defence security. Federal Bureau of Investigation (FBI) has depicted in their investigation reports[15] about the vulnerability to national security due to internal extremists and terror fugitives. Moreover, inability to detect their daily activities has been a major investigating challenge for every defence agency which, in many cases has been the cause for investigation failure. Furthermore, with the availability of ubiquitous information through various online resources, it has become an easier task for terrorists to plan and execute a massive terrorist attack. In such a scenario, it has become indispensable to extend the perspective of smart data analytics from management boundaries to include real time activity analyzation. More importantly, analyzation of data about various activities using smart data analytics is vital in determining suspicious patterns of internal extremists and terrorists among large number of people. Various innovations in ICT in terms of sensors, and internet-enabled hardware devices have made it possible to acquire every minute level of interactive activity performed by a person in the social world[16]. Data from these devices are continuously transmitted to the connected cloud or backend databases[17]. GPS Location records, Call records, and Internet-Usage records are some of the important activities that can provide important information about the possible terrorists if analyzed efficiently. As mentioned earlier, analyzation techniques are being utilized in different applications for obtaining results in efficient manner[7][18]. Researchers around the world have developed different data mining and analyzation techniques for abstracting useful information from large datasets, thereby depicting its effectiveness[19]. In the current scenario, various data mining and analyzation techniques can be collaborated to develop an efficient framework that can aid defence officials in determination of terrorists and internal extremists in time-sensitive and efficient manner. Moreover, with cloud computing as a powerful computational platform, smart data analytics has provided an optimal computing environment for data analyzation[20][21]. With such aspects into consideration, the research performed in this paper provides a comprehensive framework for determining the possible terrorist and internal extremist for an attack or incident using smart data analytics over cloud storage. The architecture is designed to analyze various interactive activities of people from distributed databases that are suspicious with respect to the attack. Investigation reports have shown that most of the time terrorist attacks or incidents are preplanned and well-organized. Moreover, terrorist/s tend to acquire sufficient information about the target location, prior to the attack. Analyzation of all such interactive activities about execution of attack using smart data analytics formulates the identification core of the system. The framework is designed to analyze the suspectible behavior of every activity over suspicion scale. Based on this, every activity is classified into two classes depending upon their respective suspiciousness. Moreover, a probabilistic parameter, named as Suspectibity Index (SI) is defined to analyze every person on the basis of their activities. Furthermore, a Two Level Decision Model based on various data mining and analysis techniques is proposed to provide efficiency in terrorist identification. Both levels consider certain activities of the people and evaluates the corresponding SI value, which provides a statistical estimation of the possible terrorist. For the sake of distinction, Table 1 shows various terminologies that are used in rest of the paper.

Table 1: System Terminology

Sl. no.	*Defence terminology*	*Terminology used*	*Description*
1.	People	Individual	Person whose activities are being considered for analyzation.
2.	Suspects	Candidate	Selected group of individuals with suspicious activities.
3.	Terrorists/ Extremists	Culprit	Selected group of candidates with high probability of being responsible for the attack.

This paper is organized as follows. Section II presents a review of various Smart Data Analysis techniques and its utility in different applications. Section III describes the proposed Architecture for Identifying the Culprit using Smart Data Mining Techniques. In Section IV, performance evaluation of the proposed framework is proposed and various results are discussed subsequently. Finally, Section V concludes the paper with some future research challenges in the current domain.

II. LITERATURE REVIEW

This section provides an overview of some important literatures in the field of Smart Data Mining and Analyzation techniques. Moreover, a sub-section is made depicting some of the application scenarios where these mining techniques have been effectively used by various researchers and developers around the world.

A. Smart Data Mining and Analyzation Techniques

Ever since the boost realized in the field of Information and Communication Technology (ICT), Smart Data has been considered as a main research area for researchers. Continuous work has been performed to develop efficient data mining techniques for enhancing the efficiency of data analyzation. Wu *et al.*[19] have discussed various advantages of data mining for smart data in terms of data storage, abstraction, and classification. Authors have proposed a HACE theorem for characterizing various features of smart data. Moreover, a data processing model for smart data is presented that incorporates various data mining techniques. Specifically, the framework indulges data aggregation, mining and analysis, user interest modelling, and security and privacy features. Fahad *et al.*[10] have surveyed various data clustering algorithms that are used for smart data analyzation. Authors have developed a categorizing framework in which various algorithms are analyzed for main characteristics. Moreover, an empirical analysis of such algorithms have been performed on the datasets for statistical comparison. Gandomi and Haider[22] has provided an intense overview of various analytics methods used for unstructured smart data. Moreover, authors have put forth various challenges for organizing unstructured text, audio, and video formats into structured form. Furthermore, various algorithms are discussed to prevent various problems in analyzing smart data. Han *et al.*[23] have surveyed various smart data analytics platforms that are useful for data analyzation. Authors have proposed a systematic smart data framework by decomposing these systems into data generation, data acquisition, data storage, and data analytics forming a sequential data value chain. Moreover, authors have discussed various challenges that needs to be addressed for handling smart data efficiently. Chen *et al.*[24] have proposed two notations for mining relationships in time based events. Moreover, algorithms, named Temporal Pattern Miner and Probabilistic Temporal Pattern Miner are presented to identify interval based sequential patterns among time series data. Experimental results showed that the proposed algorithms were efficient in determining patterns for various time based events. Ristoski and Paulheim[25] provides a comprehensive survey of various approaches for data mining and knowledge discovery in smart data. As an exemplar, authors have developed a content based recommender system by indulging sematic web mining at different stages of recommendation, thereby providing efficacy for generating recommendations. Apart from the above mentioned techniques, many researchers have provided works for mining heterogeneous data in an efficient manner[26][27].

B. Application Scenarios of Smart Data Analytics

Data mining techniques have been effectively utilized by various researchers and developers in various applications. Wang *et al.*[28] have presented various research challenges of smart data analytics in logistics and supply chain management. Authors have proposed a Supply Chain Analytics on the basis of five capability levels for smart data, named as functional, process-based, collaborative, agile, and sustainable. Further, the authors have discussed various advantages of indulging the proposed system for smart data business analytics. Sanctis *et al.*[29] have provided a survey regarding incorporation of data mining techniques for communication networks. Various application environments have been discussed in which data mining techniques have been productive.

Moreover, authors have provided specific guidelines of indulging data mining for future applications.Dubey *et al.*[30] have proposed a data mining based adaptive protection scheme for enhancing the distance relay performance in power transmission networks. Decision Tree is used as classifier model for providing supervisory control to various operations of the network. System deployment shows that the proposed system is highly reliable in practical situations. Data mining techniques have also been effectively used to analyze healthcare data. Chen *et al.*[31] have used data mining techniques for analyzing patterns of large collection of geriatric medical examination data. Moreover, authors have defined a health indicator, named as personal health index for indicating health related problems. System evaluation performed on GME data set, depicts that the proposed model is highly effective. Batra and Sachdeva[32] have proposed an architecture for analyzing medical data to provide an aid to various healthcare users. The framework is composed of two steps, namely data preprocessing and data transformation. Experiment results showed that the proposed model is highly effective and accurate in provisioning healthcare services. Yang and Chen[33] have indulged data mining techniques in identifying the correlation between the clinical information for lung disease and pathology report for diagnosing staging lung cancer. Interesting work have been performed by Gotz *et al.* in[34]. Authors have incorporated data mining models for pattern detection from retrospective clinical patient data. The proposed methodology combines visual query capabilities, pattern mining techniques and visualization techniques for identifying uncovered health oriented patterns that can affect the patients.

III. PROPOSED MODEL

The proposed strategy for identifying the culprit comprises of fours layers, namely Smart Data Collection and Storage (SDCS), Smart Data Classification (SDC), Smart Data Mining and Analyzation (SDMA) and finally, Decision Making (DM) layer. All layers performed independently, thereby provides efficient environment for the adjacent layers. Initially, necessary data about various activities with respect to the attack are acquired from different distributed databases and accumulated in a centralized cloud data storage system. Since these distributed databases consist of heterogeneous data, therefore a common data storage format is defined for centralized storage of these activities. Every acquired activity set is categorized into two classes on the basis of its suspicious behaviour with respect to the attack. Various mining techniques are implemented on the accumulated data to extract vital information about the suspicious candidates for identification of the probable culprits. Analyzation of such suspicious candidates are performed on the basis of a probabilistic estimate, named Susceptibility Index (SI). SI value provides an evaluating metric for analyzing the suspectible behaviour of the candidate. Finally, based the suspectable activity set and corresponding SI values, a two level decision making model is presented to identify the most probable culprit from the available susceptible candidates. Overall architecture of the proposed model is presented in Fig. 1.

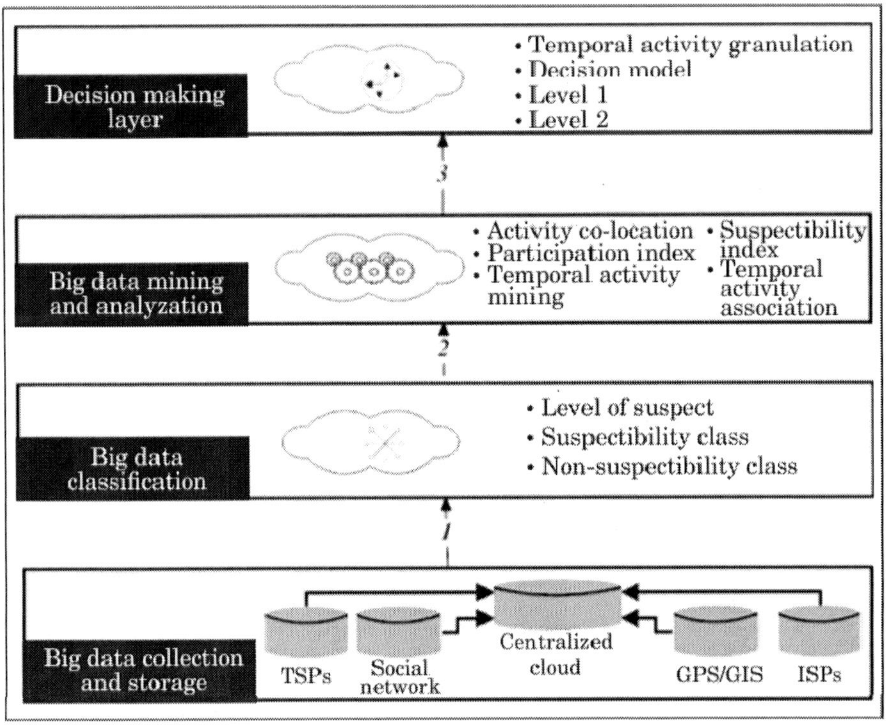

Fig. 1: Layered architecture of the proposed model.

A. Smart Data Collection and Storage (SDCS)

Data collection is the premier task of the proposed framework. SDCS layer aims at acquiring data about various activities of individuals from distributed databases and storage them in a centralized cloud database. Data about location, and time of every individual is acquired from IMEI, GPS, and GIS databases. Telecommunication data sets are acquired from telecommunication service managers while data about internet usage or website accessibility is acquired by Internet Service Providers (ISPs). These datasets comprise of heterogeneous data, so it must be stored in the common storage format for enhancing data accessibility. Henceforth, a data storage format is proposed to store heterogeneous activity sets in the cloud database. Fig. 2 shows the common data storage format for storing various activities in centralized cloud database. "PID" indicates a unique identification number of individuals. "AID" is the activity identity number for storing various activities. "Value" and "Time" are data values and time of the activity performed by an individual respectively. These activity sets are acquired from various distributed databases over a network channel. This channel is secured with Secure Socket Layer (SSL)[35] to provide data security while data collection. Moreover, since centralized database is based on cloud storage mechanism, it is also vulnerable to security attacks. Therefore,

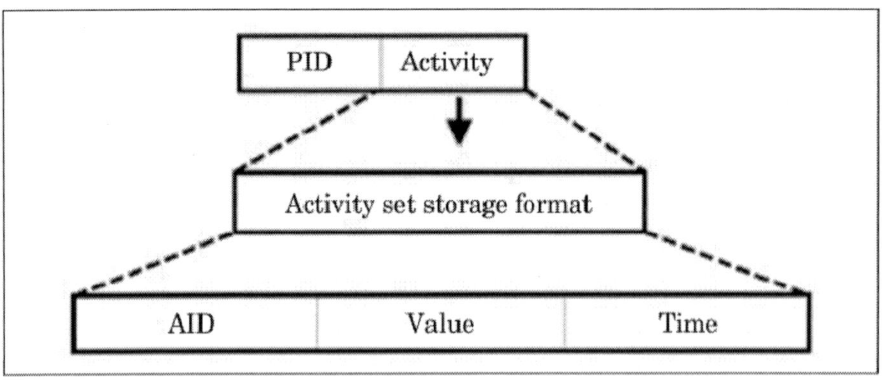

Fig. 2: Activity storage format in cloud database.

multiple number of security mechanisms are consolidated to ensure secure storage. These include data encryption, user authentication, and credential mapping[36].

B. Smart Data Classification (SDC)

The main objective of data classification layer is to categorize various activities on the basis of its suspectible behaviour with consideration to the incidence. In other words, SDC performs classifications of activities by analyzing it over suspicion scale. Specifically, two classes are defined for these activities, named as Suspectibility Class (SC) and Non-Suspectibility Class (NSC). SC comprises of those activities that give the impression of suspiciousness for the attack. On the other hand, NCS comprises of activities that are in compliance with investigating officials and do not draw any sign of suspicion. Since probability can be used to model any system effectively, therefore in this study, activity classification is performed using Bayesian Belief Network (BBN) classifier[37]. BBN is probabilistic classification technique that assigns a class to an activity on the basis of certain prefixed threshold values. These threshold values are determined by the system administrator or the domain expert prior to the deployment of the system. Fig. 3 shows an instance of classification phenomena using BBN classifier. As mentioned earlier, the probabilistic value is associated with every activity set based on which appropriate

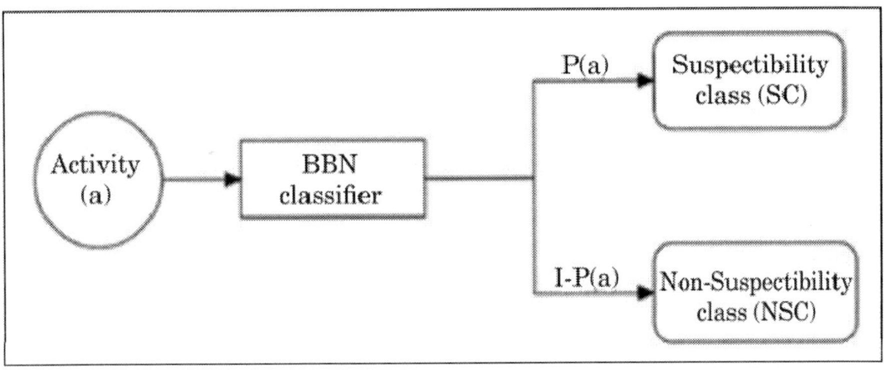

Fig. 3: Classification using BBN classifier.

class is assigned. In order to determine this probabilistic measure, every activity is analyzed for Level of Susceptibility (LoS).

Definition 1 *(Level of Suspect (LoS)): Given an activity A_I performed by an individual I in "t time of incidence Q, then level of suspect is defined as the probability of offensive measure of A_I with respect to the contextual occurrence of attack Q.*

This definition gives a probabilistic estimate to analyze every activity for suspiciousness. However, it is important to mention that "t is the prefixed time window from the occurrence of attack Q. It can be varied according to the applicational scenarios. Various types of activities that are considered for analyzation are compiled in the form of different activity sets. Table 2 shows an overview of these activity sets and related concepts.

Table 2: Activity set

Sl. no.	***Activity set***	***Sources of data collection***	***Description***	***Instances of suspectible activities***
(1)	Contextual data	GPS, GIS, IMEI Tracker Database, and Mobile No. Tracker Database.	Data about location, and place in terms of geographic coordinates.	Visiting the location of attack prior to occurrence.
(2)	Telecommunication data	Telecommunication Service Providers (TSPs).	Data about telephonic conversation, call records, and texts exchanged.	Making suspicious calls, and information exchanged through texts about attack.
(3)	Internet access data	Internet Service Providers (ISPs).	Data about web content accessed, emails, information exchanged through internet.	Accessing and sharing information through internet about the attack.
(4)	Social networking data	Social-Network Developers, and Data Managers	Data about social networking websites accessed.	Suspicious chat video calls, and other data exchanged in social network.

(a) ***Contextual data:*** Contextual Data includes data about the geographic location of an individual. Geographic coordinates are acquired from GPS or GIS databases. In cases where GPS or GIS data are unavailable, IMEI Number or Mobile Phone Tracker databases can be used to collect such data. Such kind of data provides information about the geographical location of an individual for every time instance. In other words, this dataset is useful in determining the whereabouts of every individual for analyzation purposes.

(b) ***Telecommunication data:*** Storage of data about telephonic conversation is performed in this activity set. In other words, this dataset comprises of telephonic conversation, call records, and text records of every individual. Such kind of data are acquired by various Telecommunication Service Providers (TSPs) available in the region of the attack. Moreover, in extreme cases this data set can be further enhanced to include frequency of such activities performed by the individual.

(c) ***Internet access data:*** Internet is a primary source for accessing online resources, and information. As far as an individual is concerned, acquiring suspectable resources and information is matter of concern for investigating officials. Moreover, suspicious information exchanged over internet through e-mails, and other sharing applications draws considerable attention during investigation. Therefore, this dataset comprises internet based activities performed by an individual. Regional Internet Service Providers (ISPs) can provide such kind of data in a comprehensive manner.

(d) ***Social networking data:*** Social Networking based interaction has evolved substantially over the past few years. Such kind of medium has proven to be an effective way of inter-person communication and resource exchange. Acquiring data about these social interactions formulates to constitute this activity set. With sufficient access rights, data about such activities can be acquired from the respective social-network developers.

C. Smart Data Mining and Analyzation (SDMA)

Smart Data Mining aims at extracting information about various activities of an individual from cloud database. Moreover, since data accumulated is time sensitive, therefore information must be mined for time instances to ensure efficient data analyzation. Furthermore, associations are made among various time based activities to provide an effective decision making environment for determining the most probable culprit. With all these aspects, the data mining for various activities are performed in three steps, namely Activity Co-Location Mining[38], Temporal Activity Mining[24] and Temporal Activity Association.

Definition 2 *(Activity Co-location (A_I)): Given an activity A, then individual I is said to be co-located with A only if I is in the closed proximity of activity A during its occurrence.*

A closed proximity[38] is a measure compactness between individual I and activity A. In other words, activity co-location determines the co-locative existence of every individual with the respective activity. However, mere co-location of individual with activity is not enough to determine the exact involvement of individual in the activity. Therefore, a prevalence measure is required to determine a threshold for active involvement of individual in the activity.

Definition 3 *(Participation Index (PI)): Given an Activity A and Individual I, then individual I is actively involved in the activity A only if the participation index (PI) of I for activity A is greater than* λ.

In Definition 3, PI[39] value performs an involvement analysis of an individual with the corresponding activity. Moreover, the threshold value λ is prefixed by the domain expert before the actual system deployment. Moreover, in the current scenario, time is an indispensable measure for the data analyzation, therefore every activity is mined for temporal instances using Temporal Activity Mining.

Definition 4 *(Temporal Activity Mining (TAM (A_I, Δt)): Given an Activity A_I and time space of Δt, Temporal Activity Mining determines the temporal instance (t_i) for the occurrence of activity A_I such that $t_i \rightarrow \Delta t$ and is represented as $\{t_i, A_I\}$.*

The main objective of TAM (A_I, Δt) is to associate every activity performed by individual I with the respective time instance at which it is performed. In Definition 4, t_i depicts the unit of time at which the activity A_I is performed by individual I. Based on this aspect, every activity performed by individual I is associated with its respective time unit in chronological order by using Temporal Activity Association.

Definition 5 (*Temporal Activity Association (TAA* (A_I, Δt))): Given N number of Temporal Activities (t_i, A_I^j) [$1<i=j<N$] performed by an individual I in a time space of Δt, then Temporal Activity Association (TAA* (A_I, Δt)) is defined as sequential set of all activities performed by individual I in Δt time unit and is represented as: $\{<t_1, A_I^1><t_2, A_I^2>\ldots\ldots <t_N, A_I^N>$ such that t_1, t_2, $t_N \rightarrow \Delta t$ and ($t_1<t_2<\ldots.\ t_N$).*

It can be seen from Definition 5 that TAA* (A_I, Δt)) presents a form of data granule of various activities performed by an individual within a time space of Δt. In other words, every individual is associated with every activity performed by him in given time window. Fig. 4 shows an instance of formulation of TAA* data granule for various activities.

C.1. Automated information analyzation

Data granule comprises of both suspectable and non-suspectable activities depending upon the level of suspect that each activity persists. Information Analyzation aims at determining the

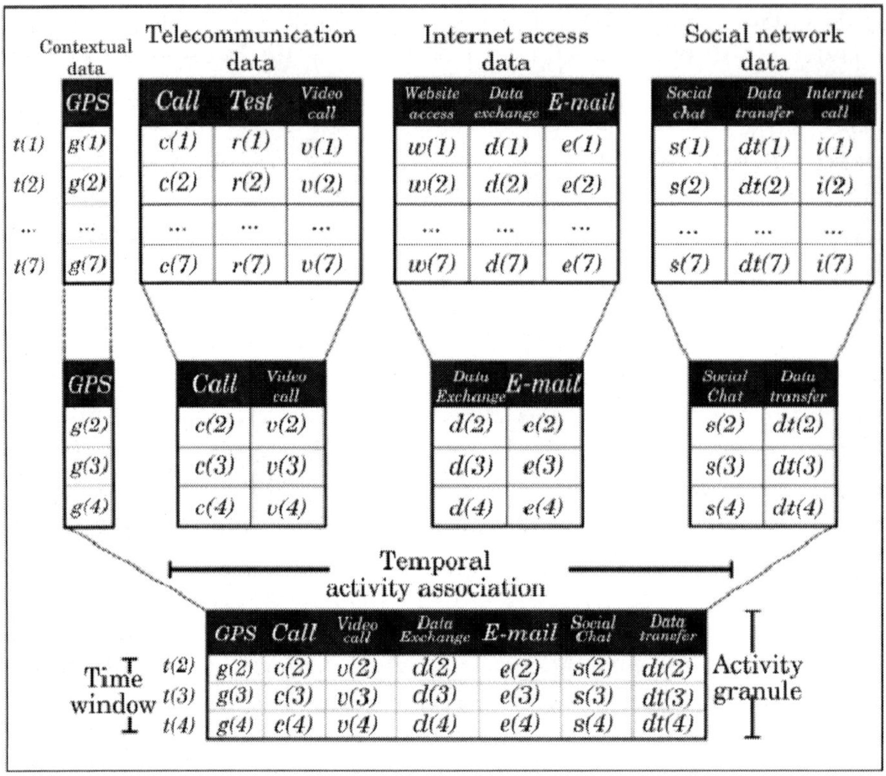

Fig. 4: Temporal activity granule.

suspectable behaviour of an individual on the basis of these activities. In other words, information analyzation will 1) provide an estimate about each individual on the basis of suspectibility 2) extract information about various activities in a given time window 3) aid in determining the most probable culprit. With these aspects, a probabilistic parameter is defined for analyzing every individual over suspectible scale, named as Suspectibility Index (SI).

Definition 6 *(Suspectibility Index (SI)): Given an individual I and temporal data granule for various activities performed by him time space of* Δt *(TAA*(*A_I*,* Δt*)), then Suspectibility Index is defined for I as a probabilistic factor depending upon the level of suspect for various activities performed in "t time with respect to the attack Q.*

Definition 6 provides a probabilistic measure to evaluate various activities performed individual on the basis of suspiciousness. Moreover, SI values can be directly related to every individual, thereby analyzing every individual for possible culprit. Specifically, Higher SI value of individual indicates more suspicious behaviour of the activities performed by him and therefore is most probable candidate for the culprit. Similarly, lower SI value shows that individual's activities are not suspicious for further investigation. Since, SI value depicts a certain degree of suspicion for an individual and thereby, presents his involvement in the occurred attack. Mathematically, SI can be represented in terms of conditional probability as shown in equation 1.

$$SI_{TAA^*(AI,\ \ddot{A}t)} = P\left(\frac{Q}{S^1US^2US^3U.....S^N}\right) \quad (1)$$

where Q denotes the occurrence of attack and S^1, S^2...S^N denotes the probabilistic suspectibility index for activity sets,which are evaluated using average weight associated method as shown in Table 3. However, since number of activities are dependent upon the time space considered for activity accumulated can be sufficiently large, therefore parallelism in data mining and analyzation can be achieved by using parallel programming paradigms like Apache Hadoop[40]and Spark[41]. These programming models works on large amount of data using two basic functions, namely Map function and Reduce functions. Therefore, development of application scenarios over these programming models will result in time sensitive data analyzation.

Table 3: Weight Associative Method

Activity set (S)	*Associated probabilistic weights for suspectibility*	*Suspectibility index evaluation for activity set S*
s_1	w_1	$\sum_{i=1}^{n} \frac{w_i}{n}$
s_2	w_2	
s_3	w_3	
...	...	
s_n	w_n	

D. Two Level Decision Model for Identification of Most Probable Culprit

Formation of data granule will aid higher officials or investigators with information about various activities from wider perspective. Many investigating reports have shown that large number of parameters in determining the suspicious behaviour of a person increases the complexity for making efficient decisions. Cognitive efforts have been considered to enhance the efficiency in decision making during investigation. This research utilizes the power of smart data analytics in analyzation of large number of activities over suspectibility scale, thereby provides a new dimension to traditional analyzation procedures for investigators. For the purpose of decision making for culprit identification, a two level decision model is proposed that indulges different activities stored in cloud and automatically determines the probable culprit/s. Furthermore, since computations are carried out in cloud environment, time sensitive results are obtained with high accuracy.

D.1.Two level decision model

An integrated data mining based methodology is proposed to enhance the decision making accuracy of the investigators in determining the possible culprits. Time is considered as an independent attribute for various activities, therefore becomes an organizational basis for the proposed system. As mentioned earlier, most of major attacks are well-organized and preplanned. In other words, culprits tend to acquire information either through online resources or physically, to execute a major attack. Based on these aspects, a two level decision model is designed in which each level performs analyzation of the intended activities, thereby aiding investigators with information intensive results.

Algorithm 1: *(Level 1) Candidate Identification Algorithm*

Input: Set of Individuals I = {1,2,3.... N}, Location of Incidence = L, Time Window = Δt, Threshold for Spatial Distance = d, Spatio-

Temporal Instances of Individual = $\{t_i, A_i\}$ [$i \rightarrow \Delta t$ and $1<I<N$]

Step 1: Determine geographical location for all instances of every individual from Spatio-Temporal Data

Step 2: Initialize j =1

Step 3: For all $t_i \rightarrow \Delta t$, Repeat

If (Distance (| L, Aj |) < d)

\\ *Geographic Location based Distance Estimation*

Then Add [j] to Candidate_Log

\\ *Candidate_Log is a storage area in Cloud*

Step 4: Increment j to j+1

Step 5: If j = N

Then Return Candidate_Log

Else Goto Step 3

Level 1

In the first level, the candidates for probable culprits are identified using the contextual information acquired from the contextual database. Since the accumulated contextual information comprises of information about geographic locations of an individual for a given time instance, therefore a spatio-temporal co-location mining (co-occurrence) algorithm is proposed to identify the possible candidates. However, it is important to mention that thresholds for time window and geographical distance are prefixed by the domain expert or administrator before the deployment of the system. Overall procedure is depicted in Algorithm 1. Spatial-Temporal instances are used in this level to determine the physical presence of the suspects. Such information analyzation will filter out the possible suspects efficiently. However, depending upon the context of the incident, other activity can also be prioritized.

In the proposed algorithm, Distance () is a function for estimating contextual distance. A temporary storage area, termed as Candidate_Log, is used to store the possible list of candidates.

Algorithm 2: *(Level 2) Culprit Identification Algorithm*

Input: Set of Candidates C = {1,2,3....M}, Temporal Activity Data Granule for Candidates TAA*(A_c, Δt), Prefixed Threshold for Suspectibility Index = λ, Time Window = Δt

Step 1: Initialize j =1

Step 2: Determine TAA*(Aj, Δt)

\\ Temporal Activity Association Granule for Candidate Activity Set

Step 3: Evaluate SI TAA*(Aj, Δt)

Step 4: If SI TAA*(Aj, Δt)> λ

\\ *Suspectibility Index Comparison for Detecting Possible Culprit*

Then Add [j] to Culprit_Log

\\ *Culprit_Log is a storage area in Cloud*

Step 5: Increment j to j+1

Step 6: If j = M

Then Return Culprit_Log and Exit

Else Goto Step 2

Level 2

In this Level, information about possible culprits for the attack are analyzed for various interactive activities. Moreover, temporal activity granule is formulated by indulging telecommunication data, internet access data, and social networking data. Every candidate is evaluated for his respective Suspectibility Index (SI) value based on the formulated data granule. Overall procedure of Level 2 is depicted in the Algorithm 2. Threshold of time window for activity analyzation can be similar to Level 1 or different depending upon the domain expert. Moreover, appropriate thresholds for suspectibility index is prefixed to enhance the identification accuracy of the system. In Algorithm 2, Culprit_Log is a storage area in the cloud which contains the final information of the possible culprits. This information is presented to investigators in the desired format. Moreover, the process for information presentation can be further feasible for investigation color coded information is presented. Highlight the information about possible culprits will provide a form of evidence to the investigators that can help them in taking future actions against the determined culprits. A complete flowchart of both levels is shown in Fig. 5.

IV. PERFORMANCE EVALUATION

This section evaluates the performance of the proposed system. As mentioned earlier, the system is deployed in three major steps. In the first step, data collected from distributed databases are classified on the basis of their suspectable behaviour, in terms of respective level of suspect. In the second step, data mining techniques are indulged to analyze these activities over temporal instances for evaluation of suspectibility index value for every person. Finally, the proposed two level decision model is used to identify the possible culprit. Based on these three steps, system deployment is performed to analyze the system performance from three aspects.

a) Determine the activity classification efficiency for the proposed model.

b) Evaluate the data mining efficiency of the system in terms of various statistical parameters.

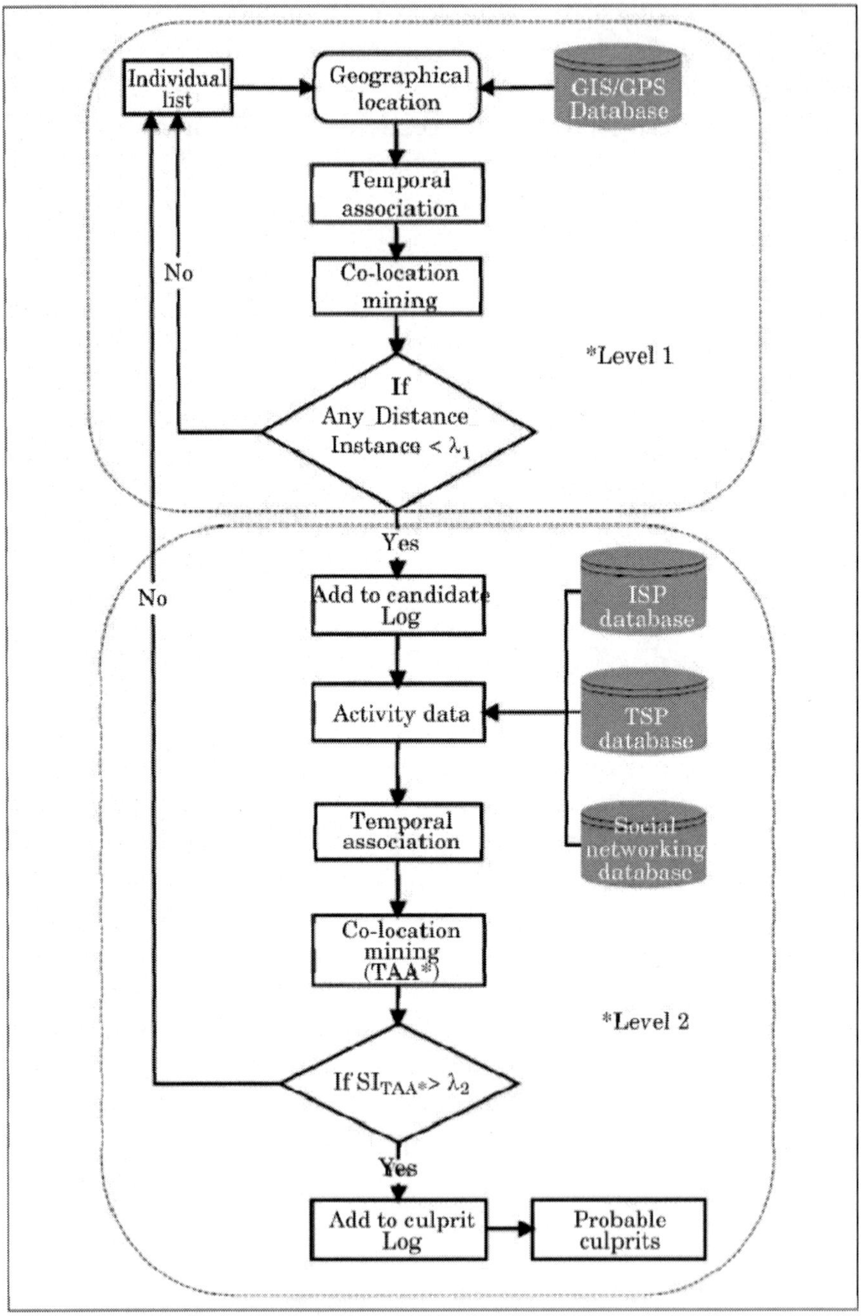

Fig. 5: Flowchart of the model

c) Assessing the identification efficiency of the proposed two level decision model for identification of possible culprits.

Table 4: IoT technology used for data accumulation

Sl. no.	*Activity set*	*IoT technology used*	*Description*
(1)	Contextual information	GPS Device, GIS Device, Tracker Sensor	Data about location, and place in terms of GPS coordinates.
(2)	Telecommu-nication	RFID Tag, Smartphone Embedded Sensors, Wireless Bug.	Data about telephonic conversation, call records, and texts exchanged.
(3)	Internet access	Sensors, Smart Routers, RFID Tag, Visual Detectors.	Data about web content accessed, emails, inform-ation exchange through internet.
(4)	Social networ-king	Sensors, RFID Tag, NFC Tag, Smart Routers.	Data about social net-working websites accessed.

Table 5: Classification results

Activity	*Sensiti-vity (%)*	*Specifi city (%)*	*Accuray (%)*	*F-Mea-sure(%)*	*Mean Error Rate (%)*	*Root Mean Square Error Rate (%)*
Contextual	96.33	87.63	98.72	91.92	3.92	3.23
Telecommunication	95.23	91.98	94.31	93.55	2.55	2.01
Internet Access	94.29	92.74	91.23	93.81	4.07	3.77
Social Networking	89.23	94.25	97.26	91.39	2.98	2.54

A. Experimental Environment

Due to the privacy constraints of TSPs and ISPs for providing real time data, the experiment is performed for monitoring 221 college students for 30 days before the commencement of the examination using Internet of Things (IoT) Technology for data accumulation. Moreover, IoT being the predominant technology for data acquisition, efficiency is believed to persist for data accumulation layer. Various sensors are embedded at different college sites, and on smart wearables of students. Table 4 depicts an overview of various IoT sensors used for data acquisition purpose. The main objective of opting this environment is to identify students performing vicious activities that can affect the normal examination procedure. These includes exam leakage, vicious information sharing, and other destructive activities. The collected data is transmitted to the connected Amazon EC2[42] cloud storage where it is further analyzed using Stata tool[43] and various results are obtained for the system. In the 30-day monitoring procedure, nearly 28923 datasets are obtained for various students. Each activity is stored in the format shown in Fig. 2 for realizing the objectives of the implementation in an efficient manner.

B. Activity Classification Efficiency

Activities performed by various students are analyzed on the basis of suspectable behaviour. List of 39 vicious activities are determined on the basis of acquired activity sets. Classification of activities into different classes is performed by the proposed system using BBN classifier. For evaluating the classification efficiency of the system, various statistical parameters are evaluated. These include Sensitivity, Specificity, Accuracy and F-measure. Moreover, various error rates in terms of Mean Error Rate (MER) and Root Mean Square Error Rate (RMSER)) are obtained for determining the overall error probability for classification. Results for the 30-day monitoring procedure are shown in Table 5. High values of Sensitivity and Specificity, averaging to nearly 94.3% and 92.9% indicates that the system is highly efficient in terms of activity classification. Moreover, the system achieved mean accuracy of 95.4% depicts the effectiveness of the system. Furthermore, low error rates for activity classification with MER averaging to 3.41% and RMSER averaging to 2.71% further enhances the decision making capability of the proposed framework.

C. Data Mining Efficiency

Data accumulated in cloud storage comprises of heterogeneous data for various activities. Every activity is associated with the corresponding temporal instances by the proposed system. Since large number of activities are under consideration, data mining efficiency concerns with the abstraction of temporal instances from the cloud database for each monitored student. In other words, data mining efficiency of the proposed is evaluated in terms of running time of the system for extracting temporal data granules of various activities. Moreover, since the activity set consists of temporally diverse data *i.e.,* some activities are continuous (for instance internet usage, and contextual data) while other are non-continuous (for instance calling, and texting), it is vital to determine the abstraction efficiency for every activity separately. Fig. 6 shows the data abstraction efficiency for the proposed system in terms of time taken by the system for extracting data about variable number of activities. Results shows that the proposed system is temporally efficient and thereby, depicts the effectiveness of smart data analytics for the current scenario. An overall running of the system is shown in Fig. 7. With such high efficiency in data analyzation, the investigation procedures adopted by the defence official will be enhanced to next level altogether.

S. No.	*Parameter*	*Value (in %)*
1	Sensitivity	88.4
2	Specificity	95.3
3	Precision	93.2
4	Coverage	96.5
5	Average Absolute Error	2.11
6	Root Average Square Error	2.76
7	Relative Absolute Error	4.47
8	Root Relative Squared Error	3.74

D. Decision Modelling Efficiency

The main advantage of using smart data analytics lies in the identification of the person with high suspectable activity set and therefore, high value of suspectibility index. The main objective for evaluating the effectiveness of automated decision making is to analyze the results for efficiency and utility perspective, in

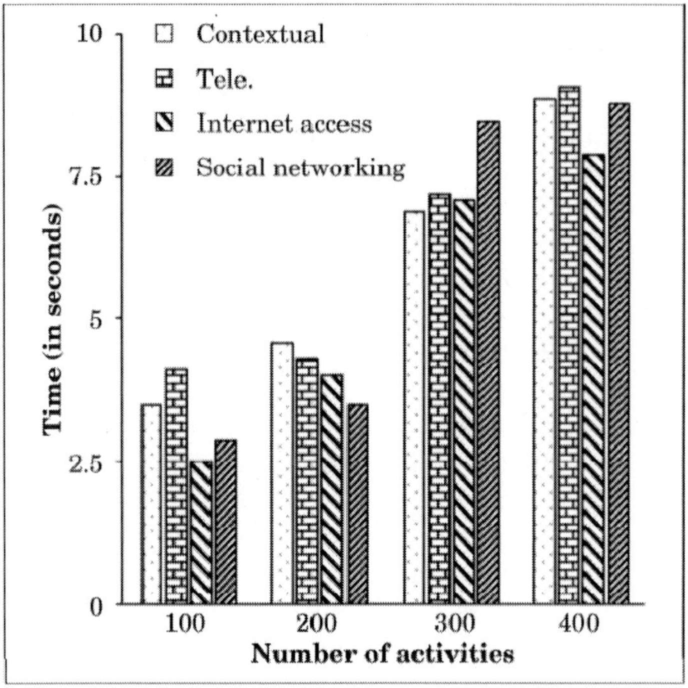

Fig. 6: Mining efficiency

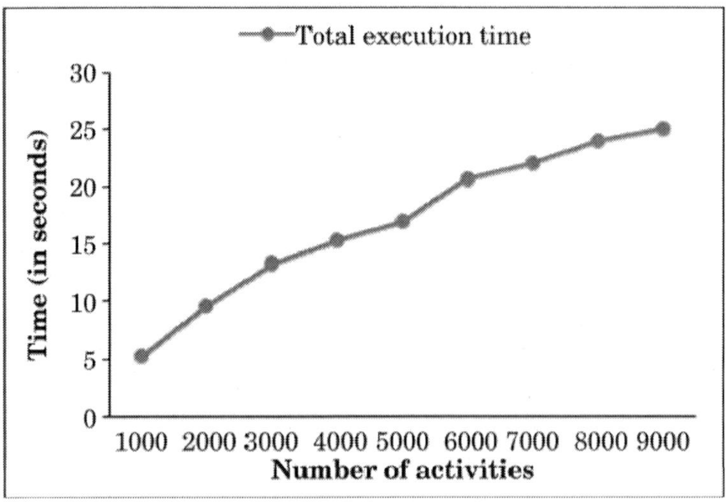

Fig. 7: Total execution time

terms of accuracy and precision. Along with these, other statistical parameters are also evaluated for evaluating the overall identification procedure. Table 6 depicts the various results for decision making that are obtained by the system. As it can be clearly seen that system persists high efficiency for the considered scenario in terms of various statistical values. Specifically, sensitivity and specificity are registered with 88.4% and 95.3% respectively, thereby depicting high accuracy in terms of suspect identification. In addition to this, high values of precision (93.2%) and coverage (96.5%) indicates that the proposed system is capable of analyzing every activity from suspiciousness, which enhances the overall decision making for identifying possible culprits. Since error rates are other important statistical parameter for evaluating any system, the proposed decision making is analyzed for error probabilities. Low values of various error indicate that the system has high resistance to errors. Based on these results, it is concluded that the proposed model based on smart data analytics is highly effective and efficient for practical scenarios and will raise the level of investigation for the defence officials.

E. Overall System Stability

In addition to the results obtained in the previous section, the proposed system is analyzed for system stability. System stability estimates the stability persistence of the system for frequency of input parameters. In the current scenario, these input parameters are set of various activities acquired by the IoT devices. In order to determine this type efficiency, a statistical measure Mean Absolute Shift (MAS) is used. MAS shift determines the overall system stability such that low value of MAS indicate high stability value and high value of MAS shows low stability value. Results for variable number of activities are shown in Fig. 8. Low Value of MAS (averaging to 0.41) indicates that the system persists stability for large number of activities.

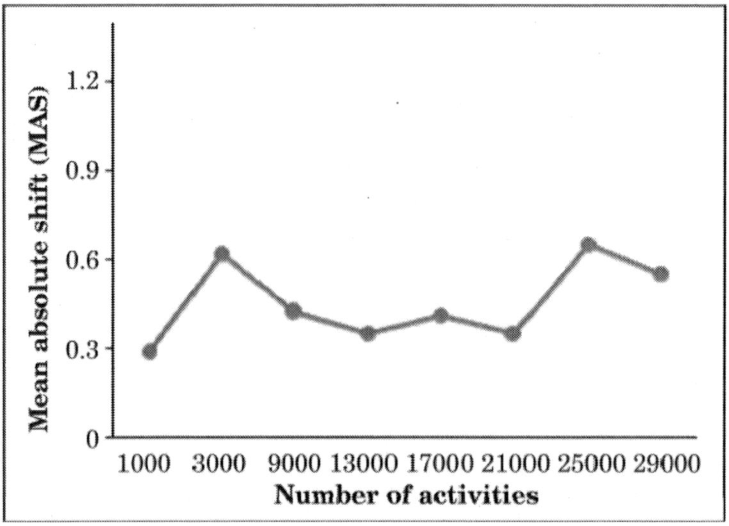

Fig. 8: System stability

F. Smart Data Analytics for Automated Decision-Making *Vs* Manual Investigation Procedure

This section provides the insight to various crucial aspects for indulging smart data analytics for defence purposes. During the experiment evaluation of the system, certain important features are determined such that it can become an important perspective for investigating officials. Following six points provides an estimate of how smart data analytics can be effective in decision making for defence personnel. Brief overview has been shown in Table 7.

Table 7: Comparative analysis

Features	*Manual investigation procedure*	*Smartdata analytics for automated decision-making*
Human biasness	Yes	No
Human error	Yes	No
Information deliverance	No	Yes
Remote access	No	Yes
Time delay	Maximum	Minimum
Availability	Minimum	Maximum

(a) Smart Data analytics has the capability of determining the suspicious pattern among large set of activities in time sensitive and efficient manner, which in case of manual investigation is a time consuming process.

(b) Absence of human biasness in automated decision making for determining the probability of suspectibility, further enhances the accuracy of the system.

(c) Accessing data remotely is another important advantage of cloud based smart data analyzation, thereby liberating the burden of storing and carrying multiple hard copies of vital data.

(d) Absence of human intervention at any stage of the implementation nullify the probability of human error, thereby enhances the overall efficiency of the system.

(e) The proposed system indulges the concept of information deliverance in the form of Temporal Activity Granule. This aids the investigators in generating official evidence for possible culprits with less time delay, which in case of manual investigations in a daunting task.

(f) Availability of information about every activity and automated analyzation are other important benefits of the proposed system as compared to manual investigation.

V. CONCLUSION

In this paper, a framework for identification of possible culprit and internal extremists using smart data analytics is presented. The proposed model indulges various activities of concern for investigating officials in consideration to the terror incident. Analyzation of these activities using the power of smart data analysis is the premier objective of the proposed model. Moreover, based on specific suspicion level, every person is evaluated for his respective suspectibility index value, thereby providing an aid to investigating officials in determination of the culprit. Moreover, a two level decision model is presented that indulges specific activities and provides a list of possible candidates for culprits. The decision model indulges various data analyzation techniques for producing results with high accuracy and efficiency. In order to validate the proposed system, it is implemented in analyzing activities of 221 students using Internet of Things (IoT) Technology. Results obtained for different layers of the model shows that the system is highly efficient and effective in determination of the possible terrorist in time sensitive manner. However, there are many important challenges that must be considered in the future research. One of the them includes the information fusion of heterogeneous data in a common data storage. Such aspect plays crucial role in consideration to cloud based data abstraction. Another important challenge that must be addressed for efficient deployment of the system is to determine the appropriate threshold values from the domain experts.

REFERENCES

[1] Takaishi, T., Nishiyama, H., Kato, N. and Miura, R. (2014). "Toward energy efficient smart data gathering in densely distributed sensor networks." *IEEE Trans. Emerg. Top. Comput.*, 2(3): 388–397.

[2] Jin, X., Wah, B.W., Cheng, X. and Wang, Y. (2015). "Significance and Challenges of Smart Data Research." *Smart Data Res.*, 2(2): 59–64.

[3] Tan, W., Blake, M.B., Saleh, I. and Dustdar, S. (2013). "Social-Network-Sourced Smart Data Analytics." *IEEE Internet Comput.*, 17(5): 62–69.

[4] Zhang, F., Cao, J., Khan, S.U., Li, K. and Hwang, K. (2015). "A task-level adaptive map reduce framework for real-time streaming data in healthcare applications." *Futur. Gener. Comput. Syst.*, 43–44: 149–160.

[5] Akter, S. and Wamba, S.F. (2016). "Smart data analytics in E-commerce: A systematic review and agenda for future research." *Electron. Mark.-Int. J. Networked Bus.*, 26: 1–22.

[6] Philip Chen, C.L. and Zhang, C.Y. (2014). "Data-intensive applications, challenges, techniques and technologies: A survey on Smart Data." *Inf. Sci. (Ny).*, 275: 314–347.

[7] Kambatla, K., Kollias, G., Kumar, V. and Grama, A. (2014). "Trends in smart data analytics." *J. Parallel Distrib. Comput.*, 74(7): 2561–2573.

[8] Yang, C., Liu, C., Zhang, X., Nepal, S. and Chen, J. (2015). "A time efficient approach for detecting errors in smart sensor data on cloud." *IEEE Trans. Parallel Distrib. Syst.*, 26(2): 329–339.

[9] Rathore, M.M.U., Paul, A., Ahmad, A., Chen, B.W., Huang, B. and Ji, W. (2015). "Real-Time Smart Data Analytical Architecture for Remote Sensing Application." *IEEE J. Sel. Top. Appl. Earth Obs. Remote Sens.*, 8(10): 4610–4621.

[10] Fahad, A., Alshatri, N., Tari, Z., Alamri, A., Khalil, I., Zomaya, A.Y., Foufou, S. and Bouras, A. (2014). "A Survey of Clustering Algorithms for Smart Data: Taxonomy and Empirical Analysis." *IEEE Trans. Emer. Topic Compu.*, 2(3).

[11] Rodríguez-Mazahua, L., Rodríguez-Enríquez, C-A., Sánchez-Cervantes, J., Cervantes, J., García-Alcaraz, J. and Alor-Hernández, G. (2015). "A general perspective of Smart Data: Applications, tools, challenges and trends." *J. Supercomput.*, [Online] doi:10.1007/s11227-015-1501-1.

[12] Vandentorren, S., Paty, A-C., Baffert, E., Chansard, P. and Caserio-Schönemann, C. (2016). "Syndromic surveillance during the Paris terrorist attacks." *Lancet (London, England)*, 387(10021): 846–847.

[13] Alan Kronstadt, K. (2011). "Terrorist attacks in Mumbai, India and implications for U.S. interests." *In: Terrorist Attacks and Counterinsurgency Practices*, Nova Science Publishers, Inc., pp. 1–20.

[14] Claassen, C.A., Carmody, T., Stewart, S.M., Bossarte, R.M., Larkin, G.L., Woodward, W.A. and Trivedi, M.H. (2010). "Effect of 11 September 2001 terrorist attacks in the USA on suicide in areas surrounding the crash sites." *Br. J. Psychiatry*, 196(5): 359–364.

[15] Bjelopera, J.P. (2013). "The Federal Bureau of Investigation and Terrorism Investigations," *CRS Repor. Cong.*

[16] Gubbi, J., Buyya, R., Marusic, S. and Palaniswami, M. (2013). "Internet of Things (IoT): A vision, architectural elements and future directions." *Futur. Gener. Comput. Syst.*, 29(7): 1645–1660.

[17] Chen, Z., Xia, F., Huang, T., Bu, F. and Wang, H. (2013). "A localization method for the internet of things." *J. Supercomput.*, 63(3): 657–674.

[18] Dobre, C. and Xhafa, F. (2014). "Intelligent services for Smart data science." *Futur. Gener. Comput. Syst.*, 37: 267–281.

[19] Wu, X., Zhu, X., Wu, G-Q. and Ding, W. (2014). "Data mining with smart data." *IEEE Trans. Knowl. Data Eng.*, 26(1): 97–107.

[20] Zhang, L.J. (2012). "Editorial: Smart services era: Global trends of cloud computing and smart data." *IEEE Trans. Serv. Comput.*, 5(4): 467–468.

[21] O'Driscoll, A., Daugelaite, J. and Sleator, R.D. (2013). 'Smart data', Hadoop and cloud computing in genomics." *J. Biomed. Inform.*, 46(5): 774–781.

[22] Gandomi, A. and Haider, M. (2015). "Beyond the hype: Smart data concepts, methods and analytics."*Int. J. Inf. Manage.*, 35(2): 137–144.

[23] Han, H., Yonggang, W., Tat-Seng, C. and Xuelong, L. (2014). "Toward Scalable Systems for Smart Data Analytics: A Technology Tutorial." *Access, IEEE*, 2: 652–687.

[24] Chen, Y-C., Peng, W-C. and Lee, S.Y. (2015). "Mining Temporal Patterns in Time Interval-based Data." *IEEE Trans. Knowl. Data Eng.*, 27(12): 3318–3331.

[25] Ristoski, P. and Paulheim, H. (2016). "Semantic Web in data mining and knowledge discovery: A comprehensive survey." *Web Semant. Sci. Serv. Agents World Wide Web*, 36(1–22).

[26] Zheng, Y. (2015). "Methodologies for Cross-Domain Data Fusion: An Overview." *Smart Data, IEEE Trans.*, 1(1): 16–34.

[27] Altiparmak, F., Ferhatosmanoglu, H., Erdal, S. and Trost, D.C. (2006). "Information Mining Over Heterogeneous and High-Dimensional Time-Series Data in *Clinical Trials Databases*," 10(2): 254–263.

[28] Wang, G., Gunasekaran, A., Ngai, E.W.T. and Papadopoulos, T. (2016). "Smart data analytics in logistics and supply chain management: Certain investigations for research and applications." *Intern. J. Prod. Econ.*, 176: 98–110.

[29] De Sanctis, M., Bisio, I. and Araniti, G. (2016). "Data mining algorithms for communication networks control: Concepts, survey and guidelines." *IEEE Netw.*, 30(1): 24–29.

[30] Dubey, R., Samantaray, S.R., Panigrahi, B.K. and Venkoparao, V.G. (2016). "Data-analytics model based adaptive protection scheme to enhance distance relay performance during power swing." *Int. J. Electr. Power Energy Syst.*, 81: 361–370.

[31] Chen, L., Li, X., Yang, Y., Kurniawati, H., Sheng, Q.Z., Hu, H.Y. and Huang, N. (2016). "Personal health indexing based on medical examinations: A data mining approach." *Decis. Support Syst.*, 81: 54–65.

[32] Batra, S. and Sachdeva, S. (2016). "Organizing standardized electronic healthcare records data for mining." *Heal. Pol. Tec.* [Online], doi:10.1016/j.hlpt.2016.03.006

[33] Yang, H. and Chen, Y.P.P. (2015). "Data mining in lung cancer pathologic staging diagnosis: Correlation between clinical and pathology information." *Expert Syst. Appl.*, 42(15–16): 6168–6176.

[34] Gotz, D., Wang, F. and Perer, A. (2014). "A methodology for interactive mining and visual analysis of clinical event patterns using electronic health record data." *J. Biomed. Inform.*, 48: 148–159.

[35] Kim, J.H., Choi, G.S. and Das, C.R. (2007). "An SSL back-end forwarding scheme in cluster-based web servers." *IEEE Trans. Parallel Distrib. Syst.*, 18(7): 946–957.

[36] Ahmad, M., Amin, M.B., Hussain, S., Kang, B.H., Cheong, T. and Lee, S. (2016). "Health Fog: A novel framework for health and wellness applications." *J. Supercomput.*, [Online] doi:10.1007/s11227-016-1634-x.

[37] Lauría, E.J.M. and Duchessi, P.J. (2006). "A Bayesian Belief Network for IT implementation decision support." *Decis. Support Syst.*, 42(3): 1573–1588.

[38] Barua, S. and Sander, J. (2014). "Mining statistically significant co-location and segregation patterns." *IEEE Trans. Knowl. Data Eng.*, 26(5): 1185–1199.

[39] Huang, Y., Pei, J. and Xiong, H. (2006). "Mining co-location patterns with rare events from spatial data sets." *Geoinformatica*, 10(3): 239–260.

[40] Wang, L., Tao, J., Ranjan, R., Marten, H., Streit, A., Chen, J. and Chen, D. (2013). "G-Hadoop: MapReduce across distributed data centers for data-intensive computing." *Futur. Gener. Comput. Syst.*, 29(3): 739–750.

[41] Liu, Y., Xu, L. and Li, M. (2016). "The Parallelization of Back Propagation Neural Network in MapReduce and Spark." *Int. J. Parallel Program.*, [Online],doi:10.1007/s10766-016-0401-1.

[42] Amazon Cloud Services. Last Accessed on March 14, 2016.[Online]. Available:https://aws.amazon.com/ec2/.

[43] Stata. Last Accessed on April 1, 2016.[Online]. Available: http://www.stata.com/

3

A Brief Review on Electric Propulsion for Spacecrafts

LEMI TÜRKER[1]*

ABSTRACT

A great extent of weight/size of a spaceship is due to propellant load. One remedy for this burden seems to be the electric propulsion. Electric space propulsion is an intensively developing field addressing new demands and challenges for long-term spacecraft operation. Plasma propulsion concepts aim to find new acceleration principles, use alternative propellants, upscale or downscale thrusters for large thrust or for very small spacecrafts etc. This article presents a short review of electric propulsion (EP) technologies for satellites and spacecraft with brief past history and novel developments in main types of electric thrusters.

Key words: Electric propulsion, Thrusters, Resistojet, Arcjet, Ion thruster, Magnetoplasmadynamic thruster.

[1] Middle East Technical University, Ankara – TURKEY.

**Corresponding E-mail*: lturker@metu.edu.tr, lturker@gmail.com

INTRODUCTION

Spaceships are apt to be used for many purposes such as space research, voyages as well as space warfare in the future. Space warfare includes ground-to-space warfare as well as space-to-space warfare such as satellites attacking satellites. As the demand for commercial and military satellites has increased, parallel to that new thrust concepts and systems have been investigated. Note that the military satellites are indispensable in war and peace times for various purposes. To launch all those systems into orbit(s) space propulsion is necessary.

A few decades ago, space propulsion was defined by either chemical thrusters or cold gas thrusters with very few exceptions. Throughout most of the 20th century, electric propulsion was considered the technology of the future for spacecraft propulsion. Electric propulsion is a generic name given to ion thrusters. Electric propulsion systems convert electrical energy into directed kinetic energy of a propellant stored onboard, thus generating a thrust in a given direction. Hundreds of electric thrusters now operating in orbit on communications satellites, and ion and Hall thrusters both having been successfully used for primary propulsion in deep-space scientific missions. The literature contains several books from the 1960s and numerous journal articles and conference papers published over the years discussing electric thruster concepts, physics, technological developments and benefits. Various empirical investigations and laboratory-based development programs of different thruster types have emerged in the literature. Every development pushes the bar higher in terms of performance and along with this, mission schedules are being made tighter.

In this short review electric propulsion (EP) for satellites and spacecraft with brief past history and novel developments in the main types of electric thrusters have been presented.

EARLY HISTORY OF ELECTRIC ROCKETS

The history of electric propulsion (EP), spans almost the whole 20th century. Roughly, it is possible to subdivide the progress of the field from its start to its evolution into the concern of large corporations. Essentially, a series of five consecutive periods can be classified:

1. The era of visionaries (1906–1945)
2. The era of pioneers (1946–1956)
3. The era of diversification and development (1957–1979)
4. The era of acceptance (1980–1992)
5. The era of application (1993–present).

However, the above rough classification does not imply that the latter eras were lacking in visionaries or pioneers. Also it does not mean that EP was not used on spacecraft until 1993 or that vital conceptual developments did not occur before the 1960s[1,2]. Some milestones are;

1903: Konstantin E. Tsiolkovsky derives his famous "rocket equation," (see eq.1) which enables one to calculate fuel consumption for space missions. In 1911 he speculated that electric fields could accelerate charged particles to produce rocket thrust.

1906: Robert H. Goddard conceived electrostatic acceleration of charged particles for rocket propulsion. He invented and patented a precursor of the ion engine in 1917.

1954: Ernst Stuhlinger figured out how to optimize the performance of the electric ion rocket engine.

1962: Work by researchers in the Soviet Union, Europe and the U.S. led to the first published description of the Hall thruster, a more powerful class of plasma rocket.

1962: Adriano Ducati discovered the mechanism behind the magnetoplasmadynamic thruster, the most powerful type of plasma rocket.

1964: NASA's SERT I spacecraft conducted the first successful flight test of an ion engine in space.

1972: The Soviet Meteor satellite carried out the initial spaceflight of a Hall thruster.

1999: NASA's Jet Propulsion Laboratory's Deep Space-1 demonstrated the first use of an ion engine as the main propulsion system on a spacecraft that escapes.

The importance and attractiveness of EP for space transportation applications was recognized by the patriarch of modern rocketry, Robert H. Goddard, a century ago as early as 1906[2]. The early idea of electric propulsion for spacecraft dates back to 1911, introduced in a publication by Konstantin Tsiolkovsky[3]. Also it was mentioned by the German Hermann Oberth in his classic book on spaceflight in 1929. In the world, the first designed and tested electric propulsion was in 1929–1931 in Leningrad. The British team of Shepherd and Cleaver in 1949 is to be mentioned too. In 1950s by the initiation of S.P. Korolev, I.V. Kurchatov and L.A. Artsimovich EP adopted a program of research and development of various electrical rocket engines.

However, the first systematic and tutorial assessment of EP systems should be attributed to Ernst Stuhlinger. His book titled "*Ion Propulsion for Space Flight*" nicely summarizes his valuable studies of the 1950s[4].

In 1973 interstellar Project Daedalus by Dr. Tony Martin considered electrically powered propulsion with a nuclear reactor, but the novel approach was rejected because of very low thrust, the huge equipment needed for the conversion of nuclear energy into electricity, and as a result a small acceleration, that would take a century long time to achieve the desired speed[4].

The demonstration of electric propulsion concept and technology was an ion engine carried on board the SERT-1 (Space Electric Rocket Test) spacecraft (launched on 20 July 1964 with a pulsed plasma thruster, PPT) and its duration of operation was just 31 minutes. A follow-up mission (SERT-2) launched on 3 February 1970 carried two ion thrusters, one of which operated for more than five months and the other for almost three months. By the early 2010s, many satellite manufacturers were able to offer electric propulsion options on their satellites, mostly for on-orbit attitude control. Also, some commercial communication satellite operators were trying to use them for geosynchronous orbit insertion in place of traditional chemical rocket engines.

EP relies on the momentum conservation law like its chemical counterpart. In principle, a force, called the thrust, is exerted on a space vehicle by means of the ejection of matter with high kinetic energy. A distinctive feature of EP lies in the fact that it achieves high propellant exhaust speeds due to a large amount of electric energy, externally stored, but can be transferred to the propellant. A large ejection velocity directly means a low propellant consumption. So, propellant mass economy is one of the main advantages of EP with respect to chemical propulsion. In the later one acceleration originates from the conversion of chemical energy into kinetic energy through an expansion process. Additional advantages of an EP system are to be mentioned which include the long operation time and flexibility. On the other hand, the main disadvantage of EP is its very low thrust level, which is related to the power source limitation[5–7].

By the early 1980s, EP gradually entered its era of commercial application, as resistojet techniques became common options for station keeping and attitude control on tens of commercial spacecraft. In the following decade, early 1990s, electro thermal arcjets were adopted for north-south station keeping (NSSK) of many communication satellites in geosynchronous earth orbit (GEO). The year 1994 evidenced the first usage of electrostatic ion thrusters for the NSSK of commercial satellites. The year 1998 witnessed their application on a planetary NASA mission. Although Hall thrusters (HT) have been used on Soviet spacecrafts since the mid-1970s, and there have been already a few applications of pulsed plasma thrusters, electromagnetic thrusters were just entering their application era on Western commercial spacecrafts. The number of electrically propelled spacecraft has gone from a few number in the 1960s to double the digits in the 1970s and 1980s and in the late 1990s the number has reached the triple-digit mark. A recent trend in research and development has been the scaling down in both power level (100 W), and physical size of many EPs for the future applications on micro-spacecraft.

On the other hand, the physics of electric propulsion thrusters was first described comprehensively in a book by Robert Jahn[8] in 1968. George Brewer[9] in 1970 published the technology of early ion propulsion systems that used cesium and mercury propellants, along with the basics of low-thrust mission design and trajectory analysis. Since that time, focus concentrated on the basics of electric propulsion and some thruster characteristics and several chapters of textbooks published in the United States on spacecraft propulsion devoted for them[10–13]. In 1989 in a book, Grishin and Leskov made an extensive presentation of the principles and working processes of several electric thrusters[14]. Various significant electric propulsion research programs were established in the 1960s at the National Aeronautics and Space Administration (NASA) Glenn Research Center, NASA's Jet Propulsion Laboratory (JPL), Hughes Research Laboratories, and at various institutes in Russia to develop this technology for deep-space prime propulsion and satellite station-keeping applications. The first experimental ion thrusters using cesium and mercury propellants were launched into orbit in the early 1960s by the U.S. and Russia. Experimental test flights of ion thrusters and Hall thrusters continued from that time into the 1980s. The first extensive and remarkable application of electric propulsion was by Russia using Hall thrusters for station keeping on communications satellites[15]. Since 1971 when the Soviets first flew a pair of SPT-60s on the Meteor satellite, over 238 Hall thrusters have been operated on 48 spacecraft to date[16]. In 1995 Japan launched the first ion thruster system intended for north–south station keeping on the communications satellite "Engineering Test Satellite (ETS) VI"[17]. Although occurrence of a launch vehicle failure did not permit station keeping by this system, the ion thrusters were operated successfully in space. In the United States the commercial use of ion thrusters started in 1997 with the launch of a Hughes Xenon Ion Propulsion System (XIPS)[18] and the first NASA deep-space mission using the NASA Solar Electric Propulsion Technology Applications Readiness (NSTAR) ion thruster was launched in 1998 on Deep Space-1[19]. Hughes/Boeing launched their second-generation 25-cm XIPS ion thruster system[20] in 2000 for station-keeping applications on the high-power 702 communications satellite[21]. Meanwhile, the Japanese have successfully used ion thrusters in order to provide the prime propulsion for the Hayabusa asteroid sample return mission[22]. The European Space Agency (ESA) has used Snecma's PPS-1350-G Hall thruster on its SMART-1 mission to the moon[23].

The Russians have been steadily launching communications satellites with Hall thrusters aboard and it seems they will continue to use these devices for future station keeping applications[16]. The first commercial use of Hall thrusters by a U.S. spacecraft manufacturer was in 2004 on Space Systems Loral's MBSAT which used the Fakel SPT-100[24]. Additional ion and Hall thruster launches have been planned in the U.S. in the near future using thrusters produced by commercial vendors[25–27]. In the past 2–3 decades, electric propulsion use in spacecraft has steadily grown worldwide. Moreover, advanced electric thrusters have emerged over that time in several scientific missions as an attractive alternative to chemical thrusters for station-keeping applications in geosynchronous communication satellites. Rapid growth has occurred in the last 10–20 years in the use of ion thrusters and Hall thrusters in communications satellites to reduce the mass of propellant for station keeping as well as orbit insertion. The U.S. and the Russians have now each flown far exceeding a hundred thrusters in communications satellites. The trend indicates that they will continue to launch more ion and Hall thrusters in the future. The use of these technologies for primary propulsion in deep-space scientific applications has also been increasing over the past decade. There exist many planned launches of new communications satellites as well as scientific missions that use ion and Hall thrusters in the coming years parallel to the acceptance of the reliability and cost benefits of these systems grows along positive direction.

Typical operating parameters for thrusters are presented in Tables 1, 2 and 3 show some recently launched spacecrafts and some planned missions both involving electric propulsion systems. The thruster types mentioned in those tables are considered in sections below.

Table 1: Typical operating parameters for thrusters[12].

Thruster	*Propellant*	*Input Power (kW)*	*Specific Impulse (s)*	*Efficiency Range(%)*
Cold gas	Various		50–75	
Chemical (mono-propellant)	N_2H_4 H_2O_2		150–225	
Chemical (bi-propellant)	Various		300–450	
Resistojet	N_2H_4 monoprop	0.5–1	300	65–90
Arcjet	N_2H_4 monoprop	0.9–2.2	500–600	25–45
Ion thruster	Xenon	0.4–4.3	2500–3600	40–80
Hall thrusters	Xenon	1.5–4.5	1500–2000	35–60
PPTs	Teflon	<0.2	850–1200	7–13

SOME FACTS ABOUT ROCKETS

In the light of the drawbacks of conventional rockets the benefits afforded by plasma engines become most striking evident. In their minds, people usually imagine a spaceship streaking through the dark void toward a distant planet, trails a long, fiery plume through its nozzles. Yet the truth is totally different: voyages to the outer solar system have been mostly rocketless affairs. Most of the fuel

Table 2: Some recently launched spacecrafts using electric propulsion.

Spacecraft name	***Launch date***	***Thruster type***	***No***	***Model***	***Propellant***	***Spacecraft customer***
BS-3A	2 Mar 2015	Ion engine	4	XIPS-25	Xenon	ABS
Satmex 7 (now: Eutelsat 115 West B)	2 Mar 2015	Ion engine	4	XIPS-25	Xenon	Satmex
BRICsat-P	20 May 2015	Vacuum arc Thruster	4	μCAT		USNA
KaiTuo-1A (XinJiShu YanZheng-2)	19 Sep 2015	Hall-effect thruster	1 1(Unnamed)	LHT-100	Xenon	
ABS-2A	15 Jun 2016	Ion engine	4	XIPS-25	Xenon	ABS
Satmex 9 (now: Eutelsat 117 West B)	15 Jun 2016	Ion engine	4	XIPS-25	Xenon	Satmex
AOBA-VELOX III	9 Dec 2016	Pulsed plasma thruster	1		PTFE	NTU KIT
Hispasat 36W-1 (Small GEO)	27 Jan 2017	Hall effect thruster	8	PPS-1350	Xenon	Hispasat

is typically consumed in the first few minutes of operation, leaving the spacecraft to coast the rest of the way to its goal. Although, chemical rockets do launch all spacecraft from Earth's surface and can make midcourse trajectory corrections, they are impractical for powering deep-space explorations due to requirement of huge quantities of fuel, such that too much to be lifted into an orbit practically and affordably. To achieve the necessary trajectories having high speeds for long, lengthy, high-precision journeys without additional fuel, seems to be unpractical. Many deep-space probes of the past have had to spend very long time although their

Table 3: Some planned missions involving electric propulsion.

Spacecraft name	*Launch date*	*Thruster type*	*No*	*Model*	*Prope-llant*	*Space craft custo-mer*	*Space craft name*
NovaSAR	2017	Resistojet Quad Confinement Thruster	1 1		Xenon		SSTL/ ADS UK
Ionozond (Ionosfere 1 & 2)	2017	Pulsed plasma thruster		APPT-95	PTFE		Roskosmos
PEGASUS	2017	Pulsed plasma thruster			PTFE		FH Wiener Neustadt
SES 15	2017	Ion engine	4	XIPS-25	Xenon		SES World Skies
BepiColombo	2018	Ion engine	4	T6	Xenon		ESA & JAXA
Eutelsat 172B	2017	Hall-effect thruster		PPS5000	Xenon		Eutelsat
GSAT-9	2017	Hall-effect thruster			Xenon		ISRO
ShiJian-13 (SJ-13)	2017	Ion engine		LIPS-200	Xenon		
VENμS	2017	Hall-effect thruster	2	IHET-300	Xenon		ISA & CNES
Neosat	2018	Hall-effect thruster		PPS5000	Xenon		ESA
Dong Fang Hong-5	2018	Ion engine		LIPS-300	Xenon		

way to planets or moons providing gravitational kicks to accelerate them in the desired direction (slingshot moves called gravity-assist maneuvers). Such long and complex flight paths is the limitations of missions. Only blasting off within a certain short time frame will ensure a precision swing while a cosmic body serving as a gravitational booster. Even worse than that, after many years of travel toward its destination, a vehicle with a chemical rocket motor would unfortunately have no fuel left for braking. Such a probe would obviously need the ability to fire its rocket so that it could slow down sufficiently enough to achieve an orbit around its target in order to perform some extended scientific observations. Otherwise, it would be limited to merely a fleeting encounter with the object it aimed to explore[1]. Indeed, New Horizons, a NASA deep-space probe launched in 2006, will get only a brief encounter the recently demoted "dwarf planet" Pluto after a trip of more than nine years.

ELECTRIC THRUSTER TYPES

A strong advantage of electric propulsion comparing to other propulsion systems (such as chemical or cold gas propulsion) follows from a direct well-controlled acceleration of the propellant to very high velocities[28]. With higher exhaust velocities, the same amount of propellant can produce a higher velocity gain $\ddot{A}V$ of the spacecraft, as given by the 'ideal' rocket equation[9,12,28]:

$$\ddot{A}V = V_{ex} Ln(m_0/m_1) \quad (1)$$

where V_{ex} is the propellant exhaust velocity and m_0 and m_1 are initial and final or dry mass of the spacecraft, respectively.

In electric thrusters electrons are introduced into a flowing inert gas, either Argon or Xenon, under the influence of either an electric field; both an electric and a magnetic field; or an electromagnetic wave in the radio or microwave frequency range. Once a plasma is created ions are extracted using electrical fields, often using grids or orifices that have been designed to produce an optimal ion beam for operation periods of more than 10,000 hours. Plasma creation and ion extraction occur concurrently with the ions being made neutral once they leave, by emitting electrons into the beam.

Electric thrusters (EP) are generally described in terms of the acceleration method used to produce the thrust. EP technologies may be divided into three broad categories according to the way thrust is generated: electro thermal, electrostatic and electromagnetic propulsion. There are, of course, many types of propulsion these days all with a specific purpose. Here are some examples:

Resistor jets and colloid thrusters.

Field-emission electric propulsion (FEEP).

Ferroelectric thrusters and pulsed plasma thrusters.

Gridded ion thrusters – Kaufman, microwave or radio-frequency.

Hall-Effect thrusters.

Magneto-plasma-dynamic thrusters.

Common EP thruster types are described in the following sections[9,13].

Resistojet

Technically, resistojets are electro thermal devices which operate such a manner that the propellant is heated by passing through a resistively heated chamber or over a resistively heated element before entering a downstream nozzle. The increase in exhaust velocity is due to the thermal heating of the propellant, which limits the I_{sp} to low levels (<500 s)[9].

Traditionally cold gas nitrogen systems have been used as they provide a simple solution, combining high reliability with low cost and heritage. However cold gas systems tend to be limited by fairly low specific impulses and poor storage densities. So, they need to be improved. One method of enhancing their performance, hence extending the mission life, is based on heating the propellant to achieve a higher exhaust velocity. When this is done by means of electrical resistance heaters it is known as a resistojet. Note that one feature of small satellites is that they are often power limited. Hence a balance must be accomplished between the propulsion system power requirements and the rest of the spacecraft.

Principally a resistojet generates thrust by heating a fluid using the Joule effect[8,27–30]. Namely, the gas is first heated electrically, passing through resistance heaters of various geometries. Then the hot gas at temperature T is expanded through a convergent–divergent solid nozzle to create thrust. The specific impulse therefore increases as square root of T. All gaseous propellants can be used, as possible as they are compatible with the heater material. The temperature in the resistojet chamber is constrained to about 3000 K due to properties of the wall material. The I_{sp} then reaches around 300 s, which is well above the value achieved with a cold gas thruster with a small increase in complexity and a high efficiency above 50%[31].

The design is very flexible and the parameters specified below can be varied over a large range to customize the thruster to different mission requirements:

The propellants might be: Nitrogen, Xenon, Butane, and other gases.

Measured performance: up to 100 s (subject to propellant and operation).

Thrust: up to 100 mN.

Operating temperature: up to 500° C.

Feed Pressure: up to 10 bar.

Redundant heaters.

K-type thermocouple to monitor thruster temperature.

Heat shield included.

The thruster has been subjected to thermal cycles from 50° C to 500° C.

Although resistojets have a low I_{sp} level, they are attractive because they can be easily integrated, they use the propellant management system of chemical thrusters and they operate at low voltage, which does not necessitate complicated power conditioning equipment. In addition, resistojets are low-cost, reliable and safe devices[31].

Gibbon *et al.*, in their article have described some of the features and limitations of usage of resistojets on small spacecraft and the evolution of the Surrey family of thrusters[32].

Traditionally in small spacecraft either cold gas nitrogen propulsion systems or hydrazine monopropellant systems have been used. The move from nitrogen to hydrazine gives an affirmative step shift in the system performance, although it also gives a step change in the cost. Surrey Satellite Technology Ltd, SSTL's, current generation of spacecraft typically require a delta V capability somewhere between that of nitrogen and hydrazine, however a hydrazine system is cost prohibitive[32].

The first flight having resistojet thruster developed at Surrey Space Centre was a 100 Watt resistojet, which was flown on the UoSAT-12 spacecraft in 1999. UoSAT-12 was a 325 kg spacecraft, which generated in the order of 60 Watts orbit average power. Hence, the 100 Watt power supply requirement of the thruster was reasonably acceptable for short durations, whilst the payloads were switched off.

The advantage of using a resistojet with nitrous oxide over a conventional cold gas propulsion system can be seen by examining the UoSAT-12 spacecraft budgets. The resistojet system used 2.1 kg of nitrous oxide to give up to 9.7 m/sec delta V on the spacecraft. There was also a cold gas nitrogen system on UoSAT-12. This uses 6.4 kg of N_2 to give the spacecraft 14 m/sec delta V. Although, the nitrous oxide resistojet system has around a third of the propellant mass, but gave two thirds the performance. The nitrous oxide system also had a much lower dry mass and lower volume[32].

A smaller, lower power resistojet thruster was designed and first experimented on ALSAT-1 spacecraft in Nov 2002. The thruster mass was reduced from 1,200 grams to 60 grams and the power consumption decreased from a single 100 Watt heater to prime and redundant 15 Watt heaters. By reducing the mass of substantial thermal insulation, major mass and volume savings were achieved on the 100 Watt unit to a simple heat shield on the 15 Watt unit. This approach has a number of advantages and disadvantages. Namely, it reduces the maximum operating temperature from 800°C to around 500°C. Hence the increase in I_{sp} is not as marked. It also reduces the mass flow rate, hence thrust. However the warm up time is faster with the smaller unit.

Arcjet

Another electro thermal thruster is known as arcjet that heats the propellant simply by passing it though a high current arc in line with the nozzle feed system. The purpose is to overcome the temperature limitation of a resistojet by passing an electrical arc directly through the gas flow. A high-current arc (100 A) is created between the conical tip of a rod, which acts as a cathode, and a divergent nozzle that serves as an anode[31]. The two electrodes are made of tungsten that has a high melting point. Thorium is often incorporated into the cathode material to enhance electron emission. Although, there is an electric discharge involved in the propellant path, plasma effects are insignificant on the exhaust velocity because the propellant is weakly ionized. The I_{sp} is limited (by the thermal heating) to less than about 700 s for most of the easily stored propellants.

Generally, arcjets operate under standard conditions at an input power level of a few kW[33–35]. The usual propellant is mostly either ammonia or hydrazine. The specific impulse is therefore around 500 s. However, an I_{sp} level above 1000 s was achieved with hydrogen and helium[36,38]. Note that low-power arcjet thrusters operating at around 100 W have also been developed for micro-satellites[38]. Water-cooled arcjets were available operated at 100 kW during short periods here on Earth, with a thrust level up to 4 N[36]. Usually the lifetime of the device is only a few hundreds hours. It has limitations determined by erosion and evaporation of the cathode material under ion bombardment in the arc chamber, especially at discharge ignition. The main handicaps of arcjet thrusters are the relatively short lifetime and the unstable character of the arc plasma.

Ion Thruster

The thermal expansion process highly limits the specific impulse to moderate values, even with light propellants. Then the only way to increase the I_{sp} level and the thrust density is to turn towards magnetic and electric interactions instead[8,28,39,40].

Category of ion thrusters employ a variety of plasma generation techniques in order to ionize a large fraction of the propellant being used. These thrusters technically utilize biased grids to electrostatically extract ions from the plasma and then accelerate them to high velocity at voltages up to or exceeding 10 kV. Ion thrusters feature the highest efficiency (from 60% to >80%) and very high specific impulse values (from 2000 to over 10,000 s) compared to other thruster types. Nowadays, many novel plasma propulsion concepts try to find new acceleration principles, upscale or downscale thrusters, use alternative propellants, in order to get large thrust or for very small spacecrafts etc. Rafalskyi and Aanesland reviewed the neutralizer-free concepts, where both positive and negative particles are extracted and accelerated from plasmas[41]. They categorically classified these concepts into three, defined by their acceleration principle: i) neutral beam generation, ii) plasma acceleration/expansion and iii) bipolar beam acceleration. They described the basic physical principles and additionally evaluate the main advantages and drawbacks in view of general space applications. They also presented further details on a rather recent concept where RF voltages are used to speed up quasi-simultaneously positive ions and electrons from the same source[41].

The neutral beam propulsion concepts have represented by only one system (CXT thruster) in which the system ions are accelerated from plasma and converted into a fast neutral beam by charge-exchange process. Although some significant progress has been achieved, total thruster efficiency remains one of the crucial parameters that needs to be improved significantly.

The biggest group of neutralizer-free plasma propulsion systems is based on plasma acceleration concepts. This group is represented by the PPT concept which has been already tested in space, by the various prospective concepts based on free plasma expansion and $\boldsymbol{J} \times \boldsymbol{B}$ acceleration (coaxial ECR, RMF, HDLT, VAT, CAT etc). The performances observed such as specific impulse and thrust efficiency for the plasma acceleration concepts are generally inferior than the performances provided by the traditional electric propulsion systems (ion and Hall thrusters). However, these types of thrusters can be easily downscaled. Moreover, they require simple control onboard and a minimal number of subsystems, all of which make them very attractive for many applications. On the other hand, the beam acceleration concepts are represented by devices based on simultaneous, alternate or quasi-simultaneous acceleration of negative and positive ions or positive ions and electrons extracted from plasma by using the polarized grids. The strong advantage of beam acceleration concepts compared to other neutralizer-free plasma propulsion systems emerges from strong technological heritage with already existing ion thrusters. Rafalskyi and Aanesland briefly described the Pegases and fullerene-filled ion–ion thruster concepts, and ion–electron concepts based on RF acceleration[41].

Hall Thruster

The Hall thrusters (HT) are some electrical propulsion devices for spacecraft that use an electric discharge with magnetized electrons to ionize and accelerate a propellant gas. The system relies on a fundamental effect discovered in 1879 by Edwin H. Hall. In this type of an electrostatic thruster a cross-field discharge, described by the Hall effect, is applied to generate the plasma. An electric field established perpendicular to an applied magnetic field enables one to accelerate ions electrostatically to high exhaust velocities, while the transverse magnetic field inhibits electron motion that would tend to short out the electric field[9,13].

In a typical HT, the electrostatic acceleration of heavy atomic ions to high velocity occurs within the core of the discharge glow, which implies the use of a magnetized plasma able to sustain internal electric fields. Electrons gain energy in the electric field, then they ionize the neutral atoms inside the channel. The propellant gas is introduced through the back of the channel (either through the anode or using a dedicated injection system).

Although, HTs provide a moderate specific impulse levels (<2000 s) the thrust-to-power ratio is about 60 mN kW^{-1} and the thrust density is >30 N m^{-2}. Note that there is no space-charge limitation on the ion current. The thrust efficiency is about 50%, but it is in excess of 60% for high-power thrusters. Losses of various origins occurs in an HT [28,42–44].

Generally Hall thrusters are very efficient and competitive electric propulsion devices for satellites. They are currently in use in a number of telecommunications and government spacecraft. Their power spans from 100W to 20 kW, with thrust ranging between a few mN and 1N and specific impulse values between 1000 and 3000 s. As mentioned above the basic idea of Hall thrusters consists of generation a large local electric field in a plasma by using a transverse magnetic field to reduce the electron conductivity. This electric field can extract positive ions from the plasma and accelerate them to high velocity without extracting grids, providing the thrust. Despite these principles are very simple in appearance but the physics behind Hall thrusters is very intricate and non-linear. The complexity is due to electron transport across the magnetic field. Also, its coupling with the electric field and the neutral atom density further complicates the picture.

The main drawback of conventional HTs is the fact that the wall material determines to a large extent (through the secondary electron emission) the discharge properties, and consequently, the performance level as well as the operational lifetime[31]. Erosion occurs when the ion kinetic energy is above the sputtering threshold of the dielectric compound.

The paper by Boeuf describes the basic physics of Hall thrusters and gives a summary of the research efforts through the years that have been devoted to the modeling and understanding of these devices. Although the predictive capabilities of the models are still not sufficient enough for a full computer aided design of Hall thrusters, nevertheless significant progress has been made both in the qualitative and quantitative understanding of these devices[45].

Electron interactions with walls as well as instabilities and turbulence contribute to the enhancement of electron transport across the magnetic field. At the optimized operating point of Hall thrusters, the electron conductivity is sufficiently small to allow efficient ion extraction by a large electric field localized close to the maximum magnetic field. The physics of anomalous cross-field transport arising from electron-wall collisions or turbulence is complex and due to this complexity the development of fully self-consistent and predictive Hall thruster models has been prevented[45].

General Hall thruster (HT) efficiency and specific impulse is somewhat less than that achievable in ion thrusters. However, the thrust at a given power is higher and the device is much simpler and requires fewer power supplies to operate. The first successfully operated HT in space dated back to 1972 (aboard the former USSR Meteor satellite)[46]. The results of various works along with details about the HT physics, architecture and operation can be found in several books and reviews[47–49].

HTs are technologically compact and robust EP devices that offer interesting features in terms of thrust-to-power ratio, efficiency and mass. In addition, the associated power unit is more basic. They, therefore represent an attractive propulsion means for satellites. Of those, low-power HTs (H"100 W) are well suited for drag compensation of observation satellites which operate on a low-altitude Earth orbit and for trajectory correction of micro satellite constellations as well. On the other hand, 1 to 2 kW class of HTs have long been employed for attitude correction and station keeping of geosynchronous satellites.

HTs also appear to be good candidates for moving space probes, such as demonstrated by the successful SMART-1 moon flyby solar-powered mission[50].

Of the many types, cylindrical geometry Hall thrusters have lower surface-to-volume ratio than conventional thrusters and, thus, the technology seems to be more promising for scaling down. The cylindrical Hall thruster (CHT) is fundamentally different from the conventional design in the way that the electrons are confined and the ion space charge is neutralized[42,51,52]. Further details can be found in the cited references.

Small Hall thrusters are ideal so that they can handle higher amounts of power to generate greater exhaust speeds and thrust levels. The work also aims to extend their operating lifetimes to the multiyear durations needed for deep space exploration.

The Plasma Physics Laboratory of UnB has been developing a thruster called permanent magnet Hall thruster (PHALL) for the UNIESPAÇO program, which is a part of the Brazilian space activities program (PNAE) since 2004[53]. Indeed the idea of using an array of permanent magnets, instead of an electromagnet, to produce a radial magnetic field inside the plasma channel of the thruster is very significant. Because it allows the development of a Hall thruster with power consumption low enough to be used in small-and medium-size satellites. The PHALL project consists on plasma source design, its construction and characterization of the Hall-type propulsion engine using several plasma diagnostics sensors. PHALL is basically a plasma source in which a Hall current is generated inside a cylindrical channel possessing an axial electric field produced by a ring anode and a radial magnetic field produced by many permanent magnets. Ferreira *et al.*, presented a brief description of the plasma propulsion engine, its diagnostics instrumentation and measured plasma parameters with a focus on possible applications of PHALL on orbit transfer maneuvering for future Brazilian geostationary satellite space missions[53]. Specifically, they showed plasma density and temperature space profiles inside and outside the thruster channel, ion temperature measurements based on Doppler broadening of spectral lines and ion energy measurements. Relying on the measured plasma parameters, they constructed an aptitude figure of the PHALL. It contained the specific impulse, total thrust, propellant flow rate and power consumption necessary for orbit raising of satellites. Based on previous studies of geosynchronous satellite orbit positioning they performed numerical simulations of satellite orbit raising from an altitude of 700–36,000 km using a PHALL operating in the 100–500 mN thrust range. The main simulation parameters were orbit raising time, fuel mass, total satellite mass, thrust and exhaust velocity. They compared their results with results obtained with known space missions performed with Hall thrusters[53].

One way to further raise the thrust density of plasma propulsion is to increase the total amount of plasma that is accelerated in the engine. Unfortunately, as the plasma density in a Hall thruster is raised, electrons collide more frequently with atoms and ions, which makes it more difficult for the electrons to carry the Hall current needed for acceleration. An alternative known as the magnetoplasmadynamic thruster (MPDT) allows for a denser plasma by forgoing the Hall current in favor of a current component (see section 2.6).

Recently, Miyasaka *et al.,* investigated interference effects on discharge characteristics for the cluster system that was initiated. For the characterization purpose of cluster operations, a side-by-side (SBS) system comprising two anode layer heads and a hollow cathode was developed. In this study, discharge characteristics for a two-head anode layer thruster system (SBS operation) and a single thruster system (single operation) were compared to investigate interference effects of multi-head operation. As the discharge currents in SBS operation increased relative to those in single operation it was observed that the discharge current oscillation amplitudes in SBS operation at coil currents increased substantially relative to those in single operation. Likely cause of increases in the discharge current and ionization oscillation amplitude should be due to plume interference of the two heads. The differences in the discharge current and ionization oscillation amplitude between same direction and opposite-direction applied magnetic fields were found to be small[54]. The results reveal that the interference from the magnetic fields and electric potentials applied by the two heads have little effect on discharge characteristics.

A mode transition phenomenon was found in Hall thrusters, which was induced by the increase of the magnetic field gradient. In the transition process, Han *et al.*, experimentaly observed that there have been obvious changes in the oscillation characteristics, including the mean value of the discharge current, the thrust, the anode efficiency, and the plume pattern. The shifting and compression of the high magnetic field causes the electron density in the discharge channel to decrease and the ionization zone to move towards the exit plane. This also corresponds to a low atom density in the discharge channel, resulting in a loss of stability of the ionization at a high magnetic field gradient, which presents the transition of the discharge mode[55].

It has been observed that Hall plasmas with magnetized electrons and unmagnetized ions display a wide range of small scale fluctuations in the lower-hybrid frequency range as well as low-frequency large scale modes. Modulational instability of lower-hybrid frequency modes is investigated by Lakhin *et al.*, for typical conditions in Hall plasma devices such as magnetrons and Hall thrusters[56]. In these conditions, the dispersion of the waves in the lower-hybrid frequency range propagating perpendicular to the external magnetic field arises from the gradients of the magnetic field and the plasma density. It is shown that such lower-hybrid modes are unstable with respect to the secondary instability of the large scale quasimode perturbations. The authors suggested that the large scale slow coherent modes observed in a number of Hall plasma devices may be explained as a result of such secondary instabilities[56].

On the other hand, Lafleur and coworkers recently have demonstrated (using particle-in-cell simulations) the definite correlation between an anomalously high cross-field electron transport in Hall effect thrusters (HETs), and the presence of azimuthal electrostatic instabilities leading to enhanced electron scattering[57]. They proposed a kinetic theory that predicts the enhanced scattering rate providing an electron cross-field mobility that is in good agreement with experiment. The large azimuthal electron drift velocity in HETs drives a strong instability that quickly saturates due to a combination of ion-wave trapping and wave-convection, leading to an enhanced mobility having many orders of magnitude larger than that of expected from the classical diffusion theory. In addition to the magnetic field strength, B_0, this enhanced mobility is a strong function of the plasma properties (such as the plasma density) and therefore does not, in general, follow simple $1/B^2_0$ or $1/B_0$ scaling laws[57].

Grimaud *et al.*, investigated the Emissive and Langmuir probes which are two widely used plasma diagnostic techniques that, when used properly, give access to a wide range of information on the plasma's ions and electrons[58]. It was shown that their use in small and medium power Hall thrusters produces large perturbations in the discharge characteristics. The investigation included some potential measurements, performed by both probes and non-invasive laser induced fluorescence (LIF) spectroscopy, highlighted significant discrepancies in the discharge profile. This phenomenon was observed both in the 200 W and the 1.5 kW-class thrusters. In order to get a better understanding of these perturbations, ion velocity distribution functions were acquired by LIF spectroscopy at different positions in the smaller thruster, with and without the probes. Emissive probes were shown to produce the highest perturbation, shifting the acceleration region upstream. Insertion of the probe was also shown to have significant effect on both the average discharge current, increasing it by as much as 30%, and its harmonic content in both amplitude and spectrum. These perturbations appeared as the probe tip possessed a threshold location between 0-5 mm downstream of the thruster exit plane[58]. Various inventions on Hall thrusters have been patented considering improvement of the technology[59–62]. Also various simulations have been performed on Hall thrusters[63–68].

Significant progress has been made in the last two decades comprising the diagnostics, modeling, and theory of Hall thrusters. Thus, the influence of electron-wall interaction of cross-field transport can now more accurately be calculated. Moreover, the genesis of the most effective oscillations, plasma instabilities and their contribution to anomalous transport characteristics are much better understood in recent years[45].

Electrospray/Field Emission Electric Propulsion Thruster

These two types of thrusters are electrostatic electric propulsion devices that generate very low thrust (<1 mN). Electrospray thrusters extract ions or charged droplets from conductive liquids which are sprayed through small needles. Then the thrusters accelerate them electrostatically with biased, aligned apertures to high energy. Whereas field emission electric propulsion (FEEP) thrusters wick or transport liquid metals (typically cesium or indium) along needles, extracting ions from the sharp tip by field emission processes. Due to their very low thrust, these devices are to be used for precision control of spacecraft position or attitude in space.

Prince considered ionic liquids in electric propulsion[69]. Due to the negligible vapor pressure, significant electric conductivities and thermal stability of ionic liquids (IL's) they attracts attention and have made them exceptionally good candidates for electrospray space propulsion applications for small space vehicles. Recently, energetic ionic liquids have been proposed for use both in electrospray thrusters and combustion, thus adding some versatility to their potential missions. The work of Prince also considers the associated physics with these fuels in single cone-jet electrosprays and it is discussed along with the recent developments with respect to these sources. Specific examples were provided including electrospray thrusters employing solutions of hydroxylammonium nitrate /water (HAN) as well as thrusters utilizing 1-butyl-3-methyl-imidazolium dicyanamide (BMIM-DCA)[69].

Ionic liquids for space propulsion, was also the topic of a chapter written by Chiu and; Dressler[70]. The chapter provides an introduction to current requirements in space propulsion, and summarizes the virtues of ionic liquid propelled electrospray thrusters. The physics associated with single cone-jet electrosprays is reviewed and recent developments with respect to ionic liquid ion sources are discussed. Specific examples of mass spectrometric measurements of charged particle emission from ionic liquid cone-jets are presented. The results include positive and negative ion emissions from certain ionic liquids ([Emim] [BF_4], [Emim] [Im] and [Emim] [NO_3])[70].

High resolution time-of-flight mass spectral analysis of vacuum electrospray ionization of ionic liquids was investigated by Ticknor and Chiu[71]. Because of their low vapor pressure and high electric conduction, ionic liquids (ILs) are recognized as ideal candidates for electrospray space propulsion systems. As an additional advantage these types of electrospray thrusters can be miniaturized with no loss of efficiency which is a significant advantage over current plasma electric thruster technology. Previously, the authors had used quadrupole mass spectrometry (QMS) to study the vacuum electrospray ionization of the ILs, 1-ethyl-3-methyl-imidazolium bis(trifluoromethylsulfonyl) imide and 1-butyl-3-methyl-imidazolium dicyanamide from an externally wetted tungsten emitter. Unfortunately, the limited mass resolution attainable with QMS, had prevented a detailed study of the fragmentation products generated in the vacuum electrospray source. To overcome this problem, the ion source was successfully coupled (*via* orthogonal injection) into a new high resolution reflectron time-of-flight mass spectrometer (RTOF-MS).

In the article some data from the RTOF-MS are presented, including a comparison to the previous QMS data and an analysis of the ionic species produced[71].

In addition to experimental studies present in the literature, also many simulation work, based on molecular dynamics (MD), exist on electrospray thruster. Borner *et al.*, have investigated an electrospray thruster for the ionic liquid (IL) EMIM-BF_4 using two coarse-grained (CG) potentials[72]. Different equilibrium properties were obtained for the two potentials and then both were used to study the electrical extrusion of the IL for different electric field strengths and mass flow rates. The MD simulations have provided the first insight into the atomistic modeling of a capillary-tip-extractor system, which constitutes the basic elements of an electrospray thruster. One of the CG potentials was found to predict the formation of the Taylor cone (the cone-jet) and other extrusion modes for similar electric fields and mass flow rates observed in the experiments of a IL fed capillary-tip-extractor system. In the study, current distributions and anion and cation behavior were characterized and estimated thrust and specific impulse values were presented which conformed reasonably well to the measurements. Moreover, inhomogeneities in the electric field as well as that of the IL space-charge were believed as the most likely causes that their amelioration would improve the agreement between modeling and experiment[72].

Borner *et al.*, also modeled (by means of Molecular dynamics simulations) the behavior of the EMIM-BF4 ionic liquid for conditions similar to those of electrospray thrusters[73]. In order to study the physics of ion extrusion, a large system composed of approximately 2160 ion pairs was introduced inside a platinum capillary and equilibrated. Also an electric field was applied to the system along the longitudinal direction. Then, the fraction of solvated and non-solvated emitted ions, as well as the internal configuration of those clusters, were analyzed. A moving-potential-wall model was adopted to generate a mass flow inside the capillary and a Taylor cone was observed in the case of an extrusion event with ionic liquid mass flow[73,74].

Field emission electric propulsion thrusters which are using liquid cesium have currently been actively developed in Europe. It is important to measure the mass flow rate of neutral cesium emitted by the thruster for studies and design purposes of thruster-spacecraft interaction. The measurement requires the characterization of the neutral cesium plume. Elias *et al.*, have managed this characterization using a specially developed setup connected to a laser-induced fluorescence velocimetry to probe the three components of the neutral cesium velocity for a field emission electric propulsion thruster employed as the representative of a flight model[75].

The results gave mappings of the plume velocity and number of density along two planes intercepting the neutral plume for four different thruster operating conditions. Mass flow rates were obtained by integration of the local flow rates. The neutral cesium mass flow rate was in the milligrams /h range; it increased with the thrust and with emitter temperature. Mean neutral velocity can be as high as 800–1000 m s^{-1}. The results show that the neutral mass flow rate has of the same order of magnitude as the ion mass flow rate computed from the thruster current. The work has provided the first direct measurement of neutral cesium mass flow rate and thruster efficiency. In other words, more generally, the first mapping of the neutral plume from this field emission electric propulsion thruster. The authors' conjecture is that the technique employed could be extended to probe dimeric cesium in the plume[75].

Other candidate metals or alloys which could replace Cs as a propellant in field emission thruster were selected *via* a literature survey and tested by Stewart and coworkers[76]. The criteria considered in the selection of the alternative propellants were a low electric resistivity /thermal conductivity ratio, low m.p., and high atomic mass. Other criteria considered include toxicity, vapor pressure, beam efficiency, wetting characteristics, cost and possible interaction with materials used in the manufacture of the thruster. Some important parameters of the propellants selected compared with those of Cs. Experimental evaluation of the wetting properties of these selected propellants was given for Ti, W, Mo, W alloy and stainless steel[76].

Buldrini *et al.*, experimentally studied the Machian mass fluctuation effect using a μN thrust balance developed for field emission thrusters[77].

Lenard *et al.*, used Indium Field Emission Thruster (In-FET) which is a highly characterized and space-proven device based on space-qualified liquid metal ion sources[78]. In another study, field-emission electric propulsion was applied as a liquid metal ion source in thrusters for electric space propulsion[79]. The effect of the residual gas atmosphere on a slit-type field ion thruster with liquid Cs propellant was searched for a long-term test of 100 days. While occasionally simulating the vacuum conditions outside a spacecraft in low Earth orbit. Of the most common possible contaminants (*e.g.*, H_2O and CO_2), H_2O was obviously by far the most serious one due to its interaction with Cs, resulting in a throttling of Cs flow after build-up of a critical number of monolayers (300–700). In contrast, an accumulation of 1700 monolayers of CO_2 had no effect on thruster emission performance. In the work, major deviations of the current-voltage emission characteristic due to gas adsorption and the related contamination of the slit area of the ion thruster were observed. Also, a recovery effect inhibited by high current ion emission was noticed[79].

Valentian and Bugeat investigated the clustering capability of field emission ion thruster by using a laboratory model of field emission ion thruster. The single emitters sustained preliminary tests on increasing the elementary thrust. Clustering showed the additivity of elementary source characteristics and the lack of interference between the ion beamlets[80].

A computational study of the ion trajectories in a field emission thruster is presented in the article by Little and Thomas[81]. In the model they developed an electrode system for accelerating Cs ions emitted from a linear array of points. It was designed to produce a collimated beam with a minimum number of ions striking the electrodes. The electric field distribution around a finite array of pin emitters was calculated for arrays containing different number of emitters. This electrostatic problem was solved in three dimensions. A modified support structure was formulated in which end effects due to finite length were negligibly small. Also the trajectories of ions, emitted from single pin emitter as well as from a sharp edge (a line source) were traced through a system of electrodes as 2-dimensional problems. The edge emitter was treated such that as if it had an infinite length, thus end effects being ignored. Finally, a 2-dimensional electrode configuration was suggested in which back-bombardment was predicted to be negligible[81].

As applications, field emission thrusters were employed in a co-operative program between ESA and NASA (The laser interferometer space antenna project (LISA)) to detect the gravitational waves by measuring distortions in the space-time fabric. LISA pathfinder was the precursor mission to LISA which was designed to validate the core technologies intended for LISA. One of the enabling technologies is the micro-propulsion system based on field emission thrusters which is necessary to achieve the uniquely stringent propulsion requirements. A consortium was established consisting of Astrium GmbH and the University of Applied Sciences Wiener Neustadt (formerly AIT). It was commissioned by ESA to develop and qualify the micro-propulsion system based on the indium needle field emission electric propulsion (FEEP) technology. Several successful tests have been performed to verify the proper FEEP operation and the thermal and mechanical design of subcomponents of the developed system. For all functional tests, the flight representative power control unit developed by SELEX Galileo S.p.A (also responsible for the micro-propulsion subsystem (MPS) development) was used. Measurements successfully have shown the exceptional stability of the thruster. An acceptance test of one thruster cluster assembly (TCA) over 3600 h has shown the stability in long term operation of the developed system. During the acceptance test compliance to all the applicable requirements were indicated that such as a thrust resolution of 0.1 μN, thrust range capability varying between

0 and 100 μN. The thrust overshoot was much lower than the required range of 0.3 μN + 3% and many others. Particularly important point was the voltage stability of the thruster (±1% over the duration of the testing) and the confirmation of the very low thrust noise. Based on the acceptance test, the lifetime of the thruster was expected to exceed 39 000 hrs, generating a total impulse bit of 6300 Ns at an average thrust level of 50 μN. A flight representative qualification model of the needle FEEP cluster assembly (DM1) equipped with one active TCA has performed a qualification program consisting of acceptance, shock, vibration and thermal vacuum test. During the performance of the last test, namely the thermal vacuum test (TVT), a performance decrease was observed. According to a preliminary analysis, this decrease in performance was not linked to the thermal conditions simulated in the TVT but it might be rather linked to secondary effects of the TVT set-up[82].

Pulsed Plasma Thruster

Actually a pulsed plasma thruster (PPT) is nothing but an electromagnetic thruster that utilizes a pulsed discharge to ionize a fraction of a solid propellant ablated into a plasma arc. The electromagnetic effects in the pulse accelerate the ions to high exit velocity and the pulse repetition rate can be used to determine the thrust level.

Williams *et al.*, investigated a liquid fueled pulsed plasma thruster which included an ionic liquid propellant and electrodes disposed to at least partially cause electrolytic decomposition of the ionic liquid propellant[83]. For these type of thrusters, the ionic liquid propellant may include a Hydroxylammonium Nitrate (HAN) -based Green Electric Monopropellant (GEM). Furthermore, the electrodes may be located in various orientations within the thruster, including parallel or coaxial orientations. In another example, a dual mode combustion thruster was provided which allows a thruster to operate selectively, either chemical mode for high thrust or in a pulsed plasma mode for high efficiency[83].

Plasma engines are also used for space propulsion as an alternative to chemical thrusters. Due to the high exhaust velocity of the propellant, they are accepted as more efficient engines for long-distance interplanetary space missions compared to their conventional counterparts. An advanced laboratory of plasma space propulsion (PlaNS) at the Institute of Plasma Physics and Laser Microfusion (IPPLM) has specialized in designing and testing various electric propulsion devices. Szelecka have made some contributions for the testing of plasma thrusters[84]. During the tests, inside of a special vacuum chamber with three performance pumps, a pseudo environment, similar to the one that prevails in space was realized. An innovative Micro Pulsed Plasma Thruster (LìPPT) with liquid propellant was built at the laboratory. Then it was used to test the second prototype of Hall effect thruster (HET) operating on krypton propellant. In the meantime, an improved prototype of krypton Hall thruster was constructed[84].

Another type of thrusters called "laser ablative pulsed plasma thruster" includes assembly of a power processing unit, capacitor unit, working fluid, working fluid supply means, cathode, anode and laser generating mechanism. The power processing unit is connected to the capacitor unit *via* the transmission line; the negative and positive output ends of the capacitor cell are respectively connected to the anode and the cathode *via* a transmission line. The capacitor unit, the transmission line, the anode and the cathode constituted the discharge circuit. In the device the gas inside the anode and the cathode can be ionized and accelerated. Thus the discharge channel is formed between the cathode and the anode. In the experiment, the working fluid supply device for fixing and supplying the working fluid was provided at one end of the discharge channel from which the working fluid was extended inside the discharge channel. There were gaps between the working fluid and the poles. The laser generating mechanism emitted laser beam ablation working fluid into the discharge channel. The laser beam conducts continuous ablation so that the produced partial ionized gases and particulate matters enter into the discharge channel to form the plasma jet moving around the discharge channel to generate thrust. The system had high specific impulse and total impulse, high working fluid utilization and high control precision[85].

The pulsed plasma thruster (PPT) is suitable for various applications, including attitude control, station keeping and formation flying due to its significant advantage with regard to the related savings of wet system mass, small volume and high specific impulse. In the work of Zhang *et al.*, in order to elaborate the mechanism of PPT operation process, the optical emission spectrum was conducted on a breech-fed PPT with tongue electrodes[86]. The results revealed that plasma plume mainly consists of C, F, C^+, F^+ and C^{2+}, beside them Cu^+ and Cu^{2+} cations, were detected in plasma which were obviously produced by electrode ablation. The plasma distribution was asymmetrical in the discharge channel, the maximum of plasma density of plasma appeared at the central axis of discharge channel and the plasma density nearby the anode was much higher than that of nearby the cathode. The composition of plasma was not symmetrical and not uniform. The distribution of F^+ and neutral particle concentrated close to the anode. The electron temperature was about 6.67 eV derived from the optical emission spectra by Boltzmann linear fitting. Evolution of the plasma emission spectrum was derived at the fourth measurement point and the results showed that there was much difference between different discharge stages for the composition of plume and the proportion of each component[86].

Haque studied a thruster system and method which provides a fault-tolerant multi-channel pulsed plasma thruster system[87]. It utilized a control unit and an embedded real time application manipulating low-level timing events with programming, providing with examples of completely flexible control techniques of a scalable micro propulsion system having many pulsed plasma thruster channels (also taking into account of aging behavior of the system and specific mission utilization requirements that may change in the mission lifetime). The system and method also covered an architecture lending itself suitable for design of a dedicated FGPA or ASIC that would tightly integrate many channels of thruster components to build a robust, resilient and versatile micro propulsion subsystem for space applications, and indirectly for advanced multi-channel spacecraft instrumentation[87].

In pulsed plasma thrusters (PPTs) wall-plasma interactions excited by ablation controlled arcs are very critical physical processes. Their effects directly determine PPT performances on the ionization processes of ablated vapor into discharge plasma. To reveal the physics involved in governing the ionization phenomena in PPT discharge, a modified model taking into account the pyrolysis effect of heated polytetrafluoroethylene propellant on the wall-plasma interactions was developed[88]. Then, the feasibility of the modified model was analyzed by creating a one-dimensional simulation of a rectangular ablative PPT. Based on this modified model, the wall-plasma interaction results were found to be more realistic than for the unmodified model. This reflects the dynamic changes of the inflow parameters during discharge in the model. Furthermore, the temporal and spatial variations of the different plasma species in the discharge chamber were numerically studied. The numerical studies indicated that polytetrafluoroethylene plasma was mainly composed of monovalent ions. The carbon and fluorine ions were concentrated in the upstream and downstream discharge chamber, respectively. The results based on this modified model were in good agreement with the experimental formation times of the various plasma species. A large number of short-lived and highly ionized carbon and fluorine species (divalent and trivalent ions) were generated during initial discharge. These highly ionized species reached their peak density earlier than the singly ionized species[88].

Martin developed and searched a circuit model for an inductive pulsed plasma thruster in order to investigate the performance of thrusters with conical coils[89]. The designed model was such that it was able to accommodate cone-angles from 0° (a straight theta-pinch coil) to 90° (a planar coil). The plasma was considered as a deformable slug that was capable of moving both radially and axially in response to the force applied by the coil. The radial equation of motion included a restoring force due to the plasma pressure. It was derived under the assumption that the electron population was isothermal, while the ions were isothermal, adiabatic, or shock-heated depending on the magnitude and sign of the radial velocity. The inductance of the coil and the plasma slug, and their mutual inductance, were determined using QuickField. A local maximum in efficiency and specific impulse was found for angles less than 90°. However, the maximum for both these quantities occurs at 90°. High pulse-rate operation was found to yield dynamic efficiencies (excluding ionization cost) as high as 60–70% for I_{sp} in the range of 3000–5000 s, even for a device with modest jet-power (5 kW). Note that this mode of operation also permits elimination of the pulsed gas valve, which would be a significant system-level simplification. An alternate mode of inductive recapture (in which the current is interrupted at the second zero-crossing) was found to result in a decrease of only 1–2% in efficiency, while keep offering other significant system-level benefits for this kind of thruster[89].

In order to gain great insight into the working process in pulsed plasma thrusters (PPT), an ionization model was developed by Huang *et al.*[90]. The ionization processes of LES-6 PPT and XPPT-1 PPT were simulated by use of the ionization model, and some parameters such as propellant utilization and electron density were obtained. The propellant utilization ratios were 16.32% (LES-6) and 81.04% (XPPT-1), and the electron densities were determined as 6.56×10^{21} m^{-3}(LES-6) and 5.83×10^{21} m^{-3}(XPPT-1). The results have showed that the model can correctly mimics the ionization process of PPT and the simulated values of the propellant utilization and electron densities fit well with the experimental values[90].

Magnetoplasmadynamic Thruster

Magnetoplasmadynamic (MPD) thrusters are electromagnetic devices that use a very high current arc (to ionize a significant fraction of the propellant) and electromagnetic forces (Lorentz **FL**

= **j**×**B** forces) in the plasma discharge to accelerate the charged propellant. Since both the current and the magnetic field are usually generated by the plasma discharge, MPD thrusters tend to operate at very high powers in order to generate sufficient force field for high specific impulse operation, and thereby also generate high thrust compared to the other technologies described above.

Magnetoplasmadynamic (MPD) thrusters are capable of accelerating quasi-neutral plasmas to high exhaust velocities using Megawatts (MW) of electric power. These characteristics obviously make such devices worthy of consideration for demanding, far-term missions such as the exploration of Mars or beyond. Assessment of MPD thrusters at the system and mission level is often difficult due to their status as ongoing experimental research topics rather than the already developed thrusters. However, in order to assess MPD thrusters' utility in later missions, some adequate characterization of performance, or more exactly, projected performance, and system level definition are required for use in analyses. Gilland and Johnston considered the most recent physical models of self-field MPD thrusters which have been examined, assessed, and reconfigured for use by systems and mission analysts. The physical models allow for rational projections of thruster performance based on physical parameters that can be measured in the laboratory. In the article by Gilland and Johnston, the models and their implications for the design of future MPD thrusters are presented[91].

The nozzle geometry has a great influence on the magnetoplasmadynamic (MPD) thruster performance and several studies have been performed using numerical simulations to optimize the design[92,93].

MPD thrusters are simple, robust and compact devices. They have the capability of generating steady-state thrust densities as high as 105 N m^{-2}, whereas state-of-the-art HTs and gridded ion engines generate £50 Nm^{-2} and £10 Nm^{-2}, respectively, when using Xe as fuel. MPD thrusters produce thrust in the range of 0.5 and 50 N and they provide specific impulses in the 1000–10 000 s range with a thrust efficiency approaching 40% when operating with H_2, He or Ar[94–96].

In an MPD thruster, the thrust mostly originates from the combination of the gradient of the plasma thermal pressure p along with the gradient of the magnetic pressure $B^2/(2ì_0)$, where $ì_0$ is the vacuum permeability. The effect of the neutral gas pressure is negligible. The regime of operation of an MPD thruster is therefore controlled by the plasma parameter $\hat{a}$ which corresponds to the ratio of the thermal to the magnetic pressure[97].

As the induced magnetic field is proportional to the discharge current I_d, the magnetic pressure is weak at low I_d. In that case, an MPD thruster operates mainly as an electro thermal device.

In MPD thrusters high thrust efficiencies and lifetime elongation have been attained by using propellants with a low ionization energy such as alkali metals. An example is the Lithium Lorentz Force Accelerator (Li-LFA) which is a steady-state MPD thruster fueled with lithium[98]. In general, a typical magnetoplasmadynamic thruster (MPDT) of this category consists of a central cathode placed in within a larger cylindrical anode. A gas, usually lithium, is pumped into the annular space between the cathode and the anode where it is ionized by an electric current flowing radially from the cathode to the anode. This current induces an azimuthal magnetic field (one that encircles the central cathode), which interacts with the same current that induced it to generate the thrust-producing Lorentz force.

Design of MPD thrusters is open to development. A variant of the self-field MPD thruster is obtained by superimposing a steady longitudinal magnetic field to the induced field. The additional **B** field is created either by magnetizing coils or permanent magnets. This propulsion device is called an applied-field MPD (AF-MPD) thruster[99, 100].

However, although MPD thrusters are very attractive devices from a standpoint of thrust and I_{sp}, they remain complicated propulsion systems in terms of their underlying physical mechanisms with a moderate energy efficiency and a short operational life. Moreover, their development and space fight qualification require huge and expensive vacuum test chambers with enormous pumping capacity that are currently rare which creates formidable technological challenges[101].

The electromagnetic-type PPTs are plasma accelerators and offer two distinctive features compared to other concepts[102–107]. They operate in short pulse mode (H"10 ìs) and they employ a solid propellant that is consumed in an ablative discharge in their most advanced form, although liquid propellants are gaining attention as they can be supplied easily[46, 47]. In the device the discharge is ignited between the two electrodes by means of a high-voltage pulse applied to a spark plug. Once initiated, the PPT discharge turns into an arc (£100 V, £10 kA). The high-current short-duration (H"10 ìs) discharge ablates and ionizes a small amount of solid propellant, which is then accelerated to high velocity. However, performances of PPT are affected by various factors including the electrical circuit, the thruster design, the nozzle geometry, the pulse waveform, and the propellant[102,104]. It is to be noted that the propellant of an ablative PPT must be nontoxic, inert, dielectric and easy to ablate and ionize.

The operating characteristics of self-field, quasi steady magnetoplasmadynamic thrusters (MPDTs) with ThO_2-W, Y_2O_3-W, and La_2O_3-W electrodes were experimentally measured. The cathode material was found to have a large effect on the discharge voltage. The La_2O_3-W cathode exhibited the lowest voltage whereas the ThO_2-W cathode showed the highest voltage over a wide discharge current range. However, the differences in the voltage characteristics became smaller at higher currents. The observations have showed that the La_2O_3-W and Y_2O_3-W cathodes had lower erosion rates than a conventional ThO_2-W cathode. For pulsed arc discharge, erosion is caused by the evaporation or the ejection of the molten cathode material, due to the spotty arc attachment on the cathode surface. The La_2O_3-W and Y_2O_3-W cathodes have high durability in this point. The test have revealed that La_2O_3-W and Y_2O_3-W cathodes are promising alternatives to conventional ThO_2-W cathodes, for quasi-steady MPDTs. In addition, they suffer less errosive damage during the startup phase in steady-state MPDTs[107].

These type of thrusters have been investigated considerably from various research point of interests. Such as the possible role of current filamentation in the operation of magnetoplasmadynamic thrusters was investigated by means of a stability analysis of a current-carrying plasma in a simplified coaxial configuration[108].

Note that magnetoplasmadynamic thrusters are known to enter a strongly unstable regime (named onset in the literature) when operated above a threshold current level for a given propellant mass flow rate. During onset, a transition from diffuse to spotty current pattern occurs which leads to intense fluctuations of thruster terminal voltage and causes severe anode damage with commonly employed anode materials. Despite the several experimental and theoretical efforts spent in the last few decades, no complete and definitive understanding of the physical nature of this phenomenon has been available yet. In a work of Giannelli *et al.*, it has been shown what sorts of conditions suitable for azimuthal symmetry breaking and the subsequent development of this instability that can actually exist in magnetoplasmadynamic thrusters. In the article, a physical coherent explanation of the complex onset has been proposed, showing that both the plasma dynamics and the voltage fluctuations can be ultimately explained in terms of the filamentation instability and its effects[108].

The expansion of a high-temperature fusion plasma through an expanding magnetic field is a process common to most fusion propulsion concepts. The propulsive efficiency of this process has a strong bearing on the overall performance of fusion propulsion. In order to simulate the expansion of a fusion plasma, a concept has been developed by Gilland *et al.*, in which a high velocity plasma is first stagnated in a converging magnetic field to high (100s of eV) temperatures, then expanded though a converging /diverging magnetic nozzle[109]. As a first step in constructing this experiment, a gigawatt magnetoplasmadynamic plasma accelerator was constructed to generate the initial high velocity plasma and has been characterized. The source is powered by a 1.6 MJ, 1.6 ms pulse forming network. The device has been operated with currents up to 300 kA and power levels up to 200 MW. Notably, these values are among the highest levels have ever been reached in a magnetoplasmadynamic thruster. The device operation has been characterized by quasi-steady voltage and current measurements for helium mass flow rates ranging from 0.5 to 27 gs^{-1}. Probe results for downstream plasma density and electron temperature are also presented in the article. The source behavior is examined in terms of current theories for magnetoplasmadynamic thrusters[109].

Propellants for Electric Propulsion

In EP systems propellant determines to a large extent the thrust efficiency and the level of specific impulse. Additionally, propellant nature, storage feasibility, injection facility and flow control of the propellant all have an effective impact on the complexity, efficiency and the overall cost of a spacecraft propulsion assembly. Therefore, in the development of an EP system selection of the proper propellant is crucial. One of the currently used propellant is Xenon in various electric thrusters, including HTs and ion engines, whatever the spacecraft type, *i.e.,* satellites *versus* exploration probes. Several advantages are associated with Xenon although it has many disadvantages. Many factors and practical issues influence the suitability of a propellant for EP[110–114].

Factors that dictate the propellant, consequently the overall, performances are primarily the mass and the ionization energy. A heavy propellant delivers more momentum at the expense of the specific impulse. A propellant having low ionization threshold with a high ionization cross-section to minimize the amount of energy necessary to create a high-density plasma is the choice of selection. Whereas, molecular propellants are generally avoided because of the available input power is lost while dissociation into smaller fragments occurs and also due to the excitation of internal vibration and rotation modes. In that sense, the iodine molecule (I_2) is an exception as it is in many other ways. The propellants must be easy to store in order to reduce the complexity of the storage tank and associated sub-systems. Hence, solid and liquid propellants possess obvious benefits over the gaseous atomic propellants like Xe and Kr which have to be stored in the supercritical fluid state, necessitating large high-pressure (200–300 bars) storage tanks.

As for the condensable propellants, they introduce specific requirements such as suitable mass flow system and the gas feeding system to operate. Thus, a liquid/ solid material with a high vapor pressure and with low melting and boiling temperatures is preferred as propellant. Note that any power consumed for evaporation and to maintain the temperature of the transfer line and injection system reduces the overall efficiency of the thruster assembly. Iodine vapor can be obtained easily from solid I_2 and the mass flow rate can be regulated thermally at a relatively low temperature (ca. 100°C)[115,116] (For comparison, a Bi feeding system operates at about 300°C[117,118]). However, I_2, is strongly corrosive for many metals and alloys[116]. On the other hand, bismuth is a low-cost propellant that offers a large thrust-to-power ratio due to its high mass and high ionization efficiency. Additionally, its storage density is six times that of xenon. However, the main drawback arises from the fact that a high temperature is required to prevent condensation.

One of the other attractive candidates for an alternative to xenon is krypton which generates a high specific impulse and less significant modifications of the thruster assembly. Other points to be considered in the propellant selection are that it must be non-radioactive (*e.g.*, radon), non-toxic and easy to handle. Condensable propellants can deposit if the surface temperature is below their melting point. Such a coating formation leads to a change in the electrical and optical properties of the components.

After all the above mentioned points one must keep in mind that there is no ideal propellant for electric propulsion systems.

EPILOGUE

Through the years, electric propulsion (EP) science and technology have been successfully developed and employed in many commercial and military satellites. The focus of interest on EP systems is still alive because of the increasing demand for all electric communication and military satellites, small satellites, and science probes. Obvious trend reveals that the quantity and the variety of efficient EP systems will significantly skyrocket in the near future in spite of several issues and challenges still remain. The lifetime and the stability of the devices must be warranted for durations that greatly exceed what has been achieved in ground-test facilities so far. New materials should be obtained and/or tested. Also, improved or modified architectures and plasma confinement technologies are to be developed.

Abreviations

AF-MPD: applied-field MPD; CG: coarse-grained; CHT: clindrical hall thruster; EP: electric propulsion; ESA: European space agency; ETS: engineering test satellite; FEEP: field-emission electric propulsion; GEM: green electric monopropellant; GEO: geosynchronous earth orbit; HT: hall thrusters; HET: hall effect thrusters; IL: ionic liquids; In-FET: indium field emission thruster; JPL: jet propulsion laboratory; LIF: laser induced fluorescence; Li-LFA: lithium lorentz force accelerator; LISA: The laser interferometer space antenna project; LìPPT: micro pulsed plasma thruster; MD: molecular dynamics; MPD: magnetoplasmadynamic; MPDT: magnetoplasmadynamic thruster; MPS: micro propulsion subsystem; MW: megawatts; NASA: national aeronautics and space administration; NSSK: North-south station keeping; NSTAR: solar electric propulsion technology applications readiness; PHALL: permanent magnet Hall thruster; PNAE: Brazilian space activities program; PPT: pulsed plasma thruster; QMS: quadrupole mass spectrometry; RTOF-MS: time-of-flight mass spectrometer; SBS: Side-by-side; SERT: space electric rocket test; TCA: thruster cluster assembly; TVT: thermal vacuum test

REFERENCES

[1] Choueiri, E.Y. (2009). New dawn for electric rockets. *Scýentifýc American*, 300(2): 58–65. Scýentýfýc Amerýcan Inc. www. Sci Am.com.

[2] Choueiri, E.Y. (2004). A critical history of electric propulsion: The first 50 years (1906–1956). *J. Propulsion and Power*, 20: 193–203.

[3] *Palaszewski, B. (*2011). *Electric propulsion for future space missions. Electric propulsion for future space missions. NASA Glenn Research Center.* http://www.jpl.nasa.gov/images/ds1/borrelly_caption3.html.

[4] Jahn, R.G. and Choueiri, E.Y. (2002). Electric propulsion, *Encyclopedia of Physical Science and Technology,* 5. New York: Academic Press.

[5] Sutton, G.P. and Biblarz, O. (2010). Rocket Propulsion Elements. New York: Wiley.

[6] Turner, M.J.L. (2009). Rocket and Spacecraft Propulsion. Chichester: Spinger.

[7] Frisbee, R.H. (2003). Advanced space propulsion for the 21st century. *J. Propul. Power*, 19: 1129–1154.

[8] Jahn, R.G. (1968). *Physics of Electric Propulsion.* New York: McGraw-Hill.

[9] Brewer, G.R. (1970). Ion Propulsion Technology and Applications. New York: Gordon and Breach.

[10] Kaufman, H.R. (1974). Technology of Electron-Bombardment Ion Thrusters, *In*: *Advances in Electronics and Electron Physics*, vol. 36, Ed. Marton L. New York: Academic Press.

[11] Turchi, P.J. (1995). Electric rocket propulsion systems. Ch. 9, *In*: Space propulsion analysis and design. Humble, R.W., Henry, G.N. and Larson, W.J. (*eds.*), New York: McGraw-Hill.

[12] Wertz, J.R. and Larson, W.J. (*eds.*) (1999). Space Mission Analysis and Design. New York: Springer.

[13] Sutton, G.P. and Biblarz, O. (2001). Rocket Propulsion Elements. New York: Wiley.

[14] Grishin, S.D. and Leskov, L.V. (1989). Electrical Rocket Engines of Space Vehicles. Moscow, Russia: Mashinostroyeniye Pub House.

[15] Boever, A.S., Kiim, V., Koroteev, A.S., Latyshev, L.A., Morozov, A.I., Popov, G.A., Rylov, Y.P. and Zhurin, V.V. (1991). State of the works of electrical thrusters in the USSR. IEPC-91-003, 22nd International electric propulsion conference, Viareggio, Italy: IEPC.

[16] Kim, V. (2001). Electric propulsion activity in Russia. IEPC-2001-005, 27th International Electric Propulsion Conference, Pasadena, California, USA: IEPC.

[17] Shimada, S., Sato, K. and Takegahara, H. (1987). 20-mN Class xenon ýon thruster for ETS-VI. AIAA-1987-1029, 19th International Electric Propulsion Conference, Colorado Springs, Colorado, USA: AIAA.

[18] Beattie, J.R. (1998). XIPS keeps satellites on track. *The Industrial Physicist*, 4(2): 24–26.

[19] Brophy, J.R. (2002). NASA's deep space-1 ýon engine. *Review Scientific Instruments*, 73: 1071–1078.

[20] Beattie, J.R., Matossian, J.N. and Robson, R.R. (1990). Status of xenon ion propulsion technology. *J. Propul and Power*, 6: 145–150.

[21] Goebel, D.M., Martinez-Lavin, M., Bond, T.A. and King, A.M. (2002). Performance of XIPS electric propulsion in station keeping of the boeing 702 spacecraft. AIAA-2002-4348, 38th Joint propulsion conference, Indianapolis, Indiana, USA: AIAA.
[22] Kuninaka, H., Nishiyama, K., Funakai, I., Tetsuya, K., Shimizu, Y. and Kawaguchi, J. (2005). Asteroid rendezvous of hayabusa explorer using microwave discharge Ion engines. 29th International electric propulsion conference, IEPC-2005-010, Princeton, New Jersey, USA: IEPC.
[23] Koppel, C.R. and Estublier, D. (2005). The SMART-1 Hall effect thruster around the moon: In flight Experience. 29th International electric propulsion conference, IEPC-2005-119, Princeton, New Jersey, USA: IEPC.
[24] Pidgeon, D.J., Corey, R.L., Sauer, B. and Day, M.L. (2006). Two years on-orbit performance of SPT-100 electric propulsion. AIAA-2006-5353, 24th AIAA International communications satellite systems conference, San Diego, California, USA: AIAA.
[25] Chien, K.R., Tighe, W.G. and Hart, S. (2005). L-3 Communications ETI electric Propulsion overview. 29th International electric propulsion conference, IEPC-2005-315, Princeton, New Jersey, USA: IEPC.
[26] Wilson, F., King, D., Willey, M., Aadland, R., Tilley, D. and de Grys, K. (1999). Development status of the BPT family of Hall current thrusters. AIAA-99-2573, 35th Joint Propulsion Conference, Los Angeles, California, USA: AIAA.
[27] de Grys, K.H., Welander, B., Dimicco, J., Wenzel, S. and Kay, B. (2005). 4.5 kW Hall thruster system qualification status. AIAA-2005-3682, 41st Joint Propulsion Conference, Tucson, Arizona, USA: AIAA.
[28] Goebel, D.M. and Katz, I. (2008). Fundamentals of Electric Propulsion. Hoboken, NJ: Wiley.
[29] Jahn, R.G. and Choueiri, Y. (2002). Electric propulsion. *Encyclopedia of Physical Science and Technology*, 5: 125–41. San Diego: Academic press.
[30] Martinez-Sanchez, M. and Pollard, J.E. (1998). Spacecraft electric propulsion—An overview. *J. Propul. Power*, 14: 688–99.
[31] Mazouffre, S. (2016). Electric propulsion for satellites and spacecraft: Established technologies and novel approaches. *Plasma Sources Sci. Technol.*, 25(033002): 1–27.
[32] Gibbon, D., Baker, A., Coxhill, Ian and Sweeting, M. (2003). The development of a family of resistojet thruster propulsion systems for small spacecraft, SSC03-IV-8. 17th Annual AIAA / USU Conference on small satellites. Logan, Utah, USA: AIAA/USU.
[33] Curran, F.M. and Haag, T.W. (1992). Extended life and performance test of a low-power arcjet. *J. Spacecr. Rockets*, 29: 444–452.
[34] Fujita, K. and Arakawa, Y. (1999). Performance computation of a low-power hydrogen arcjet. *J. Propul. Power*, 15: 144–50.

[35] Le, Q.H. and Herdricht, G. (2013). Development of a 1 kW class thermal arcjet thruster TALOS. *Proc.* of the 33rd Int. Electric Propulsion Conf. Washington, DC, USA: IEPC-238.

[36] Auweter-Kurtz, M., Golz, T., Habiger, H. and Hammer, F. (1998). High-power hydrogen arcjet thrusters. *J. Propul. Power*, 14: 764–773.

[37] Welle, R. (1997). Space propulsion applications of helium arcjets. *Proc.* of the 35th Aerospace Sciences Meeting and Exhibit, Reno, NV, USA: AIAA-0794.

[38] Horisawa, H. and Kimura, I. (2000). Very low-power arcjet testing. *Vacuum*, 59: 106-117.

[39] Choueiri, E.Y. (1998). Scaling of thrust in self-field magnetoplasmadynamic thrusters. *J. Propul. Power*, 14: 744–753.

[40] Myers, R.M., Mantenieks, M.A. and Lapointe, M.R. (1991). MPD Thruster Technology. *Proc.* of the Conf. on Advanced SEI Technologies, Cleveland, OH, USA: AIAA-3568.

[41] Rafalskyi, D. and Aanesland, A. (2016). Brief review on plasma propulsion with neutralizer-free systems. *Plasma Sources Sci. Technol.*, 25(043001): 1–14.

[42] Dannenmayer, K. and Mazouffre, S. (2011). Elementary scaling relations for Hall effect thrusters. *J. Propul. Power,* 27: 236–45.

[43] Lazurenko, A., Vial, A., Bouchoule, A., Skrylnikov, A., Kozlov, V. and Kim, V. (2006). Dual-mode operation of stationary plasma thrusters. *J. Propul. Power*, 22: 38–475.

[44] Hofer, R.R. and Jankovsky, R.S. (2001). A Hall thruster performance model incorporating the effects of a multiply charged plasma. *Proc.* of the 37th Joint Propulsion Conf. Salt Lake City, UT, USA: AIAA-3322.

[45] Boeuf, J.P. (2017). Tutorial: Physics and modeling of Hall thrusters. *J. Applied Physýcs*, 121(011101): 1–24.

[46] Kim, V., Kozubsky, K.N., Murashko, V.M. and Semenkin, A.V. (2007). History of the Hall thrusters development in USSR. *Proc.* of the 30th Int. Electric Propulsion Conf. Florence, Italy: IEPC-142.

[47] Morozov, A.I. and Savelyev, V.V. (2000). Fundamentals of stationary plasma thruster theory, Kadomtsev, B.B. and Shafranov, V.D. (*eds.*). *Reviews of Plasma Physics*, 21: 203–391. New York: Consultant Bureau.

[48] Gascon, N., Dudeck, M. and Barral, S. (2003). Wall material effects in stationary plasma thrusters. I. Parametric studies of an SPT-100. *Phys. Plasmas*, 10: 4123–4136.

[49] Choueiri, E.Y. (2001). Fundamental difference between the two Hall thruster variants. *Phys. Plasmas*, 8: 5025–5033.

[50] Koppel, C.R., Marchandise, F., Prioul, M., Estublier, D. and Darnon, F. (2005). The SMART-1 electric propulsion subsystem around the Moon: In flight experience. *Proc.* of the 41th Joint propulsion Conf. Tucson, Arizona, USA: AIAA-3671.

[51] Dannenmayer, K. and Mazouffre, S. (2011). Elementary scaling laws for the design of low and high power Hall effect thrusters. *Progress in Propul. Physics*, 2: 601–616.

[52] Shagayada, A.A. (2013). On scaling of Hall effect thrusters. 33rd International Electric Propulsion Conference, Washington, USA: IEPC-056.

[53] Ferreira, J.L., Martins, A.A., Miranda, R., Schelin, A.B., Alves, L de S., Costa, E.G., Coelho, H.O., Serra, A.C.B. and Nathan, F. (2016). Permanent magnet Hall thruster development for future Brazilian space missions. *Compt. and App. Mathematics*, 35: 711–726.

[54] Miyasaka, T., Uyama, Y., Yoshida, M., Miyake, Y., Shimizu, D., Goto, R. and Sakoda, M. (2017). Interference effects of multi-head operation of anode layer side by side (SBS) system. *Vacuum*, 136: 184–189.

[55] Han, L., Wei, L. and Yu, D. (2016). Mode transition induced by the magnetic field gradient in Hall thrusters. *Journal of Physics D. Applied Physics*, 49: 375203/1–7.

[56] Lakhin, V.P., Ilgisonis, V.I., Smolyakov, A.I. and Sorokina, E.A. (2016). Nonlinear excitation of long-wavelength modes in Hall plasmas. *Physics of Plasmas*, 23: 102304/1–7.

[57] Lafleur, T., Baalrud, S.D. and Chabert, P. (2016). Theory for the anomalous electron transport in Hall effect thrusters. I. Insights from particle-in-cell simulations. *Phys. Plasmas*, 23: 0535031–05350311.

[58] Grimaud, L., Petin, A., Vaudolon, J. and Mazouffre, S. (2016). Perturbations induced by electrostatic probe in the discharge of Hall thrusters. *Review of Scientific Instruments*, 87: 043506/1–8.

[59] Marchandise, F.R.J., Vanessa, V. and Zurbach, S. (2016). Hall effect thruster for spacecraft. Fr. Demande FR 3032325 A1 20160805.

[60] Marchandise, F.R.J., Vanessa, V. and Zurbach, S. (2016). Hall effect thruster for spacecraft. PCT Int. Appl. WO 2016120570 A1 20160804.

[61] Hruby, V., Szabo Jr, J., Gasdaska, C. and Robin, M. (2016). Hall thruster with condensable propellant US. US 9334855 B1 20160510.

[62] Welander, B.A. (2016). Hall thruster with exclusive outer magnetic core. PCT Int. Appl. WO 2016149082 A1 20160922.

[63] Fernandez, E. (2007). Simulating plasma-induced Hall thruster wall erosion with a two-dimensional hybrid model. *IEEE Trans. Plasma Sci.*, 35: 1379–1387.

[64] Lam, M., Fernandez, E. and Cappelli, M.A. (2015). A 2-D hybrid Hall thruster simulation that resolves the E_B electron drift direction. *IEEE Trans. Plasma Sci.*, 43: 86–94.

[65] Cho, S., Komurasaki, K. and Arakawa, Y. (2013). Kinetic particle simulation of discharge and wall erosion of a Hall thruster. *Phys. Plasmas*, 20: 063501/1–12.

[66] Cho, S., Watanabe, H., Kubota, K., Iihara, S., Fuchigami, K., Uematsu, K. and Funaki, I. (2015). Study of electron transport in a Hall thruster

by axial–radial fully kinetic particle simulation. *Phys. Plasmas*, 22: 103523/1–11.

[67] Smith, A.W. and Cappelli, M.A. (2010). Single particle simulations of electron transport in the near-field of Hall thrusters. *J. Phys. D: Appl. Phys.*, 43: 045203/1–11.

[68] Lopez, O.A. and Mikellides, I.G. (2016). The importance of the cathode plume and its Interactions with the ion beam in numerical simulations of Hall thrusters. *Physics of Plasmas,* 23: 043515/1–14.

[69] Prince, B.D. (2012). Ionic liquids in electric propulsion. 243rd ACS National meeting and exposition, San Diego, CA, USA: ACS IEC-6.

[70] Chiu, Yu-hui and Dressler, R.A. (2007). Ionic liquids for space propulsion. *ACS Symposium Series*, 975 (*Ionic Liquids* IV), 10: 138–160. DOI: 10.1021/bk-2007-0975.ch010.

[71] Ticknor, B.W. and Chiu, Yu-Hui (2010). High resolution time-of-flight mass spectral of vacuum electrospray ionization of ionic liquids. 240th ACS National meeting, Boston, MA, USA: ACS Phys-526.

[72] Borner, A., Li, Z. and Levin, D.A. (2013). Prediction of fundamental properties of ionic liquid electrospray thrusters using molecular dynamics. *J. Physical Chemistry B*, 117: 6768–6781.

[73] Borner, A., Li, Z. and Levin, D.A. (2012). Modeling of an ionic liquid electrospray using a molecular dynamics model. *AIP Conference Proceedings*-1501 (28th *International Symposium on Rarefied Gas Dynamics*), 2: 887–894.

[74] Borner, A., Li, Z. and Levin, D.A. (2012). Modeling of an ionic liquid electrospray using molecular dynamics with constraints. *J. Chem. Physics*, 136: 124507/1–11.

[75] Elias, P.Q., Packan, D., Bonnet, J., Ceccanti, F., Cesari, U., Tata De, M., Nicolini, D. and Gengembre, E. (2011). Optical measurements of neutral cesium mass flow rate in field emission thrusters. *J. Propul. and Power*, 27: 448–460.

[76] Stewart, D., Wilson, P.D. and Nicholas, M.G. (1980). Study on additional propellants for field emission thrusters. Report (FRI-R664, ESA-CR(P)-1395), p. 85.

[77] Buldrini, N., Marhold, K., Seifert, B. and Tajmar, M. (2006). Experimental study of the machian mass fluctuation effect using a ìN thrust balance. AIP Conference proceedings, (Space Technology and Applications International Forum STAIF), 813: 1313–1320.

[78] Lenard, R.X, Kravitz, S.H. and Tajmar, M. (2005). Recent Progress in Silicon-Based MEMS Field Emission Thrusters. (Space Technology and Applications International Forum—STAIF), AIP Conference proceedings 746 Melville, NY: American Institute of Physics, pp. 954–964.

[79] Mitterauer, J. (1991). Contamination test of a cesium field ion thruster. *J. Propul. and Power*, 7: 364–367.

[80] Valentian, D. and Bugeat, J.P. (1983). Clustering capability of field emission ion thruster. *Acta Astronautica*, 10: 697–701.
[81] Little, P.F. and Thomas, C.L. (1977). Ion optics studies for a field emission thruster. Report (CLM/RR/E1/24), p. 86.
[82] Scharlemann, C., Buldrini, N., Killinger, R., Jentsch, M., Polli, A., Ceruti, L., Serafini, L., Cara, di D. and Nicolini, D. (2011). Qualification test series of the indium needle FEEP micro-propulsion system for LISA Pathfinder. *Acta Astronautica*, 69: 822–832.
[83] Williams, S., Sawka, W.N. and McPherson, M.D. (2017). PCT Int. Appl. WO 2017023383 A1 20170209.
[84] Szelecka, A. (2016). Advanced laboratory for testing plasma thrusters and Hall thruster measurement campaign. *Nukleonika*, 61: 213–218.
[85] He, Z., Wu, J., Zhang, Y., Li, J. and Zhang, H. (2016). Laser ablation pulsed plasma thruster, *Faming Zhuanli, Shenqing:* CN 105952603 A 20160921.
[86] Zhang, H., Wu, J-j., He, Z., Li, S.l. and Zhang, Y. (2016). Plasma characteristics in a pulsed plasma thruster by optical emission spectroscopy. *Guangpuxue Yu Guangpu Fenxi*, 36: 1867–1871.
[87] Haque, S. (2016). Method and system for a programmable and fault tolerant pulsed plasma thruster. US 2016 /0047364 A1.
[88] Yang, L., Zeng, G., Tang, H., Huang, Y. and Liu, X. (2016). Numerical studies of wall plasma interactions and ionization phenomena in an ablative pulsed plasma thruster. *Physics of Plasmas*, 23: 073518/1–10.
[89] Martin, A.K. (2016). Performance scaling of inductive pulsed plasma thrusters with coil angle and pulse rate. *J. Physics D: Applied Physics*, 49: 025201/1–16.
[90] Huang, T., Wu, Z., Liu, X., Xie, K., Wang, N. and Cheng, Y. (2015). Numerical analysis on the ionization mechanism of pulsed plasma thrusters. *Gaodianya Jishu*, 41: 2958–2964.
[91] Gilland, J. and Johnston, G. (2003). MPD thruster performance analytic models, AIP Conference proceedings (Space Technology and Applications International Forum—STAIF) Albuquerque, NM, 654: 516–524.
[92] Nakata, D., Toki, K., Funaki, I., Shimizu, Y., Kuninaka, H. and Arakawall, Y. (2005). Experimental verification of the nozzle shape optimization for self-field MPD thruster. *Proc.* of the 29th Int. Electric Propulsion Conf. Princeton, NJ, USA: IEPC-163.
[93] Hoyt, R.P. (2005). Magnetic nozzle design for high-power MPD thrusters. *Proc.* of the 29th Int. Electric Propulsion Conf. Princeton, NJ, USA: IEPC-230.
[94] Kodys, A.D. and Choueiri, E.Y. (2005). A critical review of the state-of-the-art in the performance of applied-field magnetoplasmadynamic thrusters. *Proc.* of the 41st Joint Propulsion Conf. Tucson, AZ, USA: AIAA-4247.

[95] La Pointe, M.R., Strzempkowski, E. and Pencil, E. (2004). High power MPD thruster performance measurements. *Proc.* of the 40th Joint Propulsion Conf. Fort Lauderdale, Fl, USA: AIAA–3467.
[96] Choueiri, E.Y. and Ziemer, J.K. (2001). Quasi-steady magnetoplasmadynamic thruster performance database. *J. Propul. Power*, 17: 967–976.
[97] Ahedo, E. (2011). Plasmas for space propulsion. *Plasma Phys. Control. Fusion*, 53: 124037/1–18. https://doi.org/10.1088/0741-3335/53/12/124037.
[98] Tikhonov, V.B., Semenikhin, S.A., Brophy, J.R. and Polk, J.E. (1997). Performance of 130 kW MPD thruster with an external magnetic field and Li as a propellant. *Proc.* of the 25th Int. Electric Propulsion Conf. Cleveland, OH, USA: IEPC–117.
[99] Krulle, G., Auweter-Kurtz, M. and Sasoh, A. (1998). Technology and application aspects of applied field magnetoplasmadynamic propulsion. *J. Propul. Power,* 14: 754–763.
[100] Mikellides, P.G., Turchi, P.J. and Roderick, N.F. (1995). Theoretical model for applied field MPD thrusters. *Proc.* of the 31st Joint Propulsion Conf. San Diego, CA, USA: AIAA–2676.
[101] Sovey, J.S., Vetrone, R.H., Grisnik, S.P., Myers, R.M and Parkes, J.E. (1994). Test facilities for high-power electric propulsion. *J. Propul. Power*, 10: 18–24.
[102] Burton, R.L. and Turchi, P.J. (1998). Pulsed plasma thruster. *J. Propul. Power*, 14: 716–735.
[103] Molina-Cabrera, P., Herdrich, G., Lau, M., Fausolas, S., Schoenherr, T. and Komurasaki, K. (2011). Pulsed plasma thrusters: A worldwide review and long yearned classification. *Proc.* of the 32nd Int. Electric Propulsion Conf. Wiesbaden, Germany: IEPC–340.
[104] Schonherr, T. (2017). Plasma acceleration in ablative pulsed plasma thrusters. *Encyclopedia of Plasma Technology*. DOI: 10.1081/E-EPLT-120053951.
[105] Rezaeiha, A. and Schonherr, T. (2014). Review of worldwide activities in liquid-fed pulsed plasma thruster. *J. Propul. Power*, 30: 253–64.
[106] Koizumi, H., Kakami, A., Furuta, Y., Komurasaki, K. and Arakawa, Y. (2003). Liquid propellant pulsed plasma thruster. *Proc.* of the 28th Int. Electric Propulsion Conf. Toulouse, France: IEPC–87.
[107] Nakata, D., Toki, K., Funaki, I. and Kuninaka, H. (2011). Performance of ThO2-W, Y2O3-W and La2O3-W cathodes in quasi-steady magnetoplasmadynamic thrusters. *J. Propul. Power,* 27: 912–915.
[108] Giannelli, S., Misuri, T. and Andrenucci, M. (2011). Current filamentation and in magnetoplasmadynamic thrusters. *Plasma Sources Science and Technology*, 20: 035004/1–11.
[109] Gilland, J., Mikellides, P. and Marriott, D. (2009). Energy deposition *via* magnetoplasma-dynamic acceleration: I. Experiment. *Plasma Sources Science and Technology*, 18: 015001/1–12.

[110] Kieckhafer, A. and King, L.B. (2007). Energetics of propellant options for high-power Hall thrusters. *J. Propul. Power*, 23: 21–26.

[111] Szabo, J., Robin, M., Paintal, S., Pote, B. and Hruby, V. (2012). High density Hall thruster propellant investigations. *Proc.* of the 48th Joint propulsion conf. Atlanta, GA, USA: AIAA–3853.

[112] Holste, K., Gartner, W., Kohler, P., Dietz, P., Konrad, J., Schippers, S., Klar, P.J., Muller, A. and Schreiner, P.R. (2015). In search of alternative propellants for ion thrusters. *Proc.* of the 34th Int. electric propulsion conf. Hyogo-Kobe, Japan: IEPC–320.

[113] Singh, L.A. and Walker, M.L.R. (2015). A review of research in low earth orbit Propellant collection. *Prog. Aerosp. Sci.*, 75: 15–25.

[114] Garrigues, L. (2012). Computational study of Hall-effect thruster with ambient atmospheric gas as propellant. *J. Propul. Power*, 28: 344–54.

[115] Polzin, K.A., Peeples, S.R., Seixal, J.F., Mauro, S.L., Lewis, B.L., Jerman, G.A., Calvert, D.H. and Dankanich J. (2015). Propulsion system development for the iodine satellite (iSAT) demonstration mission. *Proc.* of the 34th Int. Electric Propulsion Conf. Hyogo-Kobe, Japan: IEPC–09.

[116] Szabo, J., Pote, B., Paintal, S. and Robin, M. (2012). Performance evaluation of an iodine-vapor Hall thruster. *J. Propul. Power*, 28: 848–857.

[117] Marrese-Reading, C. *et al.* (2005). The VHITAL program to demonstrate the performance and lifetime of a bismuth-fueled very high Isp Hall thruster. *Proc.* of the 41st Joint Propulsion Conf. Tucson, AZ, USA: AIAA–4564.

[118] Massey, D., King, L. and Makela, J. (2008). Development of a direct evaporation bismuth Hall Thruster. *Proc.* of the 44th Joint propulsion conf. Hartford, CT, USA: AIAA-452.

4

Acting Loads and Stiffness in High-Speed Railway Infrastructure: Theoretical Analysis *vs* Observations and Measurements

KONSTANTINOS GIANNAKOS[1*]

ABSTRACT

The existing international bibliography -German, French, AREMA methods- includes various methods for a realistic estimation of loads on track superstructure and the reactions / actions on the sleepers, through semi-analytic mathematical formulas. The magnitude of loads derived from these formulas could not justify the systematic appearance of cracks at 60% of the concrete sleepers / ties in the Greek railway network. This generated the need of a more exhaustive research program of the extensive appearance of cracks on sleepers, that would lead to the development of a new (semi-analytic) methodology for the calculation of the actions on the sleepers, which would be able to simulate and explain the phenomena that have been observed in the Greek network. In this paper a sensitivity analysis is presented for the influence of the stiffness (mainly fastening stiffness) on the estimation on Acting

[1] Civil Engineer, PhD, P.E., Fellow ASCE; Member: TRB AR050 & 060 Committees, AREMA, fib. 108 Neoreion str., Piraeus 18534, Greece

*Corresponding E-mail: kongiann@otenet.gr, kyannak@gmail.com.

and Design Loads on Railway Infrastructure. Japanese and European fastenings and Observations and Measurements on Ballasted and Slab Track are presented.

Key words: Acting Loads, Static stiffness, Dynamic stiffness, Dynamic component of the Load, Static component of the Load, Ballasted track, Ballastless (slab) track.

INTRODUCTION

The means of transportation are classified as air, maritime, fluvial and terrestrial. The terrestrial means of transport are characterized by the top of their infrastructure that is the asphalt pavement in road transport and the steel-rail, part of the railway superstructure, in railway transport, supported on the relevant substructures. The railway track superstructure is the equivalent of the road pavement and as in the case of pavements there are flexible (ballasted track) and rigid track (slab track) superstructures.

The main difference between the two types of infrastructure is that the loads in railways are applied in two discrete locations along the rails, whereas in road pavements the location of the load application is random. The track superstructure (Fig. 1) is a multilayered system that consists of the rails, sleepers/ties with their fastenings, ballast -the equivalent of a flexible pavement- and the blanket layer consisting of compacted sand and gravel, which further distributes the loads and protects the substructure from the penetration of crashed ballast particles, mud ascent and pumping. The factor of decisive importance for track's behavior is the resilience or the total static stiffness coefficient of the track defined as ρ (French, Greek literature), c (German literature) or k (American literature).

RESEARCH: OBSERVATIONS, MEASUREMENTS, ANALYSIS

The stress on the substructure plays a key role in the design and

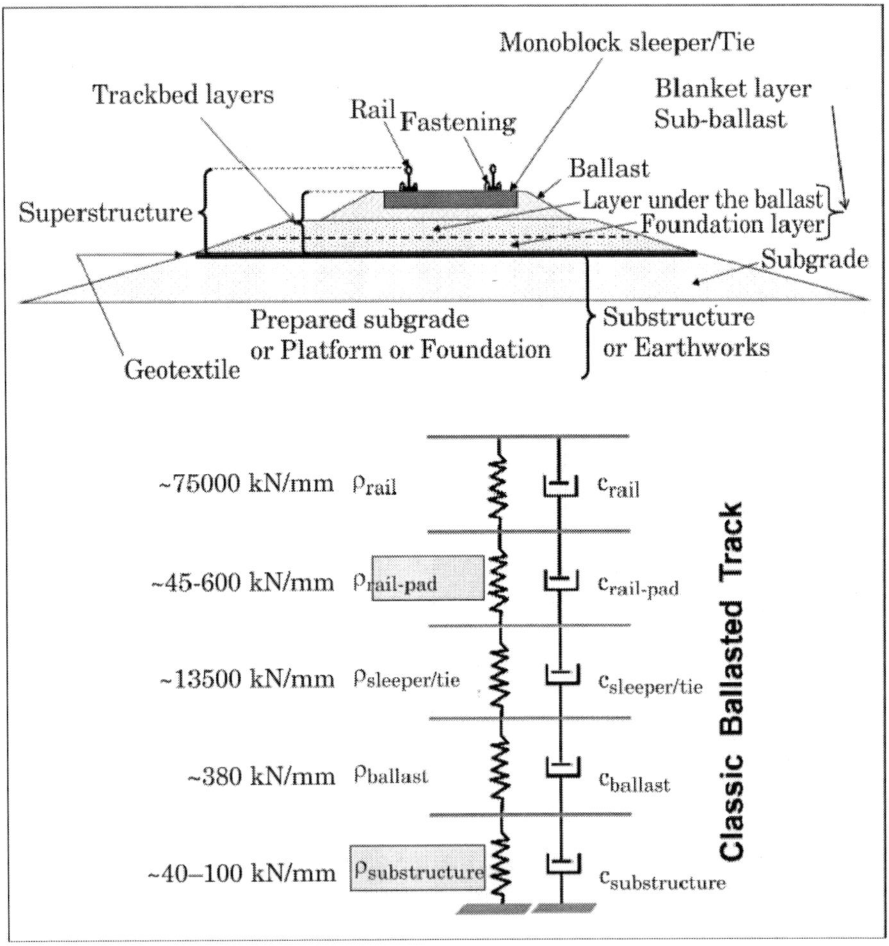

Fig. 1: Ballasted track in cross-section (upper illustration); static stiffness coefficients of each layer (lower illustration).

maintenance of High Speed railway tracks and its magnitude mainly depends on the total track stiffness coefficient. However, there is a lack of data in the international literature correlating the magnitude of stress on the track substructure and the track stiffness coefficient of High Speed lines under operation. The research performed for the Greek Railway network for the cracks observed on concrete sleepers in a percentage higher than 60% of the total number laid on track addressed this issue. The research group consisted of: (1) the National Technical University of Athens, (2) Aristotle University of Thessaloniki, School of Civil Engineering (3) the Hellenic Ministry of Environment, Land Planning, and Public Works/Central Public Works Laboratory, (4) the Hellenic Institute of Geological and Mineral Research, (5) the "Track" Research Department of the French Railways (SNCF) and (6) the University of Graz, under the coordination of the Greek Railways Organization (OSE) with the author as Coordinator and Head of the research team. The research program included theoretical analyses and measurements and tests both 'on track', in Greece and Europe, and 'in laboratory' at St-Ouen, Paris of the SNCF and at Graz University, Austria.

The findings, of this research program, highlighted the interaction between railway-vehicle and railway-track, comprising superstructure and substructure. A method (Giannakos, 2004, method) for the calculation of loads and stresses on a railway track was developed, as a result of this research. This method together with three methods found in the international literature (French, German and American) are used to calculate the loads and stresses on the track substructure after a sensitivity analysis for different cases of subgrade and condition of the rail-running-table and the results are compared and discussed for the fastenings in High Speed Lines in European and Japanese railway networks.

It should be noted that after an on-the-track investigation, professor J. Eisenmann and L. Mattner reported (1984) that the theoretical subsidence, as it is derived from the calculation of the track's vertical stiffness, coincides to the measured one. Professor J. Eisenmann (1980; 1988) ascertained also that theoretical calculations, performed by the semi-analytic methods, for the dimensioning of the superstructure correspond to the average value of the measurements on-track [see relevantly Giannakos, 2011]. Consequently, by using three times the standard deviation of the dynamic component of the Load, a 99.7% probability of occurrence is covered, in practice increased to 99.9% with five times the standard deviation, after a sensitivity analysis performed by these semi-analytic methods (easily programmed even in a spreadsheet, *e.g.*, like excel) in a very simple and fast way avoiding the sophisticated, exquisite Finite Element Method.

STIFFNESS / RESILIENCE *vs* ACTIONS ON RAILWAY TRACK

It must be noted here that in all four calculation methods the total static stiffness coefficient (resilience) of the track ρ_{total} (spring constant, [kN/mm]) is of decisive importance for the calculation of the action/reaction on each sleeper/tie. The more resilient is the track-structure the less is the acting-load (reaction) per support-point of the rail, since the load from the circulating axle is distributed in a larger area and in more adjacent sleepers. The less resilient is the track-structure the higher percentage of the circulating axle-load is acting on the rail's support-point under the wheel, whose (support-point's) reaction becomes very high. In general:

$$\frac{1}{\rho_{total}} = \sum_{i=1}^{\nu} \frac{1}{\rho_i} \tag{1}$$

where i are the layers that constitute the multilayered structure "Track" (Fig. 1), and ρ_{total} the total static stiffness coefficient of track, which must be calculated for each case.

Method cited in the French Literature

Given by Alias (1984); Prud'homme and Erieau (1976):

$$R_{total} = \left(Q_{wheel} + Q_a + 2 \cdot \sqrt{\left[\sigma^2\left(\Delta Q_{NSM}\right)\right] + \left[\sigma^2\left(\Delta Q_{SM}\right)\right]} \right) \cdot \overline{A}_{stat} \cdot 1{,}35 \tag{2}$$

which covers a probability of occurrence P = 95.5%, where: Q_{wheel} = the static load of the wheel, Q_a = load due to cant (superelevation) deficiency, $\sigma(\Delta Q_{NSM})$ = standard deviation of the Non-Suspended Masses of vehicle, $\sigma(\Delta Q_{SM})$ = standard deviation of the Suspended Masses of vehicle. The Non-Suspended Masses are the masses of the vehicle under the primary suspension (the axle, the wheels and the part of the semi-suspended electric-motor, which is supported on the axle; in the case of completely suspended electric-motors, on the bogie's frame, there is no additional mass due to the electric motor). The rest of the Vehicle's masses constitute the Suspended Masses. $\overline{A}_{stat}$ = reaction coefficient of the sleeper/tie, less than 1, which is equal to:

$$\overline{A}_{stat} = \frac{1}{2\sqrt{2}} \cdot \sqrt[4]{\frac{\rho_{total} \cdot \ell^3}{E \cdot J}} \tag{3}$$

and ρ_{total} = coefficient of total static stiffness (elasticity) of track, l = distance among sleepers, E and J = Modulus of Elasticity and Moment of Inertia of the rail.

Method cited in the German Literature

According to Eisenmann (2004; 1981b):

$$R_{\max} = Q_{wheel}\left(1 + 0.9 \cdot \left(1 + \frac{V - 60}{140}\right)\right) \cdot \overline{A}_{stat} \tag{4a}$$

which covers a probability of occurrence P = 99.7%, where: $\overline{A}_{stat}$ is given by equation (3), Q_{wheel} is the static load of the wheel, V the maximum speed.

Prof. Eisenmann in 1993 proposed a reduced factor of dynamic component:

$$R_{\max} = \left(1 + 0.9 \cdot \left(1 + \frac{V - 60}{380}\right)\right) \cdot \overline{A}_{stat} \cdot Q_{wheel} \tag{4b}$$

for V_{max}> 200 km/h, with probability of occurrence P = 99.7%.

Equation (4b) leads to a great under-estimation of the acting loads on track -than equation (4a)- with possible underestimation of the dimensioning of track elements -like *e.g.*, sleepers- as the literature describe, thus equation (4a) should be preferred for the concrete sleepers' dimensioning.

Method cited in the American Literature

According to AREMA 2012 (Hay, 1982; Selig and Waters, 2000; see also Giannakos, 2010a):

$$R_{\max} = p_{\max} \cdot \ell = \bar{A}_{stat} \cdot \left(1 + \frac{D_{33} \cdot V}{D_{wheel} \cdot 100}\right) \cdot Q_{wheel} \quad (5)$$

where D_{33} is the diameter of a wheel of 33 inches, D_{wheel} the wheel diameter of the vehicle examined in inches, $p_{\max}$ the maximum pressure per unit length of the track under the sleeper, and $\bar{A}_{\text{stat}}$ is the same as in equation (3). This method does not relate the resulting acting-load to the probability of occurrence.

Giannakos (2004) Method

According to this method which was derived as a result of the research described above (Giannakos, 2004; see also Giannakos and Loizos, 2010):

$$R_{service} = \bar{A}_{dynam} \cdot \left(Q_{wheel} + Q_{\alpha}\right) + (\mu \cdot \sqrt{\left[\sigma\left(\Delta Q_{NSM}\right)\right]^2 + \left[\sigma\left(\Delta Q_{SM}\right)\right]^2}) \quad (6a)$$

where: μ coefficient covering the probability of occurrence (μ = 2,3, or 5 for P = 95.5%, 99.7%, 99.9%), $\sigma(\Delta Q_{NSM})$ is the standard deviation of the dynamic load due to non-suspended masses m_{NSM} of each axle, $\sigma(\Delta Q_{SM})$ is the standard deviation of the dynamic load due to suspended masses m_{NSM},

$$\sigma\left(\Delta Q_{NSM}\right) = k_{1rail} \cdot V \cdot \sqrt{m_{NSM} \cdot h_{TRACK}} \quad (7)$$

$$\sigma\left(\Delta Q_{SM}\right) = \frac{V - 40}{1000} \cdot N_L \cdot Q_{wheel} \quad (8)$$

k_{1rail} coefficient of the condition of the running rail table, fluctuating (for lines with $V_{max} \geq 140$ km/h) between 0.00389 – 0.00584 for ground rail running table and 0.00779 – 0.01558 for non-ground rail running table, N_L coefficient normally equal to 0.5 – 1.2 and:

$$\bar{A}_{dynam} = \frac{1}{2\sqrt{2}} \cdot \sqrt[4]{\frac{\ell^3 \cdot h_{TR}}{E \cdot J}} \qquad (9)$$

$$h_{TR} = \rho_{dynam} = 2\sqrt{2} \cdot \sqrt[4]{E \cdot J \cdot \left(\frac{\rho_{total}}{\ell}\right)^3} \qquad (10)$$

The calculation of the track mass participating in the motion of the Non-Suspended Masses is cited in Giannakos (2010c).

The above equation (6a) is transformed in:

$$R_{max} = \frac{1}{2\sqrt[8]{2}} \cdot \sqrt[16]{\left(\frac{\rho_{total} \cdot \ell^3}{E \cdot J}\right)^3} \cdot \left(Q_{wheel} + Q_{\alpha}\right) + \left(3 \cdot \sqrt{\underbrace{\left(k_{\alpha} \cdot V \cdot \sqrt[8]{2^6 \cdot \left(m_{NSM-vehicle} + m_{TRACK}\right)^4 \cdot E \cdot J \cdot \left(\frac{\rho_{total}}{\ell}\right)^3}\right)^2}_{\sigma(\Delta Q_{NSM})} + \underbrace{\left(\frac{V-40}{1000} \cdot N_L \cdot Q_{wheel}\right)^2}_{\sigma(\Delta Q_{SM})}}\right) \qquad (6b)$$

The result of equation (11b) in kN, for a probability of occurrence 99.7%, where Q_{wheel} = the static wheel load in kN, Q_a = the load due to superelevation deficiency in kN, $m_{NSM-vehicle}$ the mass in tons (1t = 2204.62 pounds) of the Non-Suspended Masses of the vehicle, m_{TRACK} the track mass participating in their motion in tons also (for the calculation of the m_{TRACK} see Giannakos, 2013; 2012a; 2010c), ρ_{total} in kN/mm, μ the distance between the sleepers in mm, V in km/h, N_L ranging between 0.5 and 1.5 dependent on the track leveling defaults and k_a coefficient of the condition of the rail running table, ranging from $38942.43 \cdot 10^{-7}$ for ground rail running table to $155769 \cdot 10^{-7}$ for non-ground rail running table, for tracks of good condition and maybe up to $324520 \cdot 10^{-7}$ for secondary lines with rail running table in a very bad condition (Giannakos,

2004, 2014b; Giannakos and Vlassopoulou, 1994), E the modulus of elasticity [kN/mm^2], J the moment of inertia of the rail [mm^4], $\sigma(\Delta Q_{NSM})$ = the standard deviation of the dynamic load due to Non Suspended Masses and $\sigma(\Delta Q_{SM})$ = the standard deviation of the dynamic load due to Suspended Masses.

The results from this method predict an extended appearance of cracks in twin-block sleepers that was indeed observed on the Greek permanent way (over 60%). Moreover, for the estimation of the service-load, the pad stiffness is calculated through a trial-and-error procedure that ensures equilibrium among the numerous springs-components of the track system. In Feb. (2006) this method is adopted, by the International Federation of Concrete, for pre-cast concrete railway track systems design. For more details about these methods as well as about the methods in German and French Literature the interested reader may refer to Giannakos 2010c.

Comparison of Theoretical Calculations *vs.* Observations 'On-Track'

In Greece between 1972 and 1999, twin-block concrete sleepers of French technology were exclusively used, with RN fastenings, for tracks designed for V_{max} = 200 km/h and temporary operational speed V_{oper} = 120 – 140 km/h. Extended cracking was observed at a percentage of more than 60% of the sleepers laid on track. The methods cited in the international literature at that time did not provide any satisfactory justification for the appearance of the cracks, resulting in much lower values of actions on sleepers/ties than the cracking threshold, thus predicting no cracking at all. After an extensive research that included collaboration among various universities and railway organizations in Europe, the Giannakos (2004) method was developed whose results successfully predicted the extended cracking of the U2/U3 type of sleepers/ties (Giannakos, 2004; Giannakos and Loizos, 2010), calculating actions over the cracking thresh-old and in some cases over the failure threshold (Fig. 2).

This method was derived from theoretical analyses, measurements from laboratory tests performed in Greece, Austria, France, Belgium and other European countries and observations from real on-track experience. The results of the method were also presented for lines with Heavy Haul traffic that are typical in the United States (Giannakos, 2011).

STIFFNESS OF THE FASTENINGS PAD AND THE ACTING FORCES

The pad's stiffness plays a key role in the total response of the track. The pad's stiffness coefficient, ρ_{pad}, is calculated through the trial-and-error method from the load-deflection curve of the pad, provided by the producer. For the calculations the following combinations are considered based on the experience from the Greek railway network: UIC60 rail (ρ_{rail} = 75000 kN/mm), 2.60 m concrete sleeper B70 type ($\rho_{sleeper}$ = 13500 kN/mm), distance between sleepers 60 cm, ballast 2 years in operation ($\rho_{ballast}$ = 380 kN/mm), subgrade with stiffness $\rho_{subgrade}$ fluctuating from 40 kN/mm in the case of pebbly subgrade to very rigid of 250 kN/mm in the case of rocky tunnel bottom or concrete bridge with insufficient ballast depth and fastening W14 with pad Zw700 Saargummi with stiffness ρpad calculated through the trial-and-error method, wheel load 11.25 t, maximum speed 250 km/h, Non-Suspended Masses 1.5 t, height of the vehicle's centre of gravity from the rail running table 1.5 m, wheel's diameter 1 m (39.37 inch), maximum cant deficiency 160 mm, and average condition of an un-ground rail for the rail running table with coefficient ka' = 0.0116873.

The actions have been calculated also for the verification of the model (Fig. 2) for the case of the twin-block concrete sleepers that presented an extended cracking (in a percentage higher than 60%) of the total number of sleepers laid on track with the following data: UIC54 rail (ρ_{rail} = 75000 kN/mm), twin-block concrete sleeper U2/U3 type ($\rho_{sleeper}$ = 13500 kN/mm), distance between sleepers 60 cm, ballast 2 years in operation ($\rho_{ballast}$ = 380 kN/mm), subgrade with stiffness $\rho_{subgrade}$ fluctuating from 40 kN/mm in the case of pebbly subgrade to very rigid of 250 kN/mm in the case of rocky tunnel bottom or concrete bridge with insufficient ballast depth and fastening RN with pad 4.5 mm with stiffness ρ_{pad} calculated through the trial-and-error method, wheel load 10.40 t, maximum speed 140 km/h, Non-Suspended Masses 2.54 t, height of the vehicle's centre of gravity from the rail running table 1.5 m, maximum cant deficiency 105 mm, and average condition of an un-ground rail for the rail running table with coefficient ka' = 0.0116873.

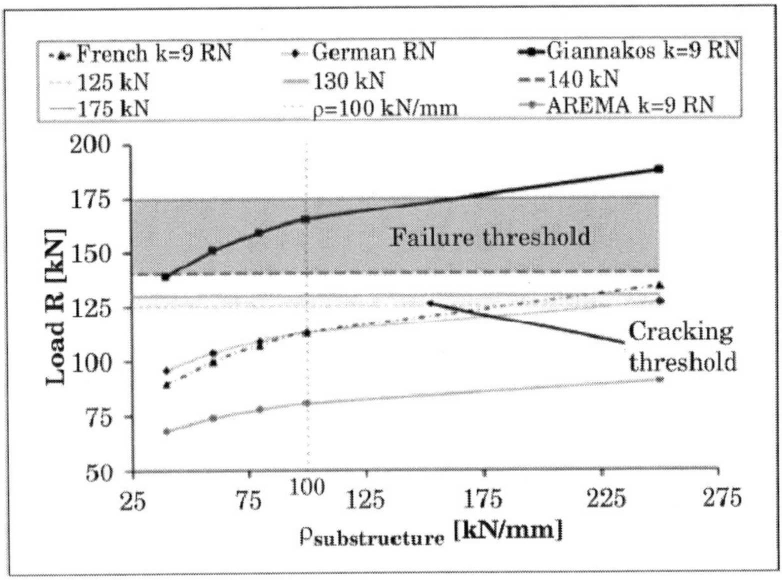

Fig. 2: Comparison of theoretical calculations (by the four methods) of the acting loads on U2/U3 sleepers with observations on track with RN fastenings.

For comparison, the same conditions were applied for the first case in combination with the Japanese fastenings (as presented in Fig. 3, see Giannakos, 2012b) with the relevant second kind pad of stiffness 60 MN/m, with actual stiffness ρ_{pad} in each case calculated through the trial-and-error method, and: UIC60 rail (ρ_{rail} = 75000 kN/mm), 2.60 m concrete sleeper B70 type ($\rho_{sleeper}$ = 13500 kN/mm), distance between sleepers 60 cm, ballast 2 years in operation

($\rho_{ballast}$ = 380 kN/mm), subgrade with stiffness $\rho_{subgrade}$ fluctuating from 40 kN/mm in the case of pebbly subgrade to very rigid of 250 kN/mm in the case of rocky tunnel bottom or concrete bridge with insufficient ballast depth, wheel load 11.25 t, maximum speed 250 km/h, Non-Suspended Masses 1.5 t, height of the vehicle's centre of gravity from the rail running table 1.5 m, wheel's diameter 1 m (39.37 inch), maximum cant deficiency 160 mm, and average condition of an un-ground rail for the rail running table with coefficient ka' = 0.0116873.

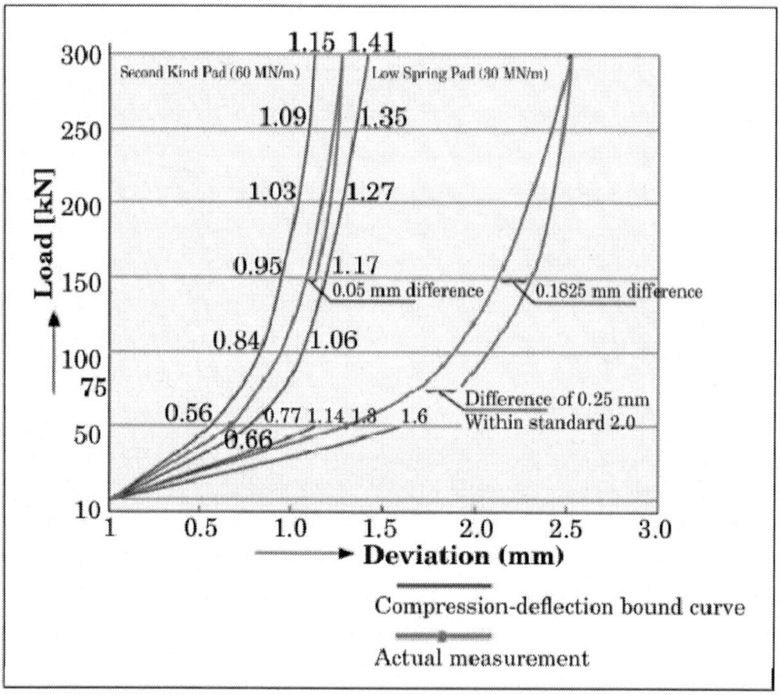

Fig. 3: Load-deflection curves of Japanese fastening pads (Giannakos, 2012b; see Acknowledgements).

The results for the Actions/Reactions on each support point (sleeper) of the track panel in the case of 2.60 m long sleeper B70 type of prestressed concrete and W14 fastening with pad Zw700 Saargummi, are depicted in Fig. 4, as derived from the four methods described above: German, French, AREMA and Giannakos (2004).

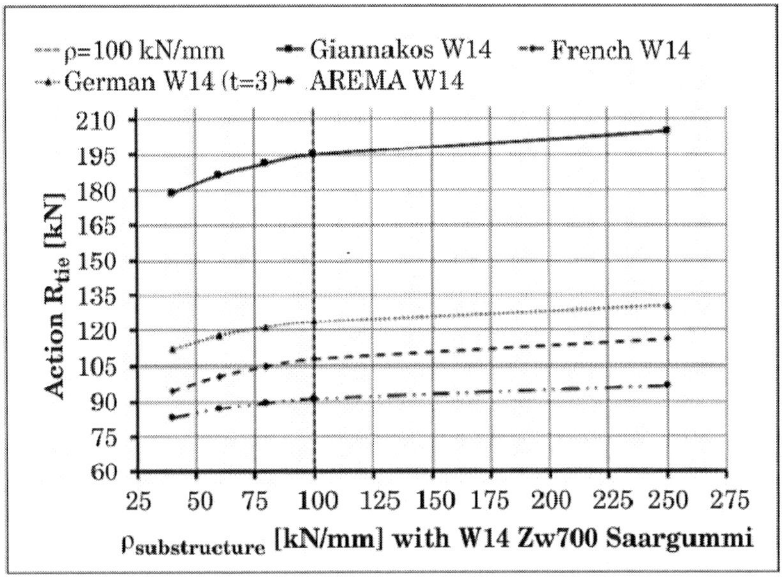

Fig. 4: Actions on the track panel calculated by the four methods for fastening W14 and pad Zw700 Saargummi.

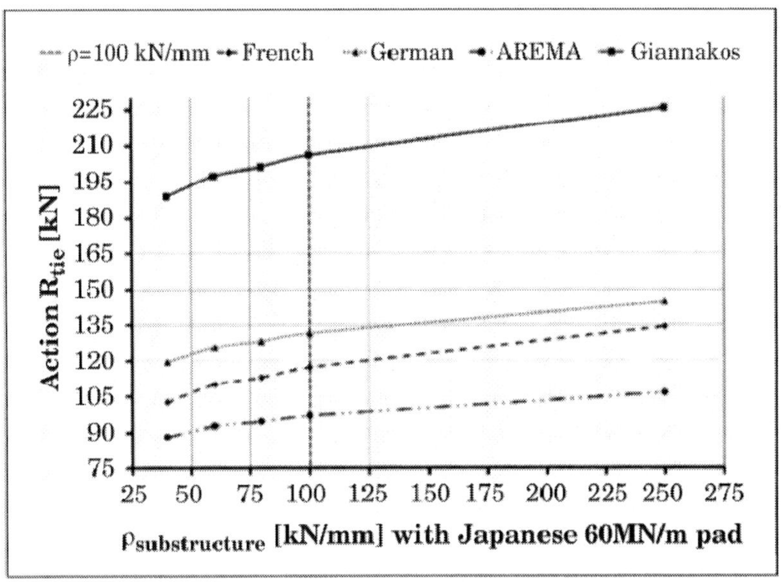

Fig. 5: Actions on the track panel calculated by the four methods for Japanese fastening with pad of second kind (60 MN/m) [Giannakos, 2012b].

The results for the Actions/Reactions on each support point (sleeper) of the track panel in the case of 2.60 m long sleeper B70 type of prestressed concrete and Japanese fastening (Giannakos, 2012b) with pad of second kind (60 MN/m) of Fig. 3, are depicted in Fig. 5, as derived from the four methods described above:German, French, AREMA and Giannakos (2004). Since there is no reference available, in this paper a toe-load of 9 kN per fastening (18 kN per rail) derived from the correct tightening of the "fastening's clip" is considered.

STRESSES ON BALLAST-BED, SUBGRADE AND DESIGN CRITERIA[1]

The average stress $p_{ballast}$ under the sleeper/tie seating surface should only be used qualitatively and not quantitatively, since, in practice, there is no uniform support of the sleeper/tie on the ballast, or uniform compaction of the ballast and the ground, and there are faults on the rail running table, imperfections on the wheels etc. The simplest way to calculate it is to divide the Action R on the tie by the "effective" tie seating surface:

$$\overline{p}_{ballast} = \frac{R_{\max}}{F_{eff-tie}} = \frac{R_{\max}}{L_{eff-tie} \cdot b_{tie}} = \frac{R_{\max}}{\left(L_{tie} - e\right) \cdot b_{tie}} \tag{11}$$

where: R_{max} the maximum reaction/action on each tie derived from each method, F_{tie} = effective tie seating surface, L_{tie} = length of the tie *i.e.* 8.5 feet or 2590 mm, e = gauge of the track (~1500 mm), $L_{eff\text{-}tie}$ calculated from Equation (12) with the assumption that the center of the tie is unsupported, b_{tie} = width of the tie at the seating surface.

$$\mathrm{L}_{\text{eff-tie}} = \left(\mathrm{L}_{\text{tie}} - \mathrm{e}\right) \tag{12}$$

The load on the ballast-bed should be equal to the sum of the mean (static) load + 1 to 3 standard deviations (probability of appearance/level of confidence P = 68.3% ÷ 99.7% depending on

[1] Giannakos 2012b, 2014e

the circulation speed and the necessary maintenance work. This implies that the action calculated from the methods cited in German and French literature as well as Giannakos (2004) method could be reduced for a probability of appearance relevant to 68.3% for the subgrade or 99.5% for the ballast.

French method: Equation 2 covers a 95.5% probability of appearance, so it is used for the calculation of the stress on ballast in Equation 11 since for the calculation of the stress on the formation a level of confidence on the order of 68.3% to 95.5%should be considered.

German method: Equation 4 is used for the calculation of R_{max} in Equation 11 using $t = 2$ (probability 95.5%) for the stress on the ballast, and $t = 1$ or 2 (probability 68.3% to 95.5%) for the stress on the subgrade.

AREMA method: This method does not use the probabilistic approach. Equation 5 is used in any case for the calculation of R_{max} in Equation 11.

Giannakos (2004) method: Equation 6 is used for the calculation of R_{max} in Equation 11, using $\mu = 2$ (probability 95.5%) for the stress on the ballast, and $\mu = 1$ or 2 (probability 68.3% to 95.5%) for the stress on the subgrade and the average stress under the tie seating surface should be calculated by the following equation (Giannakos, 2004; 2010 b):

$$\overline{p} = \overline{A}_{subsidence} \cdot \left(Q_{wheel} + Q_{\alpha}\right) + \frac{2 \cdot \sqrt{\left[\sigma\left(\Delta Q_{NSM}\right)\right]^2 + \left[\sigma\left(\Delta Q_{SM}\right)\right]^2}}{h_{TR}} \cdot C \quad (13)$$

where:

$$\overline{A}_{subsidence} = \frac{1}{2\sqrt{2}} \cdot \sqrt[4]{\frac{\ell^3}{E \cdot J \cdot h_{TR}^3}} \quad (14)$$

$$C = \frac{\rho_{total}}{\left(\frac{F_{eff-tie}}{2}\right)} \quad (15)$$

$F_{eff\text{-}tie}$ = the effective tie seating surface (for monoblock ties the central non-loaded area should be subtracted) as in Equation 12.

For conventional superstructure, which comprises of rail, fastenings, sleepers and ballast, there is an optimum life-cycle from an economic point of view. The mean stress on the subgrade (magnitude of the pressure on the contact surface under ballast-bed) plays a major role in the maintenance needs and planning and consequently on the costs. On the basis of AASHTO testing for road construction, the following formula is valid:

$$\text{Decrease in track geometry quality} = (\text{increase in stress on the ballast bed})^m \quad (16)$$

where m = 3 to 4.

When the stress on the ballast-bed is increased by 10%, then a more rapid decrease in the track's geometry from 1.33 to 1.46 times occurs with a corresponding increase of the maintenance cost.

The key parameters for the definition of the track's vertical stiffness and deformation are the quality of subgrade and elastic pad, both of which characterize the subsidence (or the stiffness) of a track, that depends on the distribution of loads between the sleeper that carries the axle and the adjacent sleepers (Eisenmann, 1988; 1981a; 1980). Among them it is the formation of the track that presents residual deformations: subsidences and lateral displacements, directly connected to the deterioration of the so-called geometry of the track, which can be nevertheless described much more specifically as quality of the track.

Minimizing or diminishing the subsidence practically minimizes the permanent deformation of the track. In order to achieve that, the mean pressure should be kept below a certain value. It is imperative to reduce as much as possible the development of vertical, primarily, as well as lateral displacements on the subgrade layer. On the contrary, the total subsidence of the track structure should acquire a high value, in order to distribute the load Q_{total} at a longer distance from its acting point and consequently to a greater number of adjacent sleepers. This will minimize the action/reaction on each sleeper. The above two requirements are contradictory.

The average stress on ballast-bed was calculated applying Equation 11 for the methods cited in French, German and American literature and Equation 11 for the Giannakos (2004) method and for a 95.5% level of confidence. The results are depicted in Fig. 6 for track equipped with W14 fastenings (European) and Fig. 7 for track equipped with Japanese fastenings with pads of 60 MN/m as in Fig. 3. The solution is the adoption of very "soft" fastening pads resulting in a high value of subsidence due to their resilient behaviour that secures non-permanent deformation and, consequently, excellent preservation of the geometry/quality of the track.

For a given quality of ballast material, as far as the ballast deformations are concerned, this is accomplished by the correct combination and usage of heavy track machinery (ballast regulator, tamping machine, dynamic stabilizer). In Giannakos (2010a) a relationship between ballast quality and life-cycle is cited. For the layers underneath the ballast a very well-executed construction is required: crushed stone material in the upper layer, with a compaction of 100% Proctor Modified or 105% Proctor Normal (Giannakos, 1999). According to the demands of the design requirement for the modulus of elasticity E_{v2} (taken from the second load step in a plate loading test) is: $E_{v2} \geq 80$ N/mm^2 (MPa) for the subgrade in the case of ballasted track. The permissible compressive stress on the formation can be established using the following equation (Esveld, 2001):

$$\bar{\sigma}_z = \frac{0.006 \cdot E_{v2}}{1 + 0.7 \cdot \log n} \tag{17}$$

where: E_{v2} modulus of elasticity taken from the second load step in a plate loading test, n number of load cycles (usually 2 million cycles).

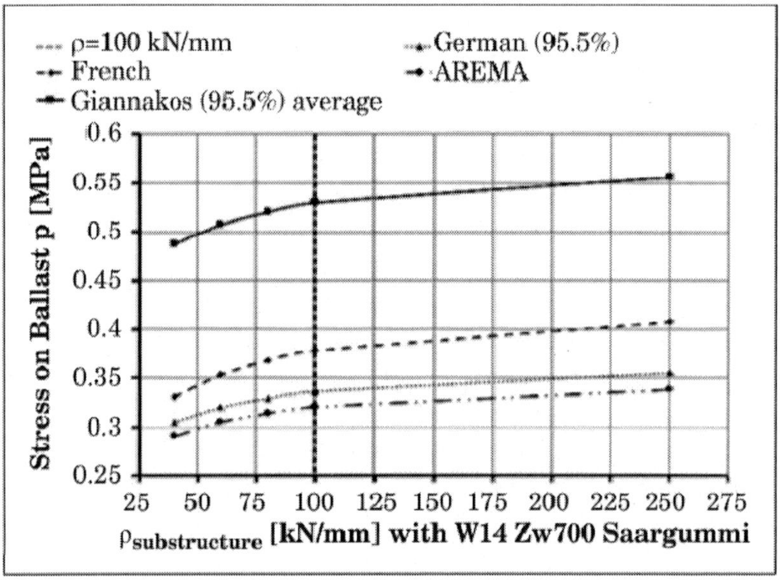

Fig. 6: Stresses on the ballast-bed calculated by the four methods for fastening W14 and pad Zw700 Saargummi.

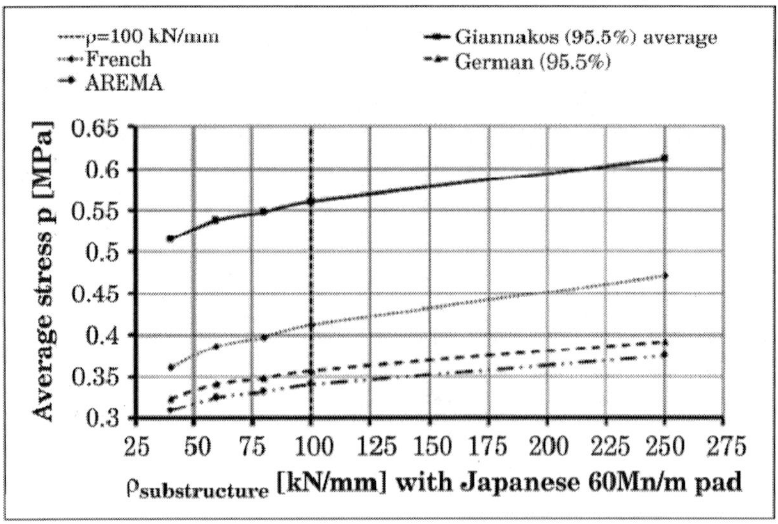

Fig. 7: Stresses on the ballast-bed calculated by the four methods for Japanese fastening with pad of second kind (60 MN/m) [Giannakos, 2012b].

For 2 million cycles and E_{v2} = 80 N/mm^2, then the permissible compressive stress for the formation should be (see also Esveld 2001):

$$\sigma_z = 0.089\ \text{MPa} \tag{18}$$

The stress on the subgrade, assuming a distribution cone of 45 degrees and a ballast-bed thickness of 30 cm underneath the lower contact surface of the sleeper to the upper surface of the subgrade, can be estimated as follows:

Sleeper seating surface S (length 2.60):

$$S_{Tie} = 1100\ \text{mm} \times 260\ \text{mm} \approx 285.000\ \text{mm}^2$$

Surface on the top of Subgrade:

$$S_{Subgrade} \approx (2600/2 + 300) \times 600 = 1600 \times 600$$

$$S_{Subgrade} = 960.000\ \text{mm}^2$$

$$\text{Relation } S_{Subgrade} / S_{Sleeper} = 3{,}368$$

Consequently

$$\bar{p}_{Subgrade} = \bar{p}_{Sleeper}/3{,}368 \tag{19}$$

And its maximum possible value is (for $\rho_{subgrade}$ = 100 kN/mm and probability of occurrence 68.3%, Giannakos method μ = 1): in the case of the quality of formation described above with E_{v2} = 80 N/mm^2. It is worth noticing that according to the most adverse results for the case of ballasted track a formation quality of E_{v2} = 80 N/mm^2 -accepted in some railway networks- could not be accepted and a subgrade's quality of at least . E_{v2} = 105 MPa with a σ_z = 0.116 MPa is required during design phase. This complies with the experience obtained from the High-Speed lines.

$$\max \bar{p}_{Subgrade} \approx 0.376 / 3.368 = 0.112 > 0.089\ \text{MPa}$$

GIANNAKOS (2004) METHOD *vs* MEASUREMENTS ON SLAB-TRACK[2]

In the article *'Entwicklung, Bemessung und Erforschung des schotterlosen Oberbaues "Rheda"'*, the measurements on a "Rheda" type slab track are cited by professor Eisenmann *et al.*, (1979), for static axle load 20 t (for train sets ICE 1 with maximum speed 250 km/h and higher). The fastening system used at that era was Ioarv 108 with pad Zwp55. The static stiffness coefficient of this pad was approximately 35 kN/mm (according to personal communication with Mr. W. Boesterling from Vossloh Gmbh, in an e-mail dated February, 2007).

The measured mean values of deflection of the rail running table for an axle-load of 20 t are cited in Table 1 below (Eisenmann*et al.*, 1979; p.34), where measurements of the deflection of the concrete slab beneath each axle of a three-axle bogie are also cited. The values presented in Table 1 are used in Giannakos (2004) method, to calculate the deflection of the rail running table.

Table 1: Measurements in a Slab Track section as cited in Eisenmann*et al.*, 1979, p. 34.

	Measurement July 1972	***Measurement Dec. 1974***	***Measurement June 1977***
Deflection of Rail Running Table/Surface	1.49 mm	1.27 mm	1.31 mm
Deflection of Concrete Slab	0.37 mm	0.27 mm	0.23 mm
Relative Deflection of Rail *vs* Slab	1.12 mm	1.00 mm	1.08 mm

In order to verify Giannakos (2004) method for slab track these five layers were used for the 1979 Rheda type slab track: rail with (1) ρ_{rail} = 75,000 kN/mm; (2) fastening pad 1 (Zwp55) with ρ_{pad} = 35 kN/mm; (3) fastening pad 2 (Zw687) with ρ_{pad} = 450 kN/mm; (4) concrete sleeper with average $\rho_{sleeper}$ = 13,500 kN/mm; for the concrete slab, a sensitivity analysis will be performed for a range

2 Giannakos 2016a.

of $\rho_{slab} = \rho_{substructure}$: 86 kN/mm, 100 kN/mm, 114 kN/mm, 171 kN/mm, 250 kN/mm (Giannakos *et al.*, 2011), to 425 kN/mm, covering the whole range of substructure.

The calculations were programmed in a computer code and calculations were performed varying the stiffness of the substructure as described by the author (in Giannakos, 2004; Giannakos and Loizos, 2010) and the probability of occurrence between 68.3% and 95.5%, with linear extrapolation for coefficient μ. The results are depicted in Figs. 7, 8 and 9 and they are presented as a function of the total static track stiffness, for the Rheda Sengeberg type Slab Track already applied in High-speed lines under operation in the Greek network.

In Fig. 8 the calculated values of deflection were derived for a probability of occurrence 95.5%. The difference is very small, however a further investigation was performed for a range of the probabilities of occurrence. The results are depicted in Fig. 9. The results of a probability of occurrence of 80% ($\mu = 1.43$) are plotted inside the area of measured values for a range of $\rho_{substructure}$ from 86 to 425 kN/mm. Fig. 9 depicts the load curve as calculated by the

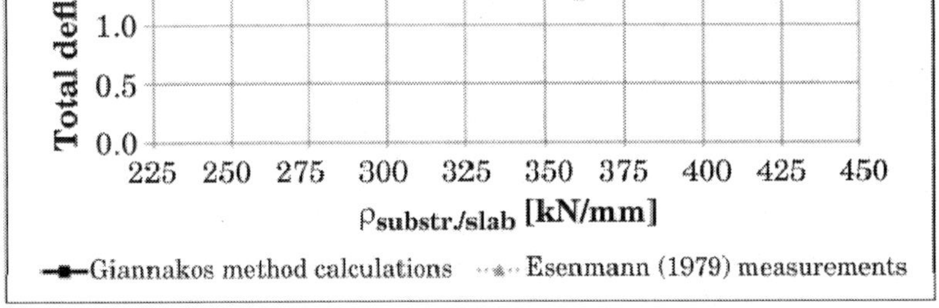

Fig. 8: Theoretical results of deflection in slab track Rheda type calculated by the Giannakos (2004) method and probability of occurrence 95.5% *vs* measurements as in Eisenmann *et al.*, 1979 [Giannakos, 2016a].

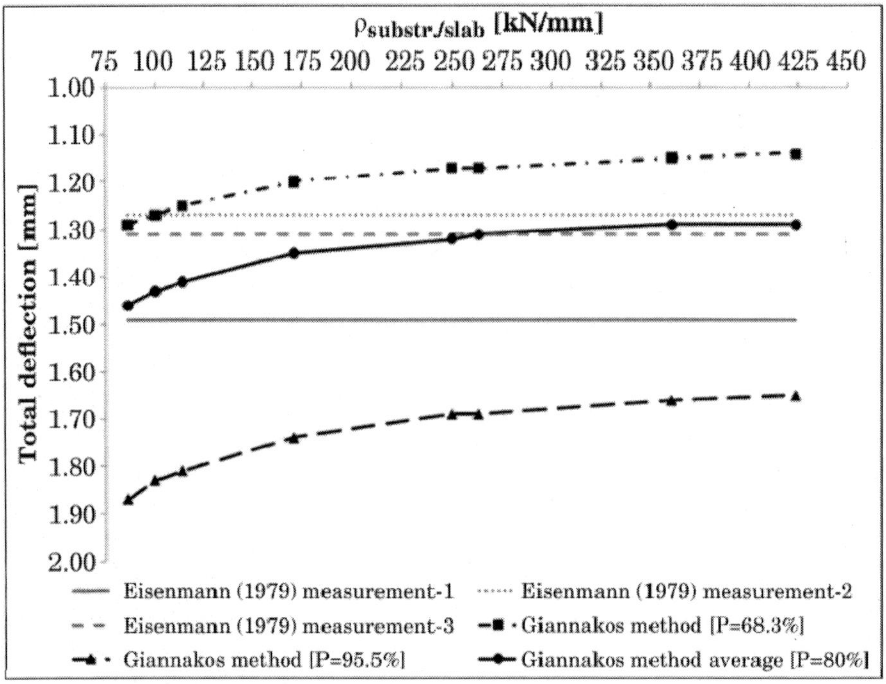

Fig. 9: Theoretical results of deflection in slab track Rheda type calculated by the Giannakos (2004) method and probability of occurrence 68.3%, 80% and 95.5% *vs* the three measurements as in Eisenmann *et al.*, 1979 [Giannakos, 2016a].

Giannakos (2004) method for a probability of occurrence 80%, in a greater scale for a more detailed depiction.

This proves that the method is also applicable for slab track. The method was also used to calculate the deflection and the actions on the slab track. For Rheda 2000 the deflections are almost the same as in the case of Rheda Sengeberg, since the total stiffness coefficients are almost identical. Rheda 2000 has a negligibly lower stiffness coefficient due to the absence of concrete sleeper ($1/\rho_{sleeper}$ = 1/13,500 equals to 0.00127–0.00151 of the ρ_{total} for a fluctuation of $\rho_{substructure}$ from 86 to 425 kN/mm). The influence of the stiffness variation of the substructure (from 86 kN/mm to 425 kN/mm) on the total deflection ρ_{total} fluctuates approximately around a percentage of 7%.

The application of Slab Track technology in a railway network creates the need for Transition Zones, which serve as interfaces between the ballastless and ballasted track sections, where significant and abrupt change in stiffness occurs. The Transition Zones guarantee a smooth stiffness transition between slab track and ballasted track, resulting in a smooth variation of the forces that act on the track (for more details on the change of elasticity in the transition zones between the ballasted and the ballastless sections of the track (see Giannakos *et al.*, 2011).

The Giannakos (2004) Method is verified *vs* measurements on-track in Slab-Track of the German railway network.

Since "the theoretical subsidence is the same as that derived from the calculation of the track's vertical stiffness" and "the theoretical calculations performed for the dimensioning of the superstructure correspond to the average value of the measurements" on-track, the use of three standard deviations of the dynamic component of the acting-loads cover a 99.7% probability of occurrence.

The sensitivity analysis performed showed that the role of the formation of the railway track (blanket layer and beneath in the case of Ballasted Track and the Frost Protection Layer in the case of Ballastless Track) is key to its overall performance therefore special attention should be paid during design and a very strict supervision during construction. For the case of the Ballastless Track an excellent quality of the top of the formation/substructure with E_{v2} = 120 MPa is expected to guarantee a satisfactory performance of the track. Under the most adverse conditions in the case of Ballasted Track a quality of E_{v2} = 80 N/mm^2 or 11.60 kips/in^2 is not expected to behave satisfactorily and a quality of E_{v2} = 105 N/mm^2 or 15.23 kips/in^2 or better should be required.

ACKNOWLEDGEMENTS

The author would like to thank Mr. Kenji Takayanagi of Mitsui and Mr. O. Haga of the JRTT for providing load-deflection curves of the Japanese fastenings on 2005 (Fig. 3).

REFERENCES

Alias, J. (1984). *La voieferree*, IIème edition, Eyrolles, Paris.

AREMA (2012). *Manual for Railway Engineering.*

Eisenmann, J. (2004). *"Die Schiene als Tragbalken"*, *Eisenbahningenieur*, 5.

Eisenmann, J. (1988). Schotteroberbau: Moglichkeiten und Perspektiven fur die Moderne Bahn. Giesel-Verlag, Isernhagen, Germany.

Eisenmann, J. (1981a). "Verhaltensfunktion des Schotters, Folgerungen fur hohe Fahrgeschwindingkeiten", *Der Eisenbahningenieur*, Darmstadt.

Eisenmann, J. (1981b). "The Rail as support and Roadway, theoretical principles and practical examples", *In*: Fastenrath, F. (*ed.*) *"Railroad Track - Theory and Practice"*, part 2, Frederic Ungar Pub. Co., NY.

Eisenmann, J. (1980). Verjormungsverhalten der Schiene. Auswirkungen auf die Oberbaubeanspruchung, Lagestabilitat und Storungsfunktion. ZEV- Glasers Annalen, Berlin, pp. 37–41.

Eisenmann, J. and Mattner, L. (1984). Auswirkung der Oberbaukonstruction auf die Schotter und Untergrund-beanspruchung. *Eisenbahningenieur*, 35(3): 99–107.

Esveld, C. (2001). *Modern Railway Track*, MRT-Productions, The Netherlands.

fib/FederationInternationale du Beton/International Federation of Concrete (2006). Precast Concrete Railway Track Systems, Task Group 6.5. (invited member K. Giannakos) of the Committee 6 for prefabrication, special edition, Switzerland.

Giannakos, K. (2016a). "Deflection of a Railway Reinforced Concrete Slab Track: Comparing the Theoretical Results with Experimental Measurements". *Engineering Structures Elsevier*, 122: 296–309.

Giannakos, K. (2016b). "Second Order Differential Equation of Motion in Railways the Variance of the Dynamic Component of Actions due to the Sprung Masses of the Vehicles". *Intl. Journal of Theoretical and Applied Mechanics*, pp. 30–37. http://www.iaras.org/iaras/journals/ijtam,

Giannakos, K. (2016c). "Modeling the Influence of Short Wavelength Defects in a Railway Track on the Dynamic Behavior of the Non-Suspended Masses", *Mechanical Systems and Signal Processing, Elsevier*, pp. 68–83.

Giannakos, K. (2015). "Mathematical analysis of the transient loads for a deformed joint or welding in a railway track". *Intl. Journal of Engineering and Mathematical Modelling*, 2: 51–62.

Giannakos, K. (2014a). "Secondary stiffness of fastening's clip: Influence on the behaviour of the railway track panel",IFSTTAR, http://tra2014.traconference.eu/papers/pdfs/TRA2014_Fpaper_17507.pdf.

Giannakos, K. (2014b). "Influence of a Bent or Battered Joint or Welding on the Dynamic Loads due to the Non-Suspended Masses of Railway Vehicles". *NAUN International Journal of Mechanics*, 8: 307–318.

Giannakos, K. (2014c). "Design Loads on Railway Substructure: Sensitivity Analysis of the Influence of the Fastening Stiffness". *International Journal of Railway*, 7(2): 46–56.

Giannakos, K. (2014d). "Ballast Specifications' Requirements Related to Ballast Hardness and Life-Cycle". *Modern Traffic and Transportation Engineering Research (MTTER) Journal*, 3(2): 37–47.

Giannakos, K. (2014e). "Actions on a Railway Track, due to an Isolated Defect". *Intl. Journal of Control and Automation*, 7(3): 195–212. http:// www.sersc.org/ journals/IJCA/vol7_no3/19.pdf.

Giannakos, K. (2013). Selected Topics in Railway Engineering, University of Thessaly, Dpt. Civil Engineering, Greece, http://giannakoskonstan tinos.com/wp.

Giannakos, K. (2012a). "Influence of the Track's Damping on the Track Mass Participating in the Motion of the Non-Suspended Masses of Railway Vehicles-Theoretical Calculation and Comparison to Measurements", volume published in honor of professor Giannopoulos, G. Aristotle University of Thessaloniki, in Greek.

Giannakos, K. (2012b). "Design Loads on Railway Substructure - Comparative parametric Investigation on the Influence of Fastening Stiffness (European and Japanese)", 2nd *International Conference on Transportation Geotechnics*- IS Hokkaido 2012, proceedings, pp. 787–792.

Giannakos, K. (2011). "Heavy Haul Railway Track Maintenance and Use of Resilient versus Stiff Fastenings", TRR2011, pp. 155–162.

Giannakos, K. (2010a). "Loads on track, Ballast Fouling and Life-cycle under Dynamic Loading in Railways". *Journal of Transportation Engineering, ASCE*, 136(12): 1075–1084.

Giannakos, K. (2010b). "Interaction between Superstructure and Substructure in railways", *Fifth International Conference on "Recent Advances in Geotechnical Earthquake Engineering and Soil Dynamics" and Symposium in Honor of Professor I. M. Idriss*, May 24-29, San Diego, CA, USA.

Giannakos, K. (2010c). "Theoretical calculation of the track-mass in the motion of unsprung masses in relation to track dynamic stiffness and damping". *International Journal of Pavement Engineering (IJPE), Special Rail Issue "High-Speed Railway Infrastructure: Recent Developments and Performance"*, 11(4): 319–330.

Giannakos, K. (2010d). *"Investigation of fastenings' stiffness on the Actions on track panel"*, performed for ObermeyerPlanen + BeratenGmbh, during the Design of the New Railway Track of Normal Gauge in the Kiato – km 2+000 position (Rododaphne), ERGA-OSE, Athens, Greece.

Giannakos, K., ObermeyerPlanen + BeratenGmbh (2008). "Calculation of Stiffness coefficients, l, in the Transition Zone between Slab Track and Ballasted Track – Slab Track Rheda 2000 type Design of the New Railway

Track of Normal Gauge in the Kiato – km 2+000 position (Rododaphne)", ERGA-OSE, Athens.

Giannakos, K. (2004). "*Actions on Railway Track*", Papazissis publications, Athens, English edition, www.papazisi.gr.

Giannakos, K. and Loizos, A. (2010). "Evaluation of actions on concrete sleepers as design loads–Influence of fastenings". *International Journal of Pavement Engineering (IJPE)*,11(3): 197–213.

Giannakos, K. and Vlassopoulou, I. (1994). Load of Concrete Sleepers and Application for Twin-Block Sleepers, Technical Chronicles. *Scientific Journal of TCG*, 14: 2, in Greek.

Hay, W. (1982). *Railroad Engineering*, John Wiley and Sons.

Prud'homme, A. and Erieau, J. (1976). "*Les nouvelles traverses en beton de la SNCF*", RGCF-2.

Selig, E. and Waters, J. (1994). "*Track Geotechnology and Substructure Management*", Thomas Telford, London, reprinted 2000.

5

Agri and Dairy Entrepreneurship and Rural Livelihood of the Sample Farmers in North 24 Parganas District, West Bengal

SAIKAT MAJUMDAR[1] & DEBARATI MAJUMDAR BHOWMICK[2]

ABSTRACTW

The Agriculture sector plays an important role in the rural economy as well as in the socio economic development of rural households. It is the back bone of Indian economy and is the dominant sector in terms of employment and playing thwe significant role in sustaining the rural livelihoods of North 24 Parganas District. It has been recognized as an instrument to bring socio-economic transformation in rural areas. With the increasing population rural people are still facing the problem of unemployment. Agri and Dairy Entrepreneurship are the solutions to many economic problems like poverty and unemployment. It is the important pillar of rural development. Youth Society is the pillar of any development. For this development their active participation, dedication is required.

[1] Department of Rural Development, University of Science and Technology, Meghalaya

[2] Department of Zoology, University of Science and Technology, Meghalaya

**Corresponding E-mail*: saikat.majumdar24@gmail.com

Therefore, it is essential to train the jobless agriculture graduates, youths and others, in Agri- business management as an Agri preneur for their betterment as well as economic stability and society's betterment.

Key words: Dairy farming, Unemployment, Poverty, Rural development.

INTRODUCTION

The Agriculture and Dairy sector plays an important role in the rural economy as well as in the socio economic development of rural households. It is the back bone of Indian economy and is the dominant sector in terms of employment and playing the significant role in sustaining the rural livelihoods of North 24 Parganas District. It has been recognized as an instrument to bring socio-economic transformation in rural areas. The dairy sector supports around 10 million members, farmers through one lakh cooperative societies existing in the country. The sector is the major source of income for an estimated 27.6 million people and the milk and its processing also provides employment. The overall contribution of Livestock Sector in total GDP is nearly 4.11% at current prices during 2012-13 (19th livestock Census- 2012, Ministry of Agriculture, Govt. of India). With the increasing population rural people are still facing the problem of unemployment. Dairy farming is the solution to many economic problems like poverty and unemployment which are the main problems in rural areas.

With this background, an attempt is made in this paper to study the Dairy Entrepreneurship and rural livelihood in North 24 Parganas district, West Bengal, with the following specific objective:

1. To improve the standard of living of farm household as well as rural people through Agri and Dairy farming.

METHODOLOGY

The study is mainly based on secondary data regarding recent trends and Development of Dairy and Agri- Preneur in India. The secondary data were collected from standard text books of related topics, journals and internet. Simple percentages were estimated in the present study. Besides, C.G.R was also estimated in the present study. The following formula was used to compute the C.G.R.

Where, x is the time variable, y is the variable for which growth rate is calculated and b is the regression co-efficient of Y on x. Now, Compound Growth percentage

$$(CGR\ \%) = (\text{antilog } `b' - 1) \times 100$$

RESULTS AND DISCUSSION

Dairy Farming in India

In India majority of rural population are still dependent upon the agriculture and allied sector especially dairy sector for their livelihood. In the stage of unemployment and low growth rate in agriculture sector it is necessary to create an environment of sustainable agriculture by providing entrepreneurship in Agriculture as well as Dairy farming, which is the important pillar of rural development.

In India agriculture is treated as a family tradition. The farming families those who are dependent upon the agriculture sector, they have to realize that it is not only their hobby; it is an important way of earning. Agriculture must be treated as an enterprise with good managerial background for the rural development as well as country's development. Sah (2009) state that developing entrepreneurship in dairy will solve the entire problem like (a) Reduce the burden of agriculture (b) Generate employment opportunities for rural youth (c) Control migration from rural to urban areas (d) Increase national income (e) Support industrial development in rural areas (f) Reduces the pressure on urban cities.

Establishment of Agri-Business Centres

Agri-Business Centre scheme was launched in April 2002 with the objective to supplement efforts of Government extension system by facilitating agri graduates and diploma holders to provide fee based extension services to farmers. During 2012-13, subsidy of 7.64 crore was released for 203 units. Cumulatively, 18.57 crore was released for 740 units. (NABARD Report, 2012-13).

Table 1: Existing no of Agri business centers in India

Year	*Agri. Graduates Trained*	*Agri-Ventures Established*
2002-03	3058	416
2003-04	1110	457
2004-05	2977	783
2005-06	2902	1415
2006-07	3149	1081
2007-08	2742	1039
2008-09	2503	824
2009-10	2564	1111
2010-11	3224	1292
2011-12	4015	2139
2012-13	3157	990
(Till 28th Feb., 2013		
C.G.R. (%)	4.71	10.77

Source: Department of Agriculture and Cooperation, Directorate of Extension, Pusa, New Delhi

The benefits of Agripreneurs are given in Table 2. The table reveals that improve cropping pattern was more in M.P. Cropping intensity was more in M.P. Employment generation was more in the Manipur (50 per cent). Manipur was followed by Tamilnadu (36.4 per cent), Bihar (33.3), A.P (30.8 per cent), Assam (25 per cent), Karnataka (17.5 per cent) respectively.

Table 2: Benefits: As per Agripreneurs (Percentages)

State	*Improved cropping pattern*	*Cropping intensity*	*Income enhance-ment*	*Improved produc-tion tech-nology*	*Produc-tivity enhan-cement*	*Employ-ment genera-tion*	*Assista-nce in marke-ting*
Karnataka	17.5	22.5	40	47.5	40	17.5	0
TN	27.3	9.1	45.5	54.5	36.4	36.4	0
AP	7.7	23.1	46.2	53.8	30.8	30.8	0
Gujarat	0	11.1	11.1	77.8	66.7	0	11.1
Maharashtra	0	0	32.7	51	49	16.3	2
Manipur	12.5	12.5	50	50	25	50	50
Assam	12.5	0	0	0	0	25	0
Orissa	0	0	25	75	25	0	0
Bihar	25	25	37.5	20.8	16.7	33.3	12.5
MP	66.7	33.3	22.2	33.3	33.3	0	0
Rajasthan	0	29	51.6	58.1	51.6	3.2	0
UP	25	27.3	70.5	31.8	25	9.1	4.5
Overall	14.4	18	42.8	44.4	36.4	16.8	4.4

(*Source*: Global Agri System Private limited Report).

Constraints of Dairy Development in Rural Area of North 24 Parganas District

1. A good number of rural populations in India are dependent on Agriculture and allied sector especially Dairy sector for their livelihood and it is their important way of survival. Due to lack of proper technical knowledge, awareness it is so difficult for dairy farmers to turn their farming in to Dairy Preneurship.
2. In the Absence of proper agri management system they are not able to establish their dairy farm.
3. Lack of awareness and proper Governmental initiatives caring the negative impact among the dairy farmers and their future generations also.
4. Sometimes they are not ready to take risk of making heavy investment and modern technologies for this farming system.

Strategy for Establishment of Agri and Dairy farming

1. Awareness generation programmes regarding agriculture and its allied sector and its future among the rural people is necessary for promoting a good and successful Dairy farm.
2. Establishment of Dairy Entrepreneurship Hubs.
3. Active participation of extension agencies and government bodies.
4. Promote various skill development programmes among the villagers.
5. There should be a good network among government officials and farmers about various extension activities.

CONCLUSION

Rural development is the dynamic process of development of the rural people through various initiatives, so that they can become self-reliant citizen of the country. For the development of the rural areas as well as whole country it is necessary to encourage the rural mass especially rural youth for take the initiatives of dairy farming because dairy sector plays a vital role for improvement of rural livelihood in North 24 Parganas District. There are many areas and sub areas in Agriculture. Within each area, enormous numbers of commodities are available. There is also much scope of improve production and productivity in Dairy Sector (Mondol and Ray, 2012). Therefore, it is required to train the jobless rural people, agriculture graduate youths and others, in Agri-business management as a Dairy entrepreneur for their betterment as well as economic stability and society's betterment.

REFERENCES

Acharya, S.S. (2007). Agribusiness in India: Some facts and emerging issues. *Agricultural Economics Research Review,* 20: 409–424

Annual Report (2006-07). Ministry of Agro and Rural Industries, Government of India.

Annual Report (2012-13). Ministry of Micro, Small and Medium Enterprises, Government of India.

Annual Report (2012-13). Department of Animal Husbandry, Dairying and Fisheries, Ministry of Agriculture, Government of India.

An Overview, Ministry of Small scales Industries.

Bairwa, S.L. and Kushwaha, S. (2012). Agro Industry scenario in India. *In:* Singh S.P. (*ed.*), "Agricultural research and Sustainable development in India", Bharti Publications, New Delhi, 110093, pp. 159–182.

Bairwa, S.L., Kushwaha, S., Meena, L.K., Lakra, K. and Kumar, P. (2014a). Agribusiness Potential of North Eastern States: A SWOT Analysis. *In*: Singh *et al.*, 2014

Agribusiness Potentials in India: Experience from hill states". EBH Publishers (India) Guwahati – New Delhi, pp. 544–556.

Dabson, K. and Markley, D. (2010). Agripreneurs- A free range of opportunity, Centre for Rural Entrepreneurship.

Entrepreneurship in India (2008). National Knowledge Commission, Government of India.

Jha Brajesh (2006). Employment, wages and productivity in Indian agriculture. Institute of Economic Growth, University of Delhi.

Mehta, M. Agri Entrepreneurship- Sustainable Livelihood, The centres for Agripreneurship Development.

National Entrepreneurship Policy. Entrepreneurship Development Institute of India, Ahmedabad, Gujarat.

Planning Commission (2007). Government of India Report of the steering committee on Agriculture and Allied Sectors for formulation of the Eleventh Five Year Plan (2007–12).

Roy, G.L. and Mondol, Sagar (2012). Rural Development, Entrepreneurship and Communication, Kalyani publication.

6

Substance in Plato's Metaphysics

Felix Agbo Okwa[1*]

ABSTRACT

The theory and conceptualization of substance in philosophy has been a perennial problem that emanated from the primary substance debate. Over the years, philosophers concerned themselves with the primary substance of the universe. Appreciating the obvious that change and permanence are evident in the world, Plato presented a well-articulated theory, the theory of forms / ideas. Plato bifurcated the world into two- universals and Particulars. He accepts the reality of permanence which he asserts are substances / ideas that exists in the world of forms; they are immutable and eternal. At the same time, he asserts that particulars do exist in the world of appearance; they are mutable, susceptible to change and a pure imitation of the substances in the world of ideas. This theory of Plato appears appealing as it seems to resolve the Heraclitus-Parmenides feud. Notwithstanding, this theory is said to have various implications for knowledge acquisition, morality and aesthetic appreciation.

***Keywords*:** Substance, Universals, Particulars, Change, Permanence.

[1] Augustinian Institute, Otukpo Road, P.O Box 584, Makurdi, Benue State, Nigeria

**Corresponding E-mail*: Okwafa@yahoo.com

INTRODUCTION

Metaphysics as often reiterated, is the queen of the sciences, little wonder then it is regarded as one of the core branches of philosophy. Metaphysicians are regarded as philosophers who attempt a holistic theorization of reality as well as the place of man in the universe. Hence, framing a logical and coherent philosophy where ideas in relation to and beyond human experience are formed and analysed is metaphysics. In this parlance of study, we are faced with perennial problems such as the problem of being, the problem of substance, the problem of change and permanence and so on.

In this work titled Substance in Plato's Metaphysics, we set out to critically address Plato's metaphysics and how he conceptualizes the idea of substance within his metaphysical postulations. To do this effectively, we have divided this work into sub-sections. First and foremost, we shall endeavor to discuss Plato's Theory of Ideas, bringing to bare the problem of change and permanence, which this theory of ideas endeavours to address. Sequel to this, we shall then engage ourselves with Aristotle's criticism of Plato's theory of ideas. In the modern period, philosophers such as Descartes, Spinoza and Leibniz tried a conceptualization of the idea of substance. For the purpose of this work however, we shall endeavor to limit ourselves to the discuss of Descartes and Spinoza's ideas of substance. We shall from these expositions then evaluate the postulations of these views as well as showcase pitfalls where observed and subsequently conclude.

PLATO'S THEORY OF IDEAS

The pre-Socratic Philosophers such as Thales, Anaximander, Anaximenes, Parmenides, Heraclitus were concerned about the origin of the world, as well as the nature of the cosmos. Little wonder they are often referred to as cosmologists. In explaining the origin and nature of the cosmos, these philosophers were fascinated about the physical realities they encountered; hence, they were divided into two main groups, the monists, who believed a single substance could serve as the origin and explanation of the cosmos, and the pluralists, who believed several basic substances could serve to explain the origin of the world.

Thales of Miletus is regarded as the first philosopher (even though the word philosopher had not yet been coined then). Thales in trying to explain the origin of the world opined that, everything that exists came out of water. Hence for him, the primary substance that there was water[1]. A disciple of Thales, Anaximander in trying to proffer a more sophisticated explanation of the origin of the world, opined that the cosmos evolved out of what he called the apeiron, a substance without distinguishable qualities for it is both infinite and indefinite[2]. For him then, this was the origin of the cosmos, for he believed it was within this struggle between the opposing sides that consequently led to the production of the cosmos.

Furthermore, yet a disciple of Anaximander, Anaximenes in trying to fathom the primary stuff the cosmos was made of believed that air was that which all things originate from. In trying to proffer justification for his claim, he thought that all other matter arose out of air by condensation and rarefaction[3]. Parmenides, the founder of the school of Eleaticism, in taking the axiom of Xenophanes to its logical conclusion believed that,

> *What is cannot have come into being and cannot pass away because it would have to have come out of nothing or to become nothing, whereas nothing by its very nature does not exist. There can be no motion either; for that is-which is not possible since it would be blocked-or a motion into something is –no- which is equally impossible since what is not does not exist. Hence, everything is solid immobile being[4].*

[1] Ridling, Z.(2001). *Philosophy Then and Now: A Look Back at 26 Centuries of Thought.* Access Foundation.p 10.

[2] Ibid, p. 10.

[3] Ibid, p. 11

[4] Ibid, p 13

Simply put therefore, according to Parmenides, change was not possible, put differently, that the very thought of change could only be but an illusion. One might then wonder, what about the change we notice in the world? For Parmenides, all these are only in our familiar world, a mere world of belief. A philosophical school of thought considered to be directly opposing this postulations of Parmenides was that of Heraclitus. For Heraclitus, everything was simply in a state of flux; that change was indeed the only reality[5].

The philosophical problem generated by these two opposing principles is often regarded as The Problem of Change and Permanence. Tracing back the history of this problem as we have just done, one easily realizes that there seems to exist features of the universe that could be regarded as unchanging, permanent and immutable. Similarly, there also exist features of the universe that are full of change, and as Heraclitus calls it, in a state of flux. The question then is, which theory seems nearer to reality than the other? Is everything in nature full of change or of permanence? The obvious problem faced herein would be the problem of how to reconcile these two indeed contradictory conclusions. The total acceptance of one invariably leads to the negation of the other.

Various philosophers have tried to resolve this problem. Empedocles is often regarded as the first philosopher to attempt a reconciliation of the issue of change and permanence. For him, there was element of truth in both positions. He therefore believed that both change and permanence are evident in nature. He opined that the four basic elements of earth, air, fire and water are in themselves permanent, experiencing neither change nor flux. However, their coming into contact, hence combining features accounts for things coming into being and going out of existence. This for him was change. Democritus in an attempt to reconcile this problem of change and permanence believed that atoms are the ultimate constitutive elements of things, they are the smallest units of matter. Hence, they cannot be divided or destroyed. He

[5] Joad, C.E.M. (1957). *Guide to Philosophy*. New York: Dover Publications, p. 270.

was of the opinion that these atoms move in void, their clashing with each other accounts for new things coming into beings while their separation accounts for things going out of being. Hence, change and permanence are accounted for.

It is in the light of this problem of change and permanence that we can fully appreciate the contributions of Plato. It is often reiterated that Plato's most significant and influential work remains his contributions to theoretical philosophy; his theory of ideas. This theory of ideas is sometimes regarded as the theory of forms. This theory of ideas comes out clearly to first and foremost address the inevitable problem of permanence and change instituted by Parmenides and Heraclitus respectively. We can assert categorically that Plato's theory of Ideas accepts essentially both assertions qualified by a limitation of their scope[6].The question however is, what are these ideas? Do they exist? If yes, where do they exists? What is the relationship between these ideas and things? How do we know these ideas if they exist?

Plato's theory of ideas rests on the axiom that ideas exists and these ideas are permanent. They are non-material substances that cannot be changed no destroyed, hence, they are eternal. In contrast, Plato critically analysis the sensible world as that which accommodates the poor copies of these eternal immutable and unchanging ideas. By implication therefore, the world is divided into two, the physical world and the world of ideas. The essences of all that are, are found in the world of ideas while their poor imitations are found in the world of particulars. This position has a lasting mark on the theory of knowledge as he claims the knowledge we gain from such a world of imitation can only be gained through experience and the senses, and since they are acquired from the imitations, they cannot suffice as knowledge as such. For example, there is the idea of "the Triangle" which is said to be found in the world of ideas and all the triangles we see are but mere imperfect copies of the eternal idea in the world of ideas[7].

---

[6] Ibid, p. 271.
[7] Stumpf, S. (2003). *Philosophy, History and Problems.* New York: McGraw-Hill Higher Education, p. 55.

This bifurcation of the world by Plato and placing one as superior, eternal and immaterial and the other of change, also attempts to solve the immanent problem of universals in philosophy. The first question we should ask at this point however is, what are ideas?

It is important to state clearly here that, C.E.M. Joad in his book "Guide to Philosophy" makes us to understand that the theory of ideas or better still ideas generally are conceived after the model of universals[8]. For Lloyd Gerson, this universals taking from the Plato's theory of ideas is taken to be a theory of *ante rem* universals as contrary to the theory of *post rem* universals[9].Put differently, Plato's theory of ideas lends total support to the existence of universals, existing yet in another world as against the backdrop that universals don't exist or exist in particular things. To this end, we can say that Plato 'reified' universals[10].

Joad further opines that the ideas in Plato's theory of ideas possess three qualities. First and foremost, the ideas are said to constitute the real world. Which by implication makes them of higher degree of reality than the obvious particular things. Little wonder then Plato accrues to these college of ideas the ultimate attributes of Good. These ideas therefore constitute the goal of human endeavour as well as the object of knowledge[11]. We can hence speak of a person as being holy, good, and beautiful simply because we know the idea of Holy, Good and Beauty and thus acknowledge that these persons show more or less in this idea of holy, good or beauty.

As stated above, Plato held that the ideas are responsible for the being of particular things. By implication, we can explain reality by getting to know the ideas of things. Hence, the knowledge of particular things should not account for knowledge. One cannot

[8] Joad, C.E.M. Op cit.,p. 277.

[9] Gerson, L.P. *Platonism and the Invention of Universals.* Unpublished work, p. 1.

[10] Ibid, p. 1.

[11] Joad, C.E.M. Op cit., p. 278.

say one knows x if what one knows is the particular. The task of the philosopher therefore is to be able to rise beyond mere appearances and transcend to the realm of ideas, a place where real knowledge bounds, here Plato believes the soul shall come face to face with ideas[12].

Though this theory seems very clear and self-explanatory, one question about what and what forms are there in the world of ideas, the explanation then becomes less obvious. For Plato himself believed not everything has its idea in the world of ideas. For if that is the case, then it would whence be but a duplicate world. Nevertheless, what is clear about Plato's theory of ideas is that, the ideas are simply the archetypes of things and they possess the characteristics of permanence, eternal, immutable and non-changing and can only be apprehended by the human mind as against the senses.

As to the question where these ideas exist, there seems to be no clear answer to the habitual abode of the universals(ideas). Simply put, Plato suggested that these ideas exist and are separate from particular things. If this is the case and they are apart or separate from the particular things, they must then have a sort of independent existence. This however is not a problem as ideas as explicated above have no tangible or particular attributes. Hence according to Edward Stumpf, the question of the location of ideas or the world of ideas is only as a consequence of our language[13].

The ideas are said to relate to particular things in basically two ways. First and foremost, the ideas are said to be the essence of all particular things. By implication, the ideas manifest themselves in the particular things. For example, the idea of beauty manifests itself in a particular things as being beautiful. Put differently, the ideas causes or manifest themselves in particular things hence causes them to imitate the idea. Hence, all things participate in the idea of beauty more or less. Secondly, a second

[12] Ibid, p. 278.
[13] Stumpf. S.Op cit., p. 56.

level of relation which is essentially derived from the first is that particular things are said to participate in ideal ideas.

The unescapable question that one might necessarily answer is, how do we come to apprehend the ideas? In response to this, Plato states that there are three different mediums through which the human mind can apprehend the ideas: Recollection, Dialectic, and the Eros, the power of love. For Plato, the human soul prior to its union with the body, the soul was acquainted with the ideas. However, at the point of that union, the soul forgets all it knew. Through recollection, therefore, the human person is able to 'retrieve' what the soul knew before its present existence.

"We cannot come by new knowledge. For, either we already know the knowledge which we wish to acquire, in which case the knowledge is not new, or we do not know the knowledge which we wish to acquire, in which case we cannot know when we acquire it"[14]. Plato provides a sort of mystical doctrine in support of this claim. He believes that the soul has a sort of pre-history, that prior to the soul being embodied, it existed in the world of ideas, knowing everything in its pure and unmixed state[15]. For Plato, at the point of its bodily incarnation, the soul forgets all about this world of ideas where it came from and knew all things in its true state. In this form, the soul is not able to through the material sense view the true state of ideas, however, it can only apprehend their "manifestations or representations in a material setting"[16].This manifestations though blurred and distorted they are, are said to remind the soul of the knowledge it had of the ideal forms before being incarnated in the human body. The question we might ask at this point however is, how can we know the real, that which is viewed as stationary and immobile and immutable?

This led Plato to believe that education or the process of learning was only but what he calls, reminiscence. Put differently, the process of learning is nothing else than the recovery of prior

---

[14] Joad, C.E.M. Op cit., p. 285.
[15] Ibid. p. 286.
[16] Ibid. p. 286.

knowledge. Through the process of dialectics, a power of abstracting the essence of things and discovering the relations of all variants of knowledge to each other[17], one according to Plato is able to gain knowledge of ideas. Finally, though the power of love which leads us step by step, we are able to acquire the real idea. For example, according to Stumpf, through the power of love, we move from the 'beautiful object to the beautiful thought and finally to the very essence of Beauty itself.

Aristotle's Criticism of Plato's Theory of Ideas

> *Misled by the admitted fact that things possess common characteristics, Plato had, he complained, attributed to the fact that a wholly unjustifiable significance, abstracting to the characteristics from the things which owned them, and then elevating the characteristics so abstracted into a separate realm of their own, where they were endowed with mystical qualities of pure being[18].*

Sequel to the above, we see that one of the most significant objection to Plato's theory of ideas is that put forward by Aristotle. Aristotle believed that Plato was misled by the fact that these 'particular' things possess similar/common characteristics. Hence, continued Aristotle, Plato abstracted these common characteristics and then crowned them with a mystical quality of being with this theory that they exist in yet another world. It is important to state that at this point that Aristotle was a student of Plato, hence, he could be said of to have a firsthand understanding of Plato's theory of ideas.

One fundamental problem faced by the theory of ideas as identified by Aristotle is captured in the fact that how possible is it that the world of ideas, a changeless, immutable and eternal world come into the world of changeful, mutable and sensible? Furthermore, Plato in his postulation stated that, while things

[17] Stumpf, S. Op cit., p. 58.
[18] Joad, C.E.M. Op cit.,p. 293.

(particular) are found in this world, their essences exist in the world of forms. The question then is, how possible is it that things could exist in a separate world as their essences? Could they be said to be? As Omoregbe puts it, 'how can the essences of things be existing independent of the things of which they are essences and in separation from them'?[19]

Furthermore, Aristotle was of the position that, the method of reasoning that led Plato to postulate a separate world owing from his misled conception that things possess similar characteristics will consequently lead to the postulation of a third world, and then to a fourth world and so on, ad infinitum.

> *Since the aim of becoming has been reached when matter has assumed its forms, the form of a thing is the reality of it and form in general is reality, or the real. Since, on the other hand, matter as is not yet what it later becomes but have the power of becoming this, it is potentiality or the potential. If we think matter without form we obtain the "first matter", which being undefined is called the qualitatively unlimited, the common substrate of all definite substance which however, is as much as it is the merely potential, never exists nor has existed in itself*[20].

Aristotle to solidify his criticism of Plato developed a theory of matter and form, a theory known as the theory of *hylemorphism*. According to him, everything that there is in this world possess two basic elements, the matter and the form. The matter according to him, is that potentiality of a thing which provides a thing the possibility of change. The form on the other hand is understood as the substance of a thing. Unlike Plato who believe the essence or form of a thing is in the world of ideas, and it is over and above the matter or particular, Aristotle believes the matter and form of a

[19] Omoregbe, J.(2006). *Metaphysics without Tears. A Systematic and Historical Study.* JOJA Educational Research and Publishers Limited, p. 141.

[20] Zeller, E. (1980). *Outlines of the History of Greek Philosophy.* Thirteenth Edition. New York: Dova Publications, Inc., p. 175.

thing must exist in order for the other to exist. Hence, the form cannot exist without the matter, and the matter cannot exist without the form[21].

Similar to the above is Aristotle's critical distinction between a substance of a thing and the accident. For Aristotle, a thing possess both the essence or substance, and the accidents[22]. The substance he believed is the nature of a thing; that which is said to exist on its own. Accidents on the other hand is the thing or quality which a thing possess, which may include size, colour, texture, weight, and so on[23].

Descartes and Spinoza on Substance

Renè Descartes was a French Philosopher and mathematician. He lived between 1596 and 1650. He is often regarded as the father of modern philosophy. Among his most famous works was the "Meditations on First Philosophy", and therein, his primary objective was the articulation of philosophy of mind as well as the possibility of certain knowledge. His task hence was to put the edifice of human knowledge upon secure foundations[24]. For Descartes, substance is that which could be understood as existing in a manner which it depends on nothing else. As put forward by Woolhouse, "By substance we can understand nothing other than a thing which exists in such a way as to depend on no other thing for its existence"[25].

It can logically be deduced that for Descartes, that which is substance and depends on no other thing for its existence is God. Even though Descartes affirms this fact, he believes also that other things, inanimate and animate could be regarded as substance,

[21] Omoregbe, J. Op cit., p. 142.
[22] Joad, C.E.M. Op cit., p. 287.
[23] Ibid, p. 287.
[24] Stokes, P.(2003). *Philosophy: 100 Essential Thinkers.* New York: Enchanted Lion Books, p. 73.
[25] Woolhouse, R.S.(1993). *The Concept of Substance, Descartes, Spinoza, Leibniz.* New York and London:Routledge Publication, p. 14.

but in this sense, created substances, for they depend in their creator in one way or the other for existence[26]. We can see clearly Descartes reechoing Aristotle's theory of substance tracing back to the unmoved mover. That which causes others to exist but itself is unmoved and uncaused. From this then, we can conclude that for Descartes, substance which is God, is indeed not an accident for it is self-subsistent and independent.

Furthermore, Woolhouse makes us to understand that for Descartes, there exists two sorts of substances that are said to exist as created substances. Hence, created substances are of two types, "some are of such a nature that they cannot exist without other things while some need only the ordinary concurrence of God in order to exist"[27].In the light of this, these created substances could be likened or termed substance, while those who depend on other things for their existence could be termed 'qualities or attributes of those substances.' It is important to state here that, this conception of Descartes' conception of substance could be said as a modification and derivation of Aristotle's theory of substance and accidents. For substances are said to exist depending only on the concurrence of God, while accidents on the substances to exist. In the light of this, we cannot talk about colour, texture, size, weight, and others without the being that harbors them.

Unlike Aristotle however, who believed that substances cannot exist without accidents and accidents cannot exist without substances, Descartes on the contrary states that "substance do not require the particular modes that they happen to have"[28]. Furthermore, though he believes substance does not need a particular mode it happens to have, substances for Descartes cannot be said to exist with no modes, "for there are certain attributes without which substances are 'unintelligible', for example, the attribute of being extended, possessing length, breadth, and depth"[29].

[26] Ibid, p. 15.
[27] Ibid, p. 16.
[28] Ibid, p. 18.
[29] Ibid, p. 19.

Sequel to the above, we can therefore state that for Descartes, there are two kinds or sorts of substances, the material and the immaterial, the body and mind, hence, mind and body are separate substances. Thought for Descartes was a principle attribute of an incorporeal substance and extension a principal attribute of a corporeal substance.

Benedict Baruch de Spinoza was a Dutch philosopher of a Jewish origin. He lived between 1632 and 1677, he was greatly influenced by Descartes and Euclid and is said to have taken rationality to its logical conclusion. Like Descartes, Spinoza was set out to put knowledge on logical foundation[30]. Spinoza's metaphysics of which we are concerned herein is espoused in his Ethics Demonstrated in Geometrical Order, a work posthumously published. In this work, Spinoza elaborates on the nature of God and of the relationship to the human mind, emotions and freedom.

> *That which is self-caused, I mean that of which the essence involves existence, or that of which the nature is only conceivable as existent. By substance, I mean that which is in itself, and is conceived through itself, in other words, that of which a conception can be formed independently of any other conception. By God, I mean a being absolutely infinite that is, a substance consisting in infinite attributes, of which expresses eternal and infinite essentiality*[31].

As stated earlier on in this work, in the Ethics, which Spinoza sets out to elaborate on the nature of God, the world, God's relation to the world, man's place in the world, and man's relation to God, he thinks clearly that of God and man and the world, God is the highest substance and so everything flows from God and consequently depends on God. Little wonder Spinoza begins his Ethics with the chapter titled "Concerning God". This logic indicates how everything follows from his conception of the

---

[30] Stokes, P. Op cit., p. 79.

[31] Benedict Spinoza (1974). "The Ethics".*In*:Elwes, R.H.M. *The Rationalists*. New York: Anchor Books, a Division of Random House, INC., p. 179.

greatest substances. Furthermore, Spinoza states that an attribute is what "the intellect perceives of a substance, as consisting its essence"[32].We see here a similitude of the Cartesian conception of the extended attribute of a corporeal substance, that which aids us to perceive it.

One striking major difference between Descartes' conception of Substance and that of Spinoza is the fact that for Spinoza, thought and extension are indeed compatible, and so can be attributes of the same substance. On the contrary however, Descartes believes thought and extension are incompatible notions. For Spinoza then, mind and body, extension and though are just different ways of conceiving the same reality. It is noteworthy to recall that for Descartes, there are two sorts or types of substances, the created substance that exist by the concurrence of God and those created substances that cannot exist without things. Spinoza on the contrary seems to be in some sense, reechoing the ideas of Parmenides, that everything in the universe is one.

Substance for Spinoza is therefore only one, and this substance we can conceive of as either nature or God[33]. Since reality is one, Spinoza believes that everything in the universe is part of God and everything happening is indeed an obvious fall out from this God or better still, everything happening is but an expression of the divine nature. We can therefore deduce and thus state that Spinoza is a core determinist[34]. His unique pantheistic view far removes responsibility or free will as it were from the human person as he believes humans only think they are free because they are conscious of their actions but unconscious of the causes of their actions. By implication, all human actions, be it "good" or "bad", is but part of the workings of this God or Nature. Finally, for Alfred Weber, Spinoza is neither an atheist nor a cosmist, but a Cosmo-theist for his cosmos is God himself and God is the cosmical substance[35].

---

[32] Woolhouse, R.S. Op cit., p. 45.
[33] Stokes, P. Op cit., p. 54.
[34] Ibid, p. 79.
[35] Ridling, Z. Op cit., p. 356.

CONCLUSION

In this work, we have been able to critically examine Plato's Theory of Ideas, Aristotle's criticism of this idea, as well as Descartes and Spinoza's idea of substance.

Substance as we know it, is regarded as that which exists on its own, self-caused, independent and immutable as well as that which causes others to be but itself uncaused. For Spinoza, substance is that which is in itself, and is conceived through itself. Substance is therefore often referred to as God, for it is only God, according to Christendom, that possess such qualities.

According to David Hume and other empiricists, metaphysics or the ideas of substance is indeed nothing to go by, for it contains nothing but sophistry and illusion. For Carnap, metaphysical statements are pseudo-statements which are utterly meaningless as they cannot be verified empirically.

In conclusion, I would like to argue in line with Aristotle when he criticized Plato saying that the essences of things as well as the particular things are said to be together. Hence, we can find the substance of a particular thing in that particular thing. I do believe that it is not possible for a substance of a thing to exist in a separate world as the thing which it is substance of. For if this is the case, then it is either the particular thing does not exist, or there exists yet another substance that exists in a particular that makes it exist, for a thing cannot exist without its essence. On the second light, as regards the meaninglessness of metaphysics, I would like to state categorically that if metaphysics is meaningless, and contains nothing but sophistry and illusion, how then do we account for things we experience but appear above causal or physical verification? Do they mean they don't exist? I therefore state emphatically at this point that, metaphysics is a veritable source of knowledge, even if it appears over and above mathematical and verifiable principles, and cannot be attested to empirically, that cannot suffice to say that it does not exist.Hence, metaphysics as it is, cannot be eliminated or regarded as utter meaningless.

REFERENCES

Benedict, Spinoza (1974). "The Ethics". *In*: Elwes, R.H.M. The Rationalists. New York: Anchor Books, a Division of Random House, INC.

Carnap, R. (1996). "The Elimination of Metaphysics through Logical Analysis of Language". *In*: Sahotra, S. (*ed.*), *Logical Empiricism at its Peak: Schlick, Carnap and Newrath*. New York: Garland Publishers.

Gerson, L.P. *Platonism and the Invention of Universals*. Unpublished work.

Hume, D. (1993). *Inquiry Concerning Human Understanding. Harvard Classics*, 37.

Joad, C.E.M. (1957). *Guide to Philosophy*. New York: Dover Publications.

Omoregbe, J. (2006). *Metaphysics without Tears. A Systematic and Historical Study.*Nigeria: JOJA Educational Research and Publishers Limited.

Ridling, Z. (2001). *Philosophy Then and Now: A Look Back at 26 Centuries of Thought*. Access Foundation.

Stokes, P. (2003). *Philosophy:* 100 *Essential Thinkers*. New York: Enchanted Lion Books.

Stumpf, S. (2003). *Philosophy, History and Problems*. New York: McGraw-Hill Higher Education.

Woolhouse, R.S. (1993). *The Concept of Substance, Descartes, Spinoza, Leibniz*. New York and London: Routledge Publication.

Zeller, E. (1980). *Outlines of the History of Greek Philosophy*. Thirteenth Edition. New York: Dover Publications, Inc.

7

An Overview to the Physical Needs of Man, The Universe and Its Twelve Categories

Ismael Tabuñar Fortunado[1]*

ABSTRACT

Abraham Maslow[1] expounded the needs of man from physiological to self-actualization in which man is motivated. One of the seven aspects of man according to Peter Holy[2] is physical wellness thus there are physical needs. To cover all the physical needs of man, the author analyzed the related literature, gathered facts and had a thought experiment. The results showed that the physical needs of man is the universe and its twelve categories. As for discussions, this research is an extension to the works of the two cited authors and eight more authors to be cited. The completeness and the categorizations may be revised or extended depending on the need and a more diversified, thorough research which the author welcomes.

***Key words*:** Needs, Privacy, Physical needs, Universe, Wellness.

[1] University of Santo Tomas, Manila, Philippines

**Corresponding E-mail*: smile.macky@yahoo.com/smile.macky.fortunado@gmail.com

INTRODUCTION

This is a compilation of the physical needs of man. Twelve categories are considered.

REVIEW OF RELATED LITERATURE

Wellness

The 7 Aspects of Wellness are seven major life areas that work together to create fulfillment and satisfaction. When you take positive steps to foster a higher level of awareness and action in each of the 7 Aspects, you build a more whole and complete way of living. The 7 Aspects of Wellness are Emotional, Physical, Social, Occupational, Intellectual, Environmental, and Spiritual (Peter Holy, 2011).

Physical Needs

The human being has needs, related to the structure and processes of the physical organism, for food, drink, sex, sleep, warmth and shelter, activity, sensory stimulation. For all practical purposes, there is virtually no genetic programming of behaviour to meet these needs, apart from minimal reflexes such as a sucking reflex in the neonate. Behaviour that satisfies physical needs is almost entirely learned through the process of socialisation: social norms prescribe the relevant behavior (John Heron, 1998).

Thought Experiment

A thought experiment or Gedanken experiment (from German) is a mental exercise which would consider a hypothesis, theory[3], or principle. Given the structure of the experiment, it may or may not be possible to actually perform it, and, in the case that it is possible for it to be performed, there need be no intention of any kind to actually perform the experiment in question. The common goal of a thought experiment is to explore the potential consequences of the principle in question (Wikipedia, 2011).

METHODOLOGY

To cover all the physical needs of man, the author analyzed the related literature, gathered facts and had a thought experiment.

We have Twelve Categories for the Physical Needs of Man

Hygiene needs

Hygiene is an old concept related to medicine, as well as to personal and professional care practices related to most aspects of living. In medicine and in home (domestic) and everyday life settings, hygiene practices are employed as preventative measures to reduce the incidence and spreading of disease. In the manufacture of food, pharmaceutical, cosmetic and other products, good hygiene is a key part of quality assurance *i.e.* ensuring that the product complies with microbial specifications appropriate to its use. The terms cleanliness (or cleaning) and hygiene are often used interchangeably, which can cause confusion. In general, hygiene mostly means practices that prevent spread of disease-causing organisms. Since cleaning processes (*e.g.,* hand washing) remove infectious microbes as well as dirt and soil, they are often the means to achieve hygiene. Other uses of the term appear in phrases including: body hygiene, personal hygiene, sleep hygiene, mental hygiene, dental hygiene, and occupational hygiene, used in connection with public health. Hygiene is also the name of a branch of science that deals with the promotion and preservation of health, also called hygienics. Hygiene practices vary widely, and what is considered acceptable in one culture might not be acceptable in another (Wikipedia, 2011).

Grooming needs

Grooming in humans typically includes bathroom activities such as primping: washing and cleaning the hair, combing it to extract tangles, and styling. It can also include cosmetic care of the body, such as shaving (Wikipedia, 2011).

Human mutual grooming plays an important role in pair bonding. In the same investigation, researchers found that individuals with more promiscuous attitudes and those who scored high on the anxiety sub-scale on an adult attachment style measure, tend to groom their partners more frequently. These findings were also consistent with some of the functions of grooming: potential parental indicator, developing trust and courtship or flirtation. (Nelson, Holly, Geher and Glenn, 2007).

Metabolic needs

For the most part, physiological needs are obvious — they are the literal requirements for human survival. If these requirements are not met, the human body simply cannot continue to function. Air, water, and food are metabolic requirements for survival in all animals, including humans (Wikipedia, 2011).

Safety needs

With their physical needs relatively satisfied, the individual's safety needs take precedence and dominate behavior. In the absence of physical safety — due to terrorist attack, war, natural disaster, or, in cases of family violence, childhood abuse, etc — people (re-)experience post-traumatic stress disorder and trans-generational trauma transfer (Wikipedia, 2011).

Security needs

In the absence of economic safety — due to economic crisis and lack of work opportunities - these safety needs manifest themselves in such things as a preference for job security, grievance procedures for protecting the individual from unilateral authority, savings accounts, insurance policies, reasonable disability accommodations, and the like (Wikipedia, 2011).

Activities

Rest and sleep – Sleep is often thought to help conserve energy (Wikipedia 2011). A relaxation technique (also known as relaxation training) is any method, process, procedure, or activity that helps a person to relax; to attain a state of increased calmness; or otherwise reduce levels of anxiety, stress or anger (Wikipedia 2011).

Excretion is the process by which waste products of metabolism and other non-useful materials are eliminated from an organism. It is an essential process in all forms of life (Wikipedia, 2011).

Physical fitness: To stay healthy it is important to engage in physical activity (Wikipedia, 2011).

Activity materials

Tools - A tool is a device that can be used to produce an item or achieve a task, but that is not consumed in the process. Informally the word is also used to describe a procedure or process with a specific purpose. Tools that are used in particular fields or activities may have different designations such as Instrument, Utensil, Implement, Machine, or Apparatus (Wikipedia, 2011). Anthropologists believe that the use of tools was an important step in the evolution of mankind (Wikipedia, 2011).

Transportation

Transport or transportation is the movement of people and goods from one location to another. Modes of transport include air, rail, road, water, cable, pipeline, and space. The field can be divided into infrastructure, vehicles, and operations. Transport is important since it enables trade between peoples, which in turn establishes civilizations (Wikipedia, 2011).

Communication

Human spoken and picture languages can be described as a system of symbols (sometimes known as lexemes) and the grammars (rules) by which the symbols are manipulated. The word "language" also refers to common properties of languages. Language learning normally occurs most intensively during human childhood. Most of the thousands of human languages use patterns of sound or gesture for symbols which enable communication with others around them. Languages seem to share certain properties, although many of these include exceptions. There is no defined line between a language and a dialect. Constructed languages such as Esperanto, programming languages, and various mathematical formalisms are not necessarily restricted to the properties shared by human languages.

A variety of verbal and non-verbal means of communicating exists such as body language, eye contact, sign language, paralanguage, haptic communication, chronemics, and media such as pictures, graphics, sound, and writing (Wikipedia, 2011).

Physical love

Love is an emotion of strong affection and personal attachment. In philosophical context, love is a virtue representing all of human kindness, compassion, and affection (Wikipedia, 2011).

"Q: What motivates people to seek out love?

A: Our primary motivation as human beings is to expand the self and to increase our abilities and our effectiveness. One of the ways we accomplish this is through our relationships with other people. We have learned in our research that it is important to feel that you have the ability to be an effective person, especially in our relationships (Arthur Aron, 2011).

Privacy

Privacy (from Latin: privatus "separated from the rest, deprived of something, esp. office, participation in the Government", from privo "to deprive") is the ability of an individual or group to seclude themselves or information about themselves and thereby reveal themselves selectively. The boundaries and content of what is considered private differ among cultures and individuals, but share basic common themes. Privacy is sometimes related to anonymity, the wish to remain unnoticed or unidentified in the public realm.

When something is private to a person, it usually means there is something within them that is considered inherently special or personally sensitive. The degree to which private information is exposed therefore depends on how the public will receive this information, which differs between places and over time. Privacy is broader than security and includes the concepts of appropriate use and protection of information (Wikipedia, 2011).

The right to privacy

It could be done only on principles of private justice, moral fitness, and public convenience, which, when applied to a new subject, make common law without a precedent; much more when received and approved by usage (Warren and Brandeis, 1890).

Companions

Friendship is a form of interpersonal relationship generally considered to be closer than association, although there is a range of degrees of intimacy in both friendships and associations. Friendship and association can be thought of as spanning across the same continuum (Wikipedia, 2011).

RESULTS

We have twelve categories for physical needs. Given are some examples:

Hygiene Needs – Water, soap, shampoo, scissors, nail cutter, toothpaste, toothbrush, towel, handkerchief, deodorant, etc.

Attending to personal hygiene needs

Certain levels of personal hygiene and grooming are required within workplaces, especially where contact with the public is required. If due to disability a person experiences difficulty attending to hygiene and grooming needs independently, there are a range of aids available. Personal hygiene and grooming aids assist people with disability to manage their personal care more independently. A variety of aids have been designed to assist people who have difficulty performing tasks independently such as brushing their hair, toileting or showering due to physical disability.

For individuals with restricted physical mobility, personal hygiene and grooming aids allow independent management of personal care both at home and within the workplace. Examples of personal hygiene and grooming aids include:

Long handled combs and brushes that allow easier reach with minimal effort.

Finger and toe nail management items such as nail brushes or emery boards on suction cups, long handled nail scissors or one handed nail clippers.

Tweezers and scissors that are adapted to meet a range of physical needs.

Long handled dressing sticks/reachers and long handled shoe horns.

Toileting aids and appliances allow people who require support in this area to manage their toileting needs more independently in the workplace. They can include toilet frames and rails, portable toilets, toilet cushions or raised toilet seats:

Toileting aids and appliances

Continence appliances can assist people to manage difficulties with urinary and bowel incontinence both at home and within the workplace. Continence appliances include sanitary pads and briefs which are worn to control continence issues as well as protectors designed for use on chairs and beds. A personal care giver may need to assist with management of these appliances in some circumstances and individuals may be eligible for assistance through the Work Based Personal Assistance program:

Continence appliances

Work Based Personal Assistance program.

For some people with disability, bathing and showering can also be difficult. For those with mobility restrictions consideration should be given to the bathroom design to ensure appropriate access is available. This will minimize the risk of injury or accident and facilitate independence.

To achieve appropriate access, door frames may need to be widened, shower hobs removed, vanity basins lowered, cupboards removed below vanities if wheelchair access is required, mirrors re-positioned or baths removed to increase bathroom space.

Commonly used appliances such as electric shavers and hairdryers can be permanently mounted on the wall for easier access and all items used on a daily basis can be left on the vanity such as toothbrushes, hairbrushes, creams and hair products.

A range of showering and bathing aids are also available to assist people with disability manage their bathing needs more independently at home in preparation for work including:

Showering and bathing appliances

Grooming Needs – Haircut, manicure, pedicure, perfume, cologne, etc.

Personal hygiene and grooming aids

Personal hygiene and grooming aids can assist with independent management of personal care both at home in preparation for work and within the workplace. Examples of personal hygiene and grooming aids include:

Long handled and curved combs and brushes that allow easier reach with minimal effort

Nail clippers or emery boards which attach to a board to allow for one handed nail care

Nail file holders which increase the grip size of a nail file for easier use

Nail or denture brushes with suction cups which allow the brush to be stuck onto a bench or sink and be used one handed

Tweezers and scissors that are adapted to meet a range of physical needs such as being long handled, angled or having a range of handle shapes

Lotion or tube squeezers to assist with squeezing toothpaste or lotion

Long handled applicators for lotion if unable to reach

Long handled pumice stones

Electric or battery powered toothbrushes to minimise hand movement required

Toothbrush grips that can be slipped over a standard toothbrush to build up grip size

Dental floss holder to allow one handed flossing

Hair dryer stands to support a hair dryer at a range of heights without having to hold the weight long handled attachments that can be added to a razor and allow shaving of legs without bending forwards.

A range of mirrors that are either handheld with the hand or finger loops and long handles for inspection or viewing purposes, along with small freestanding mirrors that sit on a benchtop.

Workplace solutions and adjustments

Being able to independently attend to personal hygiene needs to prepare for work and allow appropriate presentation, can assist with success within the workplace. Also having accessible bathroom facilities within a workplace can allow for any independent grooming that may be required by people with disability. Some things to consider within the workplace to ensure accessible bathroom design include:

Suitable height bathroom mirrors or provision of a bench based or portable mirror

Adequate turning space for wheelchairs

Provision for installation of grab rails

Suitable height toilet and toilet paper dispenser

Suitable height hand wash basin, provision of lever handles, soap dispenser and hand towels or dryer

Light weight doors that open easily and are self-closing or automated doors (Anonymous, 2012).

Metabolic Needs–Oxygen, water, food, homeostasis, etc.

Oxygen

Uptake of O_2 from the air is the essential purpose of respiration, so oxygen supplementation is used in medicine. Treatment not only increases oxygen levels in the patient's blood, but has the secondary effect of decreasing resistance to blood flow in many types of diseased lungs, easing work load on the heart. Oxygen therapy is used to treat emphysema, pneumonia, some heart disorders (congestive heart failure), some disorders that cause increased pulmonary artery pressure, and any disease that impairs the body's ability to take up and use gaseous oxygen (Wikipedia, 2012).

Safe drinking water is essential to humans and other life forms (Wikipedia, 2012)

Food

Is any substance consumed to provide nutritional support for the body. It is usually of plantor animal origin, and contains essential nutrients, such as carbohydrates, fats, proteins, vitamins, or minerals. The substance is ingested by an organism and assimilated by the organism's cells in an effort to produce energy, maintain life, or stimulate growth (Wikipedia, 2012).

Homeostasis

With regard to any given life system parameter, an organism may be a conformer or a regulator. On one hand, regulators try to maintain the parameter at a constant level over possibly wide ambient environmental variations. On the other hand, conformers allow the environment to determine the parameter. For instance, endothermic animals (mammals and birds) maintain a constant body temperature, while ectothermic animals (almost all other organisms) exhibit wide body temperature variation.

Behavioral adaptations allow ectothermic animals to exert some control over a given parameter. For instance, reptiles often rest on sun-heated rocks in the morning to raise their body temperature. Regulators are also responsive to external circumstances, however: if the same sunbaked boulder happens to host a ground squirrel, the animal's metabolism will adjust to the lesser need for internal heat production.

An advantage of homeostatic regulation is that it allows an organism to function effectively in a broad range of environmental conditions. For example, ectotherms tend to become sluggish at low temperatures, whereas a co-located endotherm may be fully active. That thermal stability comes at a price since an automatic regulation system requires additional energy. One reason snakes may eat only once a week is that they use much less energy to maintain homeostasis.

Most homeostatic regulation is controlled by the release of hormones into the bloodstream. However, other regulatory processes rely on simple diffusion to maintain a balance.

Homeostatic regulation extends far beyond the control of temperature. Homeostasis includes regulation of the pH of the Blood at 7.365 (a measure of alkalinity and acidity). All animals also regulate their blood glucose, as well as the concentration of their blood. Mammals regulate their blood glucose with insulin and glucagon. The human body maintains glucose levels constant most of the day, even after a 24-hour fast. Even during long periods of fasting, glucose levels are reduced only very slightly. Insulin, secreted by the beta cells of the pancreas, effectively transports glucose to the body's cells by instructing those cells to keep more of the glucose for their own use. See Dynamic equilibrium. If the glucose inside the cells is high, the cells will convert it to the insoluble glycogen to prevent the soluble glucose from interfering with cellular metabolism. Ultimately this lowers blood glucose levels, and Insulin helps to prevent hyperglycemia. When insulin is deficient or cells become resistant to it, diabetes occurs. Glucagon, secreted by the alpha cells of the pancreas, encourages cells to break down stored glycogen or convert non-carbohydrate carbon sources to glucose *via* gluconeogenesis, thus preventing hypoglycemia. The kidneys are used to remove excess water and ions from the blood. These are then expelled as urine. The kidneys perform a vital role in homeostatic regulation in mammals, removing excess water, salt, and urea from the blood. These are the body's main waste products.

Another homeostatic regulation occurs in the gut. Homeostasis of the gut is not fully understood but it is believed that Toll-like receptor (TLR) expression profiles contribute to it.

Intestinal epithelial cells exhibit important factors that contribute to homeostasis: (1) They have different cellular distribution of TLR's compared to the normal gut mucosa. An example of this is how TLR5 (activated by flagellin) can redistribute to the basolateral membrane, which is the perfect place where flagellin can be detected. (2) The enterocytes express high levels of TLR inhibitor Toll-interacting protein (TOLLIP). TOLLIP is a human gene that is a part of the innate immune system and is highest in a healthy gut; it correlates to luminal bacterial load. (3) Surface enterocytes also express high levels of Interleukin-1 receptor (IL-1R) -containing inhibitory molecule. IL-1R are also referred to as single immunoglobulin IL-1R (SIGIRR). Animals deficient in this are more susceptible to induced colitis, implying that SIGIRR might possibly play a role in tuning mucosal tolerance towards commensal flora. Nucleotide-binding oligomerization domain containing 2 (NOD2) is suggested to have an effect on suppressing inflammatory cascades based on recent evidence. It is believed to modulate signals transmitted through TLRs, TLR3, 4, and 9 specifically. Mutation of it has resulted in Crohn's disease. Excessive T-helper 1 responses to resident flora in the gut are controlled by inhibiting the controlling influence of regulatory T cells and tolerance-inducing dendritic cells.

Sleep timing depends upon a balance between homeostatic sleep propensity, the need for sleep as a function of the amount of time elapsed since the last adequate sleep episode, and circadian rhythms that determine the ideal timing of a correctly structured and restorative sleep episode (Wikipedia, 2012).

Safety Needs– Constitution, laws, clothing, shelter, medicine, etc.

Law is a system of rules and guidelines which are enforced through social institutions to govern behavior, wherever possible. It shapes politics, economics and society in numerous ways and serves as a social mediator of relations between people. Contract law regulates everything from buying a bus ticket to trading on derivatives markets. Property law defines rights and obligations related to the transfer and title of personal and real property. Trust law applies to assets held for investment and financial security, while tort law allows claims for compensation if a person's rights or property are harmed. If the harm is criminalised in legislation, criminal law offers means by which the state can prosecute the perpetrator. Constitutional law provides a framework for the creation of law, the protection of human rights and the election of political representatives. Administrative law is used to review the decisions of government agencies, while international law governs affairs between sovereign states in activities ranging from trade to environmental regulation or military action. Writing in 350 BC, the Greek philosopher Aristotle declared, "The rule of law is better than the rule of any individual".

Legal systems elaborate rights and responsibilities in a variety of ways. A general distinction can be made between civil law jurisdictions, which codify their laws, and common law systems, where judge-made law is not consolidated. In some countries, religion informs the law. Law provides a rich source of scholarly inquiry, into legal history, philosophy, economic analysis or sociology. Law also raises important and complex issues concerning equality, fairness and justice. "In its majestic equality", said the writer Anatole France in 1894, "the law forbids rich and poor alike to sleep under bridges, beg in the streets and steal loaves of bread." In a typical democracy, the central institutions for interpreting and creating law are the three main branches of government, namely an impartial judiciary, a democratic legislature, and an accountable executive. Law distinguishes itself from policy as laws are the standard rules and regulations that are compulsory. Policies are objectives that an organization or a government sets for itself. To implement and enforce the law and provide services to the public, a government's bureaucracy, the military and police are vital. While all these organs of the state are creatures created and bound by law, an independent legal profession and a vibrant civil society inform and support their progress (Wikipedia, 2012).

Clothing is a term that refers to a covering for the human body that is worn. The wearing of clothing is exclusively a human characteristic and is a feature of nearly all human societies. The amount and type of clothing worn depends on functional considerations (such as a need for warmth or protection from the elements) and social considerations.

Physically, clothing serves many purposes, including

Protection from uncomfortably hot or cold weather protection during hazardous activities such as hunting, hiking, cooking and the production of arts and crafts protection from very hazardous situations such as fire or the effects of warfare or terrorism social identification of the social class of strangers by means of informal clothing styles or uniforms identification of members of a particular team, group or political affiliations.

Deception involving the use of disguise

Social intimidation or reassurance by associating particular forms of dress code with functions such as religious or military activities that may be beneficial or harmful to the observer. Ordinary clothes also provide some protection from minor risks such as insect bites, splinters and limiting the transmission of a range of hazards such as germs or harmful UV radiation. Clothing can and has in history been made from a very wide variety of materials. Materials have ranged from leather and furs, to woven materials, to elaborate and exotic natural and synthetic fabrics.

Not all body coverings are regarded as clothing. Articles carried rather than worn (such as purses), worn on a single part of the body and easily removed (scarves), worn purely for adornment (jewelry), or those that serve a function other than protection (eyeglasses), are normally considered accessories rather than clothing, as are footwear and hats (Wikipedia, 2012).

Shelter is a basic architectural structure or building that provides cover (Wikipedia, 2012).

Medicine is the science and art of healing. It encompasses a variety of health care practices evolved to maintain and restore health by the prevention and treatment of illness in human beings.

Contemporary medicine applies health science, biomedical research, and medical technology to diagnose and treat injury and disease, typically through medication or surgery, but also through therapies as diverse as psychotherapy, external splints and traction, prostheses, biologics, ionizing radiation and others (Wikipedia, 2012).

Security Needs– Money, savings account, employment, insurance, etc.

Money is any object or record that is generally accepted as payment for goods and services and repayment of debts in a given country or socio-economic context. The main functions of money are distinguished as: a medium of exchange; a unit of account; a store of value; and, occasionally in the past, a standard of deferred payment. Any kind of object or secure verifiable record that fulfills these functions can serve as money (Wikipedia, 2012).

Savings accounts are accounts maintained by retail financial institutions that pay interest but cannot be used directly as money (for example, by writing a checque). These accounts let customers set aside a portion of their liquid assets while earning a monetary return. For the bank, money in a savings account may not be callable immediately and therefore often does not incur a reserve requirement freeing up cash from the bank's vault to be lent out with interest (Wikipedia, 2012).

Work is to be employed, especially as a means of earning one's livelihood: (Anonymous, 2012).

Insurance is a form of risk management primarily used to hedge against the risk of a contingent, uncertain loss. Insurance is defined as the equitable transfer of the risk of a loss, from one entity to another, in exchange for payment. An insurer is a company selling the insurance; the insured, or policyholder, is the person or entity buying the insurance policy. The amount to be charged for a certain amount of insurance coverage is called the premium. Risk management, the practice of appraising and controlling risk, has evolved as a discrete field of study and practice (Wikipedia, 2012).

Activities –BASE Jumping, Bungee Jumping, Falconry, Gliding, Hang Gliding, Helicopter Flights, Hot Air Ballooning, Indoor Skydiving, Kites and Power Kites, Microlights, Model airplanes and helicopters, Model Rockets, Paragliding and Paramotoring, Parascending, SCAD - Suspended Catch Air Device, Skydiving, Wing Walking, Aeroplane flying, Air Sphering, Outdoor Land Activities, Activity Holidays, Adventure Racing, Airsoft, Archery, Assault courses and obstacle courses, Athletics, Backyard Sleepovers, Baseball, Basketball, Baton Twirling, Battle Reenactments, Beach Activities, Beachcombing, Birdwatching,

BMX biking, Bushcraft and Survival, Camping, Canyoning and Canyoneering, Capoeira, Carnivals, Cave biking underground, Caving and potholing, Cheerleading, Circus Skills, Clay Pigeon Shooting, Climbing, Concerts, Festivals and Gigs, Conkers, Conservation, Cookout, Crazy Golf and Mini Golf, Pitch and Putt, Cricket, Croquet, Cycling on the Road, Den Building and Bivouacs, Dodgeball, Dog Scootering, Drag Racing, Driving Experiences, Eclipse Sphering and Eclipse Zorbing, Exploring, Footbags, Football and Soccer, Free Running and Parkour, Fruit Picking, Gap Year Travelling, Gardening, Geocaching, Gladiator Training, Go Karting, Golf, Greyhound Racing, Grow Your Own Vegetables, Go Ape forest high wire adventures ropes courses, Hockey, Horse Boarding, Horse Racing, Horse Riding, Jogging and running, Jousting, Kite Boarding, Kite Buggying, Lacrosse, Land Yachting, Landboarding, Landscape Painting and Drawing, Laser Tag, Live Action Role Playing Games, Marathon Running, Monster Truck Racing, Motocross and dirt biking, Motor Racing, Mountain Biking, Mountain Boarding, Mountaineering, Multi Use Games Areas, Nascar, Netball, Off Road Motor Sports, Rallying and 4x4, Open Air Theatre, Orienteering, Outdoor Movie theatres and cinemas, Outdoor Photography, Paintballing, Parks - Chess, Ping Pong, picnics, football, sunbathing..., Picnics, Piggy Back Fights, Pony Trekking, Polo, Quad Biking, Remote Control Cars, Rock Climbing, Roller Coasters and Theme Parks, Roller Skating and Roller Blading, Rope Swings, Rugby, Safari, Sandboarding, Scavenger Hunts, Skate boarding, Skid Pan Driving, Skipping, Sightseeing, Soap Box Kart racing or Extreme Gravity Racing, Soft Martial Arts - Tai Chi, Chi Kung, Sphering, Steam Train driving and model railways, Stock Car Racing and Demolition Derby, Street Hockey, Street Improvisation and Drama, Street Luge and Downhill Skateboarding and Downhill Skating, Tank Driving, Team Building Outdoor Activities, Throw and Catch an American mini football, frisbee or frisbee golf, Tracking and wildlife watching, Tractor Pulling, Trail Running, Trampolining, Treasure Hunting and Metal Detectors, Tree Climbing, Treehouses, Triathlon, Ultimate Frisbee, Unicycling, Volleyball, Walking, Walk the dog, Wash the car, Watch the sunrise or sunset, Water Fights, Young Drivers -

Driving experiences for 11 year olds and over, Zorbing, Outdoor Water Activities, Blackwater rafting, Boating, Pedalos and Punts, Body Boarding, Bore Surfing, Bridge Jumping, Canal narrow boats, Canoeing, Cave Diving, Coasteering, Crabbing, Dragon Boat Racing, Exploring Rock Pools, Fishing, Free Diving, Hovercrafting, Hydrospeeding and Riverboarding, Jet Skiing, Kayaking, Kitesurfing, Model Boats, Octopush Underwater hockey, Pond Dipping, Powerboating, Raft Building, Rib Riding, River Bugging, Rowing, Sailing, Scuba Diving, Skim Boarding, Snorkelling, Surfing, Swimming, Tall Ship Crewing, Tombstoning, Wakeboarding, Water Parks and flumes, Water Polo, Water Skiing, Water Walkerz water sphering, Waveskiing, Whale Watching, Whitewater Rafting, Wild Swimming, Windsurfing, Yacht Charters, Yachting, Zap Cat Racing, (Anonymous 2012) rest, sleep, excretion, exercise, sports, eating, ...

Activity materials– Tools, chemical elements, etc.

Tools

One can classify tools according to their basic functions:

Cutting tools, such as the knife, scythe or sickle, are wedge-shaped implements that produce a shearing force along a narrow face. Ideally, the edge of the tool needs to be harder than the material being cut or else the blade will become dulled with repeated use. But even resilient tools will require periodic sharpening, which is the process of removing deformation wear from the edge. Other examples of cutting tools include gouges and drill bits.

Moving tools move huge and tiny things. For example, concentrating force tools: the hammer moves a nail, the maul moves a stake, or a whip moves flesh on a horse. These operate by applying physical compression to a surface. In the case of the screwdriver, the force is rotational and called torque. Writing implements deliver a fluid to a surface *via* compression to activate the ink cartridge. Also grabbing and twisting nuts and bolts with pliers, a glove, awrench, etc. All these tools move items by some kind of force. Also trucks, rockets and airplanes move larger items and particle accelerators move very small items.

Tools that enact chemical changes, including temperature and ignition, such as lighters and blow torches. Guiding, measuring and perception tools include the ruler, glasses, set square, sensors, straight edge, theodolite, microscope, monitor, clock, phone, printer.

Shaping tools, such as molds, jigs, trowels.

Fastening tools, such as welders, rivet guns, nail guns, or glue guns.

Information and data manipulation tools, such as computers, middleware, IDE, spreadsheets

Some tools may be combinations of other tools. An alarm-clock is for example a combination of a measuring tool (the clock) and a perception tool (the alarm). This enables the alarm-clock to be a tool that falls outside of all the categories mentioned above.

There is some debate on whether to consider protective gear items as tools, because they do not directly help perform work, just protect the worker like ordinary clothing. They do meet the general definition of tools and in many cases are necessary for the completion of the work. Personal protective equipment includes such items as gloves, safety glasses, ear defenders and biohazard suits.

Chemical elements

A chemical element is a pure chemical substance consisting of one type of atom distinguished by its atomic number, which is the number of protons in its nucleus. Familiar examples of elements include carbon, oxygen, aluminum, iron, copper, gold, mercury, and lead.

As of November 2011, 118 elements have been identified, the latest being ununseptium in 2010. Of the 118 known elements, only the first 98 are known to occur naturally on Earth. Of these, 80 are stable or essentially so, while the others are radioactive, decaying into lighter elements over various time scales from fractions of a second to billions of years. Those elements that do not occur naturally on Earth have been produced artificially as the synthetic products of man-made nuclear reactions.

Hydrogen and helium are by far the most abundant elements in the universe. However, iron is the most abundant element (by mass) making up the Earth, and oxygen is the most common element in the Earth's crust. Although all known chemical matter is composed of these elements, chemical matter itself constitutes only about 15% of the matter in the universe. The remainder is dark matter, a mysterious substance which is not composed of chemical elements since it lacks protons, neutrons or electrons.

The chemical elements are thought to have been produced by various cosmic processes, including hydrogen, helium (and smaller amounts of lithium, beryllium and boron) created during the Big Bang and cosmic-ray spallation. Production of heavier elements, from carbon to the very heaviest elements, proceeds by stellar nucleosynthesis, and these were made available for later solar system and planetary formation by supernovae, which blast these elements into space. The high abundance of oxygen, silicon, and iron on Earth reflect their common production in such stars, after the lighter gaseous elements and their compounds have been subtracted. While most elements are generally viewed as stable, a small amount of natural transformation of one element to another also occurs in the present time, through decay of radioactive elements as well as other natural nuclear processes.

Relatively pure samples of isolated elements are uncommon in nature. While all of the 98 naturally occurring elements have been identified in mineral samples from the Earth's crust, only a small minority of elements are found as recognizable, relative pure minerals. Among the more common of such "native elements" are copper, silver, gold, carbon (as coal, graphite, or diamonds), sulfur, and mercury. All but a few of the most inert elements, such as noble gases and noble metals, are usually found on Earth in chemically combined form, as chemical compounds. While about 32 of the chemical elements occur on Earth in native uncombined form, most of these occur as mixtures. For example, atmospheric air is primarily a mixture of nitrogen, oxygen, and argon, and native solid elements occur in alloys, such as that of iron and nickel.

When two distinct elements are chemically combined, with the atoms held together by chemical bonds, the result is termed a chemical compound. Two thirds of the chemical elements occur on Earth only as compounds, and in the remaining third, often the compound forms of the element are most common. Chemical compounds may be composed of elements combined in exact whole-number ratios of atoms, as in water, table salt, and minerals as quartz, calcite, and some ores. However, chemical bonding of many types of elements results in crystalline solids and metallic alloys for which exact chemical formulas do not exist. Most of the solid substance of the Earth is of this latter type. The substances that form Earth's crust, mantle, and core do not have precise chemical empirical formulas.

The history of discovery and use of the elements began with primitive human societies that found native elements like copper and gold, and extracted (smelted) iron and a few other metals from their ores. Alchemists and chemists subsequently identified many more, with nearly all of the naturally-occurring elements known by 1900. The properties of the chemical elements are often summarized using the periodic table that organizes the elements by increasing atomic number into rows ("periods") in which the columns ("groups") share recurring ("periodic") physical and chemical properties. Either in its pure forms, or in various chemical compounds or mixtures, almost every element has at least one important human use. Save for short half-lived radioactive elements, all of the elements are available industrially, most to high degrees of purity.

Around two dozen of the elements are essential to various kinds of biological life. Most rare elements on Earth are not needed by life (exceptions being selenium and iodine), while a few quite common ones (aluminum and titanium) are not used. Most organisms share element needs, with a few differences. For example, ocean algae use bromine but land plants and animals seem to need none, and all animals require sodium, but some plants do not. Just six elements—carbon, hydrogen, nitrogen, oxygen, calcium, and phosphorus—make up almost 99% of the mass of a human body (see composition of the human body for a complete list). In addition to the six major elements that compose most of the human body, humans require consumption of at least a dozen more elements in the form of certain chemical compounds (Wikipedia, 2012).

Transportation–Aviation, Aircraft, Fixed-wing aircraft, Airship (dirigible), Autogyro, Balloon, Blimp, Helicopter, Human-powered aircraft Parachute (downward air transport only), Rocket, Projectile (goods only, normally explosives), Supersonic transport, Zeppelin, Animal-powered transport, Animals domesticated for transport, Camel, Dog, Donkey (burro), Elephant, Homing pigeon, Horse, Mule, Llama, Ox, Pigeon (goods only), Reindeer, Yak, Animal-powered vehicles, Carriage, Cart, Chariot, Horse-drawn boat, Sled, Stagecoach, Cable transport, Aerial tramway, Cable car (railway), Chairlift, Detachable chairlift, Elevator, Funicular (inclined plane), Gondola lift, List of aerial lift manufacturers, Paternoster, Conveyor transport, Conveyor belt, Escalator, Moving walkway (moving sidewalk, travelator, and the inclined moving sidewalk, a moving ramp), Human-powered transport, Baby transport, Bicycle, Boda-boda, Buggy (cart), Human-powered aircraft, Ice skate, Kick scooter, Punt (boat), Rickshaw, Roller skates, Shopping cart, Skateboard, Ski, Snakeboard, Unicycle, Watercraft rowing, Wheelbarrow, Wheelchair, Hybrid transport, Amphibious vehicle, Hybrid vehicle, Moped, Motorized bicycle, Military transport, Air force transport, Military aircraft, Army transport, Armoured fighting vehicle, Armoured personnel carrier, Jeep, Landing craft, Limbers and caissons (military), Mega Tank, Mini-Tank, German Panzer, Navy transport, Aircraft carrier, Escort carrier, Naval ship, PT boat, Submarine, U-boat, Torpedo boat, Naval Tank ship, Motorized road transport, Automobile (car), Car body styles, Auto rickshaw, Bus, Midibus, Minibus, School bus, Trolleybus, Minivan, Motorcycle, Share taxi, Truck, Trucking industry in the United States, Unimog, Van, Motorized off-road transport, All-terrain vehicle, Engineering vehicle, Hovercraft, Ice boat, Snowmobile, Sport utility vehicle, Tank, Traction engine, Tractor, Pipeline transport, Natural gas, Petroleum, Pneumatic tube, Sanitary sewer, Slurry, Water, Rail transport, Accessibility, Glossary of rail terminology, High-speed rail, Locomotive, Maglev (transport), Monorail, Mountain railway, Cable car (railway), Funicular, Rack railway (cog railway), Multiple unit, Diesel multiple unit, Electric multiple unit (EMU), People mover, Personal rapid transit, Rail tracks, Rail transport by country, Rapid transit (metro, underground, subway); see also List of rapid transit systems, Train, Tram, light rail (streetcar, trolley); see also List of tram and light-rail transit systems, Steam Train, Ship transport, Barge, Boat, Jet Ski, Jetboat, Lifeboat (rescue), Lifeboat (shipboard), Narrowboat, Punt (boat), Wherry, Ferry, Horse-drawn boat, Hydrofoil, Sailing, Ship, Tank ship, Yacht, Space transport, Interplanetary spaceflight, Rocket, Space Shuttle, Space station, Spacecraft, Spacecraft propulsion, Transport on the Moon and Mars, Lunar rover (various, manned and unmanned, Moon, 1971–1973), Nomad rover (unmanned test vehicle, has not been in space, 1997), Opportunity rover (MER-B – unmanned, Mars, 2004), Sojourner (unmanned, Mars, 1997), Spirit rover (MER-A – unmanned, Mars, 2004), Space transport launched from the surface of the Moon and Ascent stage of Apollo Lunar Module, manned, six times, 1969-1972 (return to Earth in the Apollo program) (Wikipedia, 2012), ...

Communication– Body language, sign language, television, radio, telephone, mail.

Human communication

Human spoken and picture languages can be described as a system of symbols (sometimes known as lexemes) and the grammars (rules) by which the symbols are manipulated. The word "language" also refers to common properties of languages. Language learning normally occurs most intensively during human childhood. Most of the thousands of human languages use patterns of sound or gesture for symbols which enable communication with others around them. Languages seem to share certain properties although many of these include exceptions. There is no defined line between a language and a dialect. Constructed languages such as Esperanto, programming languages, and various mathematical formalisms are not necessarily restricted to the properties shared by human languages.

A variety of verbal and non-verbal means of communicating exists such as body language, eye contact, sign language, paralanguage, haptic communication, chronemics, and media such as pictures, graphics, sound, and writing.

Convention on the Rights of Persons with Disabilities also defines the communication to include the display of text, Braille, tactile communication, large print, accessible multimedia, as well as written and plain language, human reader, and accessible information and communication technology.

Nonverbal communication

Nonverbal communication describes the process of conveying meaning in the form of non-word messages. Research shows that the majority of our communication is nonverbal, also known as body language. Some of nonverbal communication includes chronemics, haptics, gesture, body language or posture; facial expression and eye contact, object communication such as clothing, hairstyles, architecture, symbols infographics, and tone of voice as well as through an aggregate of the above.

Speech also contains nonverbal elements known as paralanguage. These include voice lesson quality, emotion and speaking style as well as prosodic features such as rhythm, intonation and stress. Likewise, written texts include nonverbal elements such as handwriting style, spatial arrangement of words and the use of emoticons to convey emotional expressions in pictorial form.

Oral communication

Oral communication, while primarily referring to spoken verbal communication, can also employ visual aids and non-verbal elements to support the conveyance of meaning. Oral communication includes speeches, presentations, discussions, and aspects of interpersonal communication. As a type of face-to-face communication, body language and voice tonality play a significant role, and may have a greater impact upon the listener than informational content. This type of communication also garners immediate feedback.

Written Communication and Its Historical Development

Over time the forms of and ideas about communication have evolved through progression of technology. Advances include communications psychology and media psychology; an emerging field of study. Researchers divide the progression of written communication into three revolutionary stages called "Information Communication Revolutions".

During the first stage, written communication first emerged through the use of pictographs. The pictograms were made in stone, hence written communication was not yet mobile.

During the second stage, writing began to appear on paper, papyrus, clay, wax, etc. Common alphabets were introduced and allowed for the uniformity of language across large distances. A leap in technology occurred when the Gutenberg printing-press was invented in the 15th century.

The third stage is characterized by the transfer of information through controlled waves and electronic signals.

Communication is thus a process by which meaning is assigned and conveyed in an attempt to create shared understanding. This process, which requires a vast repertoire of skills in interpersonal processing, listening, observing, speaking, questioning, analyzing, gestures, and evaluating enables collaboration and cooperation (Wikipedia, 2012).

Physical Love–Hugs, kisses, taps, marriage, kindness, caring, giving flowers, etc.

Privacy Needs–Space and time

Companions–Accountants, Actuaries, Advocates, Architects, Archivists, Pilots, Chefs, Dentists, Diplomats, Engineers, Financial analysts, Journalists, Lawyers, Optometrists, Nurses, Pharmacists, Philosophers Physicians, Professors, Psychologists, Scientists, Social Workers, Surgeons, Veterinarians, Bookkeeper, Credit manager, Lawspeaker, Jurist, Ombudsman, Solicitor, Solicitor-Advocate, Advocate General, Agricultural scientists, Archaeologists, Astronomers, Astrophysicists, Astrobiologists, Biophysicists Biologists Biotechnologists Bioinformatician, Botanists Cognitive scientists, Ecologists, Entomologists, Evolutionary biologists, Geneticists, Herpetologists, Immunologists, Ichthyologists, Lepidopterists, Marine biologists, Medical scientists Microbiologists, Mycologists, Neuroscientists, Ornithologists, Paleontologists, Pathologists, Pharmacologists, Physiologists, Zoologists, Chemists, Analytical chemists, Biochemists, Inorganic chemists, Organic chemists, Physical chemist, Earth scientists, Geologists, Glaciologists, Hydrologists, Limnologists, Meteorologists, Mineralogists, Oceanographers, Paleontologists, Seismologists, Volcanologists, Informaticians, Computer scientists, Library scientists, Management scientists, Mathematicians, Statisticians, Military scientists, Physicists, Psychologists, Abnormal psychologists, Behavioral psychologists, Biopsychologists, Clinical psychologists, Comparative psychologists, Cognitive psychologists, Developmental psychologists, Educational psychologists, Evolutionary psychologists, Experimental psychologists, Forensic psychologists, Health psychologists Medical psychologists, Neuropsychologists, Psychopharmacologists, Psychophysicists, Social psychologists,

Social scientists, Anthropologists, Ethnologists, Communication scientists, Criminologists, Demographers, Economists, Geographers, Political economists, Political scientists, Sociologists, Technologists, Department head, Senior Manager, Project Manager, Senior Architect, Designer, Architect, Intern Architect, Architectural technologist, Educational technologist, Engineering technologist, Industrial technologist, Medical Technologist, Radiologic technologist, Surgical technologist, Software technologist, (Wikipedia, 2012) friends, families, pets, companions, neighbors, lovers, love ones, groupmates, best friends, office mates, playmates, acquaintances, students, husbands, wives, teachers, supervisors, sons, daughters, parents, leaders, workers, brothers, sisters, priest, masters, managers, elders, children, siblings, doctors, firemen, policemen, etc.

DISCUSSION

Some things may be categorized to two or more groups, example is water. Water is grouped under metabolic needs for nourishment, under hygiene for cleansing, under grooming, under physical fitness material for swimming and under transportation for water transportation. Other examples may be distinguished depending on the use.

The categories may be put into debate for its redundancy like Hygiene and Grooming may be combined, Safety and Security may be combined, Transportation and Communication may be combined, Physical love may be combined to Activities, so on and so forth.

This is an overview, so as not to be mistaken to be fully complete. All examples are not stated. Some examples regarding cultures may vary for example for hygiene, grooming, physical love, etc.

These physical needs are essential to other aspects of wellness. Example is communication. It is essential to social, emotional, intellectual, occupational, environmental and spiritual wellness.

CONCLUSION

This research is a compilation of researches. This states the different categories of physical needs with supporting statements for the need of the category. This theory may be further developed by various authors. This is one of the steps for social awareness. The author arranged the physical needs into categories to strengthen human growth. The twelve physical needs of man are hygiene needs, grooming needs, metabolic needs, transportation, communication, safety needs, security needs, activities, activity materials, physical love, privacy needs and companions.

ENDNOTES

[1]Abraham Harold Maslow (April 1, 1908 – June 8, 1970) was an American professor of psychology at Brandeis University, Brooklyn College, New School for Social Research and Columbia University who founded humanistic psychology and created Maslow's hierarchy of needs ("Dr. Abraham Maslow, Founder Of Humanistic Psychology, Dies". *New York Times*. June 10, 1970. Retrieved 2010-09-26. "Dr. Abraham Maslow, professor of psychology at Brandeis University in Waltham, Mass., and founder of what has come to be known as humanistic psychology, died of a heart attack. He was 62 years old.") (Wikipedia, 2011)

[2]Peter Holy is a certified wellness advisor for the 123 Feel Better Company. He is also a contributing author to Insight Journal Online Magazine. Peter is an expert in Physical Wellness, and also specializes in Emotional and Intellectual aspects. Through his Spiritual approach to the 7 Aspects of Wellness, Peter focuses on creating harmonious lifestyles that support the mind, power the body, and nurture the spirit (Insight Journal Online Magazine 2011)

[3]"[C]onjectures or hypotheses ... are really to be regarded as thought "experiments" through which we wish to discover whether something can be explained by a specific assumption in connection with other natural laws." —Hans Christian Ørsted("First Introduction to General Physics" ¶16-¶18, part of a series of public lectures at the University of Copenhagen. Copenhagen 1811, in Danish, printed by Johan Frederik Schulz. In Kirstine Meyer's 1920 edition of Ørsted's works, vol. **III** pp. 151–190.) "First Introduction to Physics: the Spirit, Meaning, and Goal of Natural Science". Reprinted in German in 1822, Schweigger's *Journal für Chemie und Physik* **36**, pp. 458–488, as translated in Ørsted 1997, pp. 296–298 (Wikipedia, 2011).

REFERENCES

Book

Ørsted Hans Christian (1997). *Selected Scientific Works of Hans Christian Ørsted*, pp. 296–298. Princeton ISBN 0-691-04334-5. Translated to English by Jelved Karen, Jackson Andrew D.and Knudsen Ole(translators 1997).

Journals

Warren and Brandeis (1890). "The Right to Privacy". *Harvard Law Review*, IV(5): 193.

Nelson, Holly and Geher, Glenn (2007-09-15). Mutual Grooming in Human Dyadic Relationships: An Ethological Perspective.

Newspaper

New York Times (June 10, 1970) Abraham Maslow.

Magazine

Insight Journal Online Magazine (2011). Peter Holy from http://www.anxiety-and-depression-solutions.com/contributors/peter_holy.php.

Websites

Anonymous (2012). Attending to Personal Hygiene Needs from http://jobaccess.gov.au/Advice/JobRequirement/Pages/Attending_to_personal_hyg.aspx

Anonymous (2012). Outdoor activities Ideas List for Teenagers from http://www.activeoutdoors.info/activeoutdoors/Article35.html

Anonymous (2012). Personal Hygiene and Grooming Needs from http://jobaccess.gov.au/Advice/ProductOrSolutionOne/Pages/Personal_hygiene_and_groo.aspx

Anonymous (2012). Work from http://dictionary.reference.com/browse/work

Arthur Aron (2011). **Q: What motivates people to seek out love?** from http://health.howstuffworks.com/relationships/love/why-do-we-fall-in-love.htm

Heron John (1998). Physical Needs from http://www.co-cornucopia.org.uk/coco/articles/cathars/forword.htm

Peter Holy (2011). The seven aspects of wellness from http://www.anxiety-and-depression-solutions.com/articles/health_and_wellness/7_aspects_of_wellness_intro.php#

Wikipedia (2011). Abraham Maslow from http://en.wikipedia.org/wiki/Abraham_Maslow

Wikipedia (2012). Chemical element from http://en.wikipedia.org/wiki/Chemical_element
Wikipedia (2012). Clothing from http://en.wikipedia.org/wiki/Clothing
Wikipedia (2011). Communication from http://en.wikipedia.org/wiki/Communication
Wikipedia (2012). Food from http://en.wikipedia.org/wiki/Food
Wikipedia (2011). Friendship from http://en.wikipedia.org/wiki/Friendship
Wikipedia (2012). Homeostasis from http://en.wikipedia.org/wiki/Homeostasis
Wikipedia (2011). Hygiene from http://en.wikipedia.org/wiki/Hygiene
Wikipedia (2012). Insurance from http://en.wikipedia.org/wiki/Insurance
Wikipedia (2012). Law from http://en.wikipedia.org/wiki/Laws
Wikipedia (2012). List of professions from http://en.wikipedia.org/wiki/Profession
Wikipedia (2011). Love from http://en.wikipedia.org/wiki/Love
Wikipedia (2012). Medicine from http://en.wikipedia.org/wiki/Medicine
Wikipedia (2012). Money from http://en.wikipedia.org/wiki/Money
Wikipedia (2012). Needs from http://en.wikipedia.org/wiki/Needs
Wikipedia (2012). Outline of transport from
http://en.wikipedia.org/wiki/List_of_transportation_topics
Wikipedia (2012). Oxygen from http://en.wikipedia.org/wiki/Oxygen
Wikipedia (2011). Personal Grooming from http://en.wikipedia.org/wiki/Personal_grooming
Wikipedia (2011). Physical Fitness from http://en.wikipedia.org/wiki/Physical_fitness
Wikipedia (2011). Physiological Needs from http://en.wikipedia.org/wiki/Physiological_needs
Wikipedia (2011). Physiological Needs and Safety Needs from http://en.wikipedia.org/wiki/Maslow%27s_hierarchy_of_needs
Wikipedia (2011). Privacy from http://en.wikipedia.org/wiki/Privacy
Wikipedia (2011). Relaxation from http://en.wikipedia.org/wiki/Human_relaxation
Wikipedia (2011). Safety from http://en.wikipedia.org/wiki/Maslow%27s_hierarchy_of_needs
Wikipedia (2012). Savings Account from http://en.wikipedia.org/wiki/Savings_account
Wikipedia (2011). Security from http://en.wikipedia.org/wiki/Maslow%27s_hierarchy_of_needs
Wikipedia (2011). Sleep from http://en.wikipedia.org/wiki/Sleep
Wikipedia (2011). Thought experiment from http://en.wikipedia.org/wiki/Thought_experiment.
Wikipedia (2011). Tools from http://en.wikipedia.org/wiki/Tools
Wikipedia (2011). Transportation from http://en.wikipedia.org/wiki/Transportation
Wikipedia (2012). Universe from http://en.wikipedia.org/wiki/Universe
Wikipedia (2012). Water from http://en.wikipedia.org/wiki/Water

8

Boko Haram and Ethno-Religious Hypocrisy in Nigeria: Building on a Faulty Foundation

OKAFOR SAMUEL, O.[1*]

ABSTRACT

Every social phenomenon in human social existence is subject to human thinking, imagination and ideological expression. This vulnerability of social phenomenon to human manipulation especially, in the modern era, becomes a loop hole for individuals and groups to purwsue their interest at the detriment of the ultimate goal of the modern society and human existence. Religion as one of the social phenomenon that lives with human existence had become a smoke screen for individuals and groups who are in pursuit of multifaceted selfish interests ostensibly for the creation of a society that will please God. While individuals use some verses of the holy books to settle individual scores against non adherents, some use it as an umbrella to pursue their political interests, motivating the youth to violently undermine the existing system as unholy and heretic; yet groups with emerging ideology, conceptualization and redefinition of some verses in the holy books, hide themselves under the cloak of religion to pursue some global agenda. All these put

[1] Department of Sociology & Anthropology, University of Nigeria, Nigeria
**Corresponding E-mail*: samuelokey200@gmail. com

together have resulted to high level of underdevelopment and other negative social consequences across Asia, Middle East and African continents. Nonetheless, the same situation at the international level has emerged as a form of Neocolonization of the third world nations. BokoHaram (Jama'atuAhles-SunnahLidda' AwatiWal Jihad) is one of the many sub groups who have appeared under the umbrella of religion to pursue unjust cause and perpetuate mayhem against the modern society thereby creating an orbit for the setting in of underdevelopment and cultural cum political imperialism in Nigeria. This paper focused on unraveling of the susceptibility of religion to individual and group ideology (using Boko Haram as a case study) and the unseen roles of this to underdevelopment and neocolonialism. In view of the present situation domestically and at the global level, the paper recommends Nigerian government should choose a stand as a sovereign nation in their relationship with the Islamic nations of all categories to avoid being used as a religious dope for hidden agenda by these nations. The Islamic world should checkmate the tendencies of proliferation of illicit ideologies in their domain in order to save the image of the religion and save the world peace; and the Nigerian Muslims should leave the shackles of religion and consider the interest of black man in their judgment of unwholesome activities under the umbrella of religion in order not to be building the ground for future imperialists and racists who are bound to dominate the world via religion.

Key words: Boko Haram, Islam, Neocolonialism, Terrorism and underdevelopment.

INTRODUCTION

Religion as a social phenomenon lacks objectivity and consistency and therefore, becomes what group or individuals call it at a given context. While some individuals and groups use religion for political, economic and other ulterior motives, others use it as a psychological tool to neutralize the burdens of this life, falling in the category of adherents who reflect the Karl Marx's definition of religion as the opium of the masses. Whatever is the direction of interest in religion; there are benefits from it as well as hazards from it both at individual level and group levels.

Religion though is an individual or group thing with some level of privacy, raises concern in the modern society where human rights are endangered because of individual or group imposition of their belief, interpretation and assumptions on the masses who does not share similar views. This always leads to the state of anarchy in the society, which may be invisible to the majority. In a situation in which a particular individuals has set themselves as the only right thinking and perfect individuals to determine the destiny of the society or even a generation, there is already a loophole for individual excessiveness, right abuse and other antisocial behaviors which are detrimental to development and human existence in general.

Islam as one of the world popular religions originating from Arabian Peninsula is, one of the social phenomenon which has created opportunity for the above mentioned antisocial attitudes among many individuals and groups across the globe. Islam surfaced with the aim of countering polytheistic attitude among the Arabs in favour of monotheism (Omeire, 2006). This by implication points to the fact that Islam was meant for homogeneous existence of humanity and peaceful coexistence. Although there were some fundamental issues associated with it in the time of Muhammad such as violent strategies to conquer his kinsmen from Mecca, who were hostile to his new found faith (Boer, 1969)); in essence, this situation was a reaction to time and explicit violent attitude towards Islam by the people of Mecca, which in the Newton's law of action and reaction, required a strategy to survive by Muhammad. Again, Muhammad, while in Medina did not aspire to impose his new found faith on the inhabitants instead, his leadership qualities and ability to organize the Muslim community, attracted people around him and made him to be accepted as socio-political leader among the people of Medina (Glubb, 1971). While Muhammad was exercising his faith with his converts, other citizens of Medina and Mecca were still exercising their faith in the same environment, indicating that Muhammad's revelation in the cave of mount Hira was for him and those who accepted his teachings at the time (Mawdudi, 1981).

In view of some issues surrounding Islam in the time of Muhammad, the subsequent followers of Prophet Muhammad ventured into deep interpretations of his life time and circumstances surrounding the development of Islam. These deep interpretations were not with some level of individual and group bias as can be found between the Sunni and Shi'as. While some individuals and groups were struggling to impose their own view as supreme and representing the absolute view of Prophet Muhammad, the vestiges of such struggles spread out among the individuals and groups, who have ulterior motives and used that as a loophole to achieve their political, economic and other objectives (Milton-Edwards, 2000; Eickelman, 1998). The spread of the incoherence within Islam sprang up Islamic militants and ideologists, who later subscribed to terrorism as the justifiable means of influence and domination.

The falling of Islam into the pinhole of ideology in the subsequent times gave room for Islamic militancy with ceaseless mutations and observance of terrorism which subsequently became a strategy for empire builders and cultural imperialists hiding under the smoke screen of Religion to perpetuate evil and mayhem across the globe (Khouri, 2008; Li and Schuabi, 2004; Chaliand and Blin, 2007; Matusitz, 2008; Schmid and Jongman, 1988).

Islam is not the only culprit to the vestiges of religion falling to ideology as many other religions such as Christianity have falling into the same situation in the past such as Zionism and recently in some parts of China where individuals who form a caucus end up in forcing family members and other individuals to be converted or be kill or maimed even in the public places such as restaurants and bars.

Boko-Haram is one of the outcomes of the ever growing religion (Islamic) ideologies, which subsequently turned to terrorist organization. The origin and surfacing of Boko-Haram had been suspected to be connected to the frequent visit of Mammar Gadafi of Libya, Osama Bin Laden and other religious merchants in the early 90s, who were bent to plunge Nigeria into neocolonialism *via* religion, cultural cum economic imperialism. Indeed Boko-Haram appearing with much indices of terrorism has hit educational structures, commerce and Industries, population displacement, peace and the inter-ethnic relation in the Northern part of Nigeria, which has resulted to underdevelopment of the areas affected. Their activities have been a major setback to socio-economic activities in Nigeria in all the areas affected by its activities, and to the image of Nigeria on the global scene (Walker, 2012; Start, 2014; Campbell, 2014).

THE MUTANT NATURE OF RELIGIOUS (ISLAMIC) IDEOLOGY AND RELIGIOUS (ISLAMIC) MILITANCY

The complications bound to surface in human, other than divine interpretation of religious interests engulfed Islam after the death of Prophet Muhammad. These complications were largely due to common sense judgement, un-specificity of Muhammad's position about how and who will succeed him and, vested interests of individuals and groups within the Muslim faithful then. The death of Muhammad which led to the internal discontents among the adherents of Islam about who will succeed him, eventually sowed the seed of ideological rivalries among the Muslims till date (Mawdudi, 1981). While majority of the adherents opted for Abu Bakr from the Quraish tribe and the right hand man of Muhammad while he was alive, others prefer Ali, who incidentally was Prophet Muhammad's son in-law and cousin; he also like Abu Bakr involved in the religious activities as assistant to Muhammad while he was still living (Omeire, 2006; Boer, 1969; Mawdudi, 1981). Though Abu Bakr eventually became the first caliph after the death of Muhammad with Ali surrendering to him for the unity of the Muslims, this initial rivalry laid the foundation for the major division among the Muslims, which later resulted to the age long known two camps in Islam (Sunni and Shi'as).

The ideological rivalry in Islam gave room for different forms of human identity expressions under the umbrella of Islam such as fundamentalists, confused elements, opportunists and faithful adherents. These identity expressions surfaced in the groupings Khouri (2008) classified into seven groups, who are operating now in the Middle East. Among these ideological forces *are Mainstream Islamists, Terrorist groups, American led western hegemony, Anti American-anti imperial defiance, Home grown Arab democracy and the rule of law, Tribal loyalties and Pan Arabism.* In his own classification, Khouri maintained that these ideological groups show some level of violence of which in any case is focused towards a particular group or personalities deemed as a threat to the interest of the ideological group itself. For the Muslim Brotherhood, Hamas and Hezbollah, which were referred to as the mainstream Islamists by Khouri, the focus for violence were simply Israel and Western elements. Terrorist groups in this classification such as the group led by Osama Bin Laden, Abu Musab Al-zarqawi, Fateh el-Islam in Lebanon, etc, see violence at all cost as the means of expressing political will. The American led hegemony, which had their foothold in places like Libya, Qatar, Egypt and Jordan, have the focus of making the Middle East friend to Western nations with yet focus on the Israel as their collective enemy (Adoni, 2007; Abu-Amir, 1993; Carapico, 2002). Anti-American- Anti-imperial defiance group such as Syria, Sudan, Hamas in Palestine, and Hezbollah in Lebanon, are politically aligned; seeing America in particular and secularism in general as the enemy of the Arab world, drawing sympathies from Iran, Latin America and Muslims from Europe and other parts of the world (Craig, 2000; Ebrahim, 1980). For the home grown Arab democracy and the rule of law, the problem of the Middle East and Islam, which worth giving priority is the sick government at home which is harboring corruption, autocratic regime, police state, mismanagement, etc. To this group, getting rid of the poor and irresponsible government at home is the beginning of Arab and Islamic liberation (Edelman, 2001; Faqir, 2001; Fuller, 2002).

The tribal loyalties are more of culturally inclined than religiously inclined, focusing on bringing to prominence the cultural values of the Arab world through political control in places such as Kuwait, Yemen and Jordan. Among the pan Arabian, the interest is more of the mainstream Islamists, having America and Israel as the enemy in focus (Craig, 2001; Barak, 2002).

Beyond the seven classifications of politico-religious ideologies by Khouri and other scholars, there are numerous other ideological and political groups who still subscribe to religion (Islam) as their umbrella of operation in the Middle East and beyond. Of course, the classification above is limited to time and space as there are many other groups who have sprang up after 2008 and also, others that are operating in other parts of Asia, Africa and elsewhere (Martin, 2010; Stakelbeck, 2011).

Observing the background of each of these groups operating under the umbrella of Islam anywhere in the world, there is always a common thing among them; this is, the belief that any other group existing before the group itself is a heretic and must be eliminated by hook or crook; involving bloodshed, terror and destruction of lives and properties. Even the populists among the groups and the sub groups, who subscribe to changing government through electoral process, there are still evidence of violence at the background which is justified by the resistance to the perceived oppression from the incumbent regimes (Hamzeh, 2000; Ismail, 2000; Morgan, 2004).

Ideology in itself is a complicated issue as far as human bias is concerned, making it difficult for there to be consensus where there are diverse interests. It simply come from individuals as a concept into conceptualization and later move from disintegrated ideas into a composite of ideas and later to ideology. In such a situation most people with diverse experiences, levels of understanding and sentiments, stumble into freedom to express such without consideration of other people's right of existence. While at some point some individuals developing and spreading such ideologies under the umbrella of religion were more dedicated to the ideal interest of religion, most of them were miscreants and hoodlums who may have been rejected by the mainstream religion in question and even the initial organization that nurtured them. Again some of these ideological organizations in Islam started as genuine socio-political revolutions, but were hijacked by the hoodlums who were interested in their selfish ends.

Owing to the fact that the easiest way to achieve ulterior motive is through barbaric actions and sentiments, terrorism becomes the inseparable part of religion ideologies especially in Islam among the Islamic sects and their mutants. Among the 64 active terrorist organizations (both domestic and international) listed by U.S department of states as at 2011, more than 50% were the vestiges of religion mostly, Islamic ideologies while more than 60% of the terrorist organizations listed were Islamic origin among others (U.S State Department, 2011). The foundation of ideological proliferation within religion especially, Islamic world, gave birth to the incessant Islamic militancy, which are now the global security issue.

The Boko-Haram (Jama'atu Ahles-Sunnah), Alqaiada in the Islamic Maghreb, Alshabaab, Alqaida and Taliban are all bearing the same hallmark of religion ideology and sharing regional and international link in their operation (Walker, 2014; U.S Department, 2011; Jackson, 2005; Martin, 2010; Gunaratna, 2002); the more the vulnerability of religion to ideology, the more the religious militancy and consequently, terrorist organizations.

POLITICS, OBNOXIOUS INTERESTS AND RIDDLES ABOUT TERRORISM

The concept and conceptualization of social phenomenon is good as well as bad when it comes to the issue of divergence in interests among individuals and groups. While some scholars overtly conceptualize certain phenomenon for the sake of operationalization and empirical verification, others covertly conceptualize to suit their interests and secrete agenda. Terrorism which in itself is the use of violence to create fear for political, religious or ideological reasons has been given different interpretations by different individuals and groups. Although some scholars try to operationalize it for empirical verification, others try to conceptualize it ostensibly to sheer away from attaching a social stigma to some activities by certain group of people.

Terrorism is one of the most tri*via*lized issues in open discussion among some religious groups but covertly encouraged by the majority of adherents of some of these religious groups (Jackson, 2005). This stems from the so called holy war (jihad), among the Muslims for instance (Omeire, 2006). Jihad is an Arabic word meaning "struggle". According to the Qur'an (where jihad appears more than 41 times), Muslims have the duty of fighting enemies and invading non Muslim territories to spread Islam (Yoel, 2004; Imre, Mooney and Clarke, 2008). More than any other thing, jihad is focused to eliminate the so called people of the book such as the Jews, Christians and non Muslims of all categories. The jihad in the Quran had a profound implication for terrorism which is the modern form of it. While the jihad started with crude weapons and implements with specific targets among the faithful, it graduated into modern terrorism with modern weapons and indiscriminate attacks (Jackson, 2005; Martin, 2010; Ansari, 1984; Gerges, 2005).

As the ideological proliferation continued among the religious groups especially, in the Muslim world, so the incidents of terrorism continued to grow unabated. From 1975-1984, the number of reported terrorist attacks increased from ten per week to about ten per day, with 10% of the world countries (mostly middle east) accounting for the 60% of the world terrorist incidents (Risks International, 1985; Jenkins, 1985; Li and Schaub, 2004). According to Bakker (2007), Braziel (2008), Li and Schaub (2004), more than 80% of the arrested terrorists in Europe, America and elsewhere outside the Middle East, between 1985 and 2007 were all Muslims. Of paramount interest is the fact that most of the arrested terrorists attributed their motivation for attack to the Quran injunctions on jihad. According to Islam and Shahin (2001), Muhammad Atta, a leader of the 9/11 attacks, carried with him writings from Quran that urged him and others to stay firm in the desire to carry out the attacks and pursue the rewards of martyrdom.

Although majority of the conflicts involving the Palestinian Liberation Organization and other Islamists groups are attributed to poverty and anti Israeli sentiments, the reality on the ground show the difference. According to the interview conducted by Stakelbeck (2011) with the Al-Qaida prisoners, their response show that Islamic ideology drive them to terrorist attack order than poverty or anti Jewish sentiments. Similarly, some of the members of Hamas operating in Palestine have indicated through interview that, the driving force behind their terroristic acts were *verses* of the Quran, which they rehearsed and meditated on, before their action (Jaffer, 2000).

Some of the scholars such as Hafez (2007); Roy (1994); Khan (2001); Moustafa (2000) and Zeghal (1999), prefer to attribute terrorism (modern jihad) to the radicalization of Muslim Brotherhood by SayyidQutb in early 90s, a circumstance which according to them, set a pace for the radical Islamic ideologists about jihad; evidences show that jihad itself is a phenomenon which has its root in the Quran. This has a common ground for all the interpretations by the individuals as well as groups in Islam, with the ultimate focus on fighting the non Muslims at all cost by the Muslim faithful (Kapel, 2002; Gerges, 2005; Anderson and Sloan, 2003; Also see Quran 9:111). The extent to which the Quran injunctions on jihad affect the psychology of the common Muslim can at least be indicated through the way they overtly or covertly respond or support the issue of terrorism. According to the 2006 Gallup poll involving over 50,000 interviewees in various nations, 90 million Muslims (7% of the 1. 3 billion world Muslim population), indicated that the 9/11 attack on U.S was justifiable (Rand Corporation, 2011). Among the 2. 4 million Muslims living in America as at 2008, 15% of the under 30 think that suicide bombing was justifiable for the defense of Islam. Similarly, 6% of the older adults accepted the same thought (Pew Research Center, 2007; 2009).

According to the findings of the survey by the program on International Attitude (PIA) in university of Mary land (2006-2007), 55% of the Egyptians see the U.S war on terrorism as economic and political domination of the Middle East by the U.S, 92% saw it as a goal of U.S to weaken and divide the Muslims. About 90% of the Egyptians indicated that they subscribe to the Al-Qaida's attempt to confront U.S in order to affirm the dignity of the Islamic people while, 56% indicated that they share the Al-Qaida attitude to U.S. The overt and covert supports for terrorism among majority of Muslims in the name of fighting the infidels and crusaders operate both at general and specific levels. While generally, the attitude to terrorism related incidents may help to decipher the individual position in encouraging or discouraging terrorism, on a specific level, such can be identified through the way individuals and groups in political authorities or other public institutions approach or react to the incidents of terrorism. Chief among these are the political institutions and the media institutions, which stand as the ultimate determinants of the common man understanding and guide to perspective about the issue of jihad, Islamism and terrorism.

Among the Islamic nations such as Saudi Arabia, Iran, Iraq, Syria, Egypt, Pakistan, Lebanon, Palestine, Libya, Sudan, Jordan, Turkey, etc, the issue of terrorists had been tri*via*lized when it is against the perceived enemy of the state and Islam but had been viewed as abomination when it affects the potentates or Islamic community depending on whether it is Sunni or shi'a dominated perhaps, observing partly the Quran injunction in K2:190-191 (Yoel, 2004). Most of the Islamic nations are connected with the already classified terrorist organizations and their elements either directly or in proxy (Winer and Roule, 2002). Instances abound in the above-mentioned nations their direct and indirect involvement in the act of terrorism. For instance, while Taliban and Hakani Network are busy butchering the innocent civilians both in Pakistan and Afghanistan, Pakistani government is busy providing them with safe haven and diplomatic arguments. Pakistani government has been suspected of using her intelligent agency to covertly manage international mujahedeen forces many among them, who are Sunni extremists. Pakistan is also suspected of involvement in the development of Islamic state both abroad and their presence in the neighboring Afghanistan (Gall, 2016). United States of America had been cooperating with Pakistan in the fight against terrorists but Pakistan had been the power house for the development and training of terrorists *via* the terrible Madrasa institution. The institution had produced terrorists who operated in Afghanistan, India, China, Europe, Syria, Iraq, and even in U.S and Africa.

In Pakistani cities of Waziristan, Quetta, Rawalpindi etc, the world most dreaded terrorists such as the leaders of Al-Qaeda, Haqqani Network, Taliban, Islamic State, etc and their organizations are flourishing under the nose of Pakistani security intelligence (Gall, 2016). Pakistan is not alone in the business of hatching, developing and spreading Sunni extremists. Qatar and Turkey had been suspected in the offering of a safe haven to these terrorists and granting them a safe passage into their target countries such as Syria, Iraq, Palestine, China, Europe, America and Africa. While Qatar uses her posture as a trusted ally to America, Europe and other countries to grant the terrorists a safe passage into their nations of targets; Turkey on the other hand as a gate way to the West from Middle East had been offering a safe passage for terrorists from the West into Syria, Iraq and Palestine or even from Middle East into other parts of the world.

Iranian government, since her revolution in 1979 had been suspected of involvement in terrorism covertly, using sub organizations and her military intelligent agents who act in disguise per adventure they are caught. The notorious instances of Iranian involvement in terrorism missions included the bombing of Jewish settlement in Argentina of which Iran denied involvement and later used diplomatic channel to seek for the release of the arrested suspects over the incidence. Iran was the chief sponsor of the bombing of the U.S. marine base in Lebanon in 1984 which claimed the lives of many. Iran has consistently built and supported terrorist organizations such as Hamas, Hezbollah, etc, with weapons, logistics and diplomatic arguments in their terrible activities resulting in the loss of lives and properties (Bangstad, 2002; Gilseman, 1990). Turkey and Qatar have been covertly providing a fertile ground and safe haven for the Islamist extremists who carry out operation on the soil of other countries. They do this under cover of right of exile for the individual members of the terrorist organizations involved (Martin, 2010). Most of the Sunni extremists trained in Pakistani Madrasa institution for war, melt into the countries of their targets such as Syria, Iraq, Palestine, America, Europe and Africa *via* Qatar and Turkey, who officially award these elements authentic passports (Gall, 2016; Gunaratna, 2007). Saudi Arabia is the highest buyer of weapons of all kinds from the international market almost on yearly basis a situation, which had been questioned by political and war analysts. Most of these weapons melt into religious war against their Shi'as opponents and the perceived infidels in proxy, in different parts of the world. Bin laden's mission against America is suspected to have received the blessings of Saudi Arabia as a nation and that of other Sunni Muslim nations leaving a doubt in the mind of U. S. government about the financial and military aids to these nations in an attempt to combat terrorism (Ganor, 2002; Alexander, 2004).

The riddles of terrorism in the political and religious interests among some nations does not end with the political class, it also involves the public media in most of these nations who present the issue of terrorism in an inverted manner to continue to sustain religious and political sentiments about jihad instead of the objective realities of the terror. Commentators use this channel to champion the course of jihad in disguise, tri*via*lizing the issue of jihad/terroristic activities and taking terrorism for socio-political reaction to "West" and Arab socio-political relationship disequilibrium (Berger, 2004). Some of the instances of the falsehood of media channels in presenting the realities of terrorism include the interpretation given to Osama Bin laden's attack on U.S. While some commentators presented it as the punishment to U.S. for her policies in the Arab world (Salih, 2001; Salama, 2001;

Muhyii, 2001); others still perceived it as the hand work of FBI and Israel, which they wanted to blame on the Muslims to justify every aggression against Muslims anywhere (Fahmi, 2001; Diaa, 2001; 2003; Edward, 2001; Salim, 2005). This by implication was orchestrated to encourage the hatred against the "West" and non Muslims, among the Arab nations by the teleguided media institutions. Similarly, Hamas, Hezbollah, and other terrorist groups operating in the middle East have been justified by the media commentators, encouraging them on the ground that they are the defender of Islam against the crusaders (possibly the Jews and the West), who are perceived as the enemies of Islam and the Arab nations in general (Abdallah, 2005; Khuturat, 2001; Mada, 2001; Said, 2001; Karim, 2001; Ibrahim, 2001).

The hypocrisy and riddles about terrorism among some nations has trickled down to West African nations and Nigeria in particular. While some components of Salafist ideologists from Saudi Arabia is suspected to have given a germinating ground for Boko Haram extremists, the inter regional network among Pakistan, Qatar, Turkey, Somalia and Sudan facilitated the network between other mujahedeen forces and Boko Haram including, materials (both human and otherwise) and logistics for operation. To worsen the mater, the hypocrisy among Nigerian Muslims, who refused to call spade a spade continued to fan the amber of Boko-Haram terror activities. Indeed, evidences abound on the wavering position of the Northern Cabal an Islamic body that is dominated by the Sunni Muslims (Start, 2014; Campbell, 2014; Mauro, 2014). While the fire of Boko-Haram was consuming the innocent citizens of the country, the Northern Cabal and Arewa Consultative Forum (ACF), mostly dominated by the Sunni Muslims were busy seeking for amnesty from the Federal government of Nigeria to the Boko-Haram insurgents an argument, which the justified with comparing Boko-Haram to Niger Delta Militants. Among the Muslims sympathizing with Boko Haram in the Nigerian army, the case get worsen day by day as they sabotage their colleagues at the battle front and even sell off the ammunitions from the federal government to the group. Worst still, the politicians from the Northern part of the country within Muslim origin who pretended they know nothing about Boko Haram, were courageous enough to argue in favour of the group in the national house of assembly demanding they be granted Islamic republic. All these instances point to the relationship between political forces and religious interest. While politics (which in its raw definition is the quest for power and control) gets sophisticated in the face of modernity and post modernity, it has spread its tentacle to every other social phenomenon and institutions. Politics of culture surfaces as the globalization agenda in which North America and Western Europe want to dominate the world; politics of race surfaces in form of argument about the superior race; military politics surfaces in the quest for nuclear power; economic politics surfaces in the quest to have upper hand in the world economic resources and control over global exchange channels; in the same manner, politics of religion surfaces in the way one religious group struggle to have influence every over other religions.

RELIGION, A SACRED PHENOMENON OR ENCAPSULATION OF CULTURAL AND ECONOMIC IMPERIALISM?

Perhaps, the most important aspect of religion as a social phenomenon is the fact that it justifies the belief of man that there are other phenomenon in existence beyond his physical control, which demands for his total surrender and allegiance. In effect, this is the reason why individual is the measure in the issue of belief especially, in the modern time. In a household, family and even community, belief is a matter of what an individual has been convinced of and is sure of its validity to his quest for protection, happiness and comfort.

Before, during and after the time of Mohammad, individuals and groups have been exercising their faith in what so ever they believed in, making it (Islam), an option among other faiths that existed side by side with it (Omeire, 2006; Onyeidu, 2001). Sadly enough, Islam later became one of the religions or perhaps the only religion that has issues with human rights where ever it appears as a dominant religion, contravening the 1948 United Nations human right charter (Article 217 [iii] A). In most Islamic countries, the religion is overtly promoted in the constitution against the individual's right to freedom of worship while in others; it is covertly promoted in the constitution and *via* government policies.

In places like Iran, Sudan, Saudi Arabia, Iraq, Pakistan, Eritrea, Mauritania, etc, government which is dominated by Islam have technically ripped the citizens of the right of freedom of worship hence people being forcefully converted or technically face the threat of elimination as a minority group either by omission or commission (Pellot, 2014). Though there are other countries such as China, Russia and North Korea, who control the religion *via* government policies, these countries are more or less pursuing physical security measures against perceived outside influence order than forcing people to be converted to a particular religion. We are not justifying any form of right abuse by any government however; the interest here is the problem of turning religion into an instrument of oppression and subjugation of individuals in the society by the few especially, men who control the government powers in these nations.

The foundation some religions such as Islam laid for itself, using threats to convert individuals and groups, has created opportunities both for the extremists and some nations, especially the heads of Shi'as (Iran) and the Sunni (Saudi Arabia). While collectively these two nations culturally influence and dominate any country they have conquered; individually, they build political empires abroad using the influence of religion. These subsequently translate into economic exploitation in the else while country dominated through the influence of religion (Efraim, 2006).

On the surface, religions sound as plausible as a mere religion however, at the core of the agenda by the nations controlling these religions is neocolonialism and imperialism agenda. This agenda is focused to reduce the countries that have been dominated into perpetual servants to the interest of the top nations on the ladder of vertical relationship such as the case between Saudi Arabia, Iran, Qatar, Pakistan, etc, and other developing nations.

Neocolonialism *per se* goes beyond the surface argument of who influences which policy in developing nations; this is further entrenched in certain bilateral agreements which covertly service the interest of the nation that held the upper hand in the relationship. This is observable in the case of some Islamic nations and their allies in the developing nations. Multinational corporations from some Islamic nations into the developing nations that had been dominated by Islam have only menial jobs reserved for the indigenes. In addition, in most of these corporations, the black man in the case of Africa is seen as a nuisance irrespective of his conversion (Renold, 2015; Singh, 2000). Among the Muslim nations, most policies of the government virtually aim to enforce the Arab identity on the non-Arabs and strip the non-Arabs their autochthonous cultural identities such as mother tongue replaced by Arabic. The indigenous traditions in most of these nations, political system and the belief system are subverted in favour of the Arab traditions and cultures embedded in the Islamic religion. On the external policies, the focus of some of the Islamic nations is to continue to dominate other groups across the globe through jihadist conquest and pseudo bilateral relations with other nations. These covert strategies for engendering neocolonialism are what are obtainable in the developing nations in their relationship with the wealthy Islamic nations (Leonid and Andrey, 1997). These policies both internally and externally have caused many nations where Islam is introduced, to become Arab dominated both as the herdsmen and the ruling elites. Perhaps the astonishing example is the Egypt (the nub of Africa), which was once the home of black man but today is totally regarded as Arab nation. The same goes for other North African nations that have turned to the home of Arab population and culture. The so called Arab nations having their enclave at the Arabian Peninsula, have participated in the colonization and neocolonization using Islam as a smoke screen to eliminate other cultures and groups where ever they set in. In the past it was religion and trade in the front, sward at the middle and the migrants at the back, while in the present stage they forward their pretentious aids to the poor countries followed by the bilateral relations and terroristic activities of the Islamic militants while policy of total domination come from behind the stage to initiate cultural and economic imperialism.

BOKO HARAM AND ETHNO-RELIGIOUS HYPOCRISY IN NIGERIA

After criminalizing Boko-haram by Nigerian government, U. S. and European Union, accepting the group became a crime while supporting it was seen as a grave offence. This made those who sponsored and continued to sponsor it to hide at the background and resort to covert strategies. After months and years of criminalizing and declaration of war against Boko-Haram, the group still receives moral, logistics and technical supports. Due to limited access to some classified information, most scholars reduce their arguments about terrorists like the Boko-Haram within the ambit of everyday assumptions about criminal activities such as that, Boko-Haram is sustained by kidnapping for ransom and bank robbery as the root of their financial supply. It is a normal thing to try to link social phenomenon to the nearest empirical assumption at worst, to avoid summing it to mere literary argument however; the matter with Boko-Haram is heavier than what can be simply attached or attributed to everyday crime and criminal activities. The evolution of Boko-Haram, method of operations, engagement for and against it, and the position of prominent individuals and groups both at home and abroad have implication to the understanding of what Boko-Haram is all about and how to approach it as a problem.

What later became Boko-Haram was once a conglomeration of youth who have been intoxicated by the ideological proliferations that was common with Islam, having the Alhaji Muhammadu Ndimi mosque in Maiduguri as their starting point. Preferably to them, the point of becoming a true Muslims outside the perceived corrupt

Nigerian Muslims that were worshiping with them was to embark on *hijra* a term, used to qualify Prophet Mohammad's withdrawal from Mecca to Medina. Thus, they withdrew from their meeting point in Maiduguri to Kanama in Yobe state making Yobe, the Medina while Maiduguri remains their Mecca. After a community related conflict that exposed the group then led by Muhammadu Ali to the police and Nigerian army, the group was decimated including their leader Muhammed Ali. However, the group was not incapacitated (Walker, 2012). The remnants of the group who came back from Yobe to Maiduguri were later epoxied by Mohammed Yusuf. He succeeded in raising a new mosque for the remnants of Mohammed Ali's group and the newly deceived youth and other members of the Islamic community. The mosque (IbnTaimiyyah Masjid), was sponsored financially and logistically by the sympathetic members of Muslim community and wealthy muslims who took the financial responsibility. Only few who saw Yusuf's move as denying them popularity and stepping on their toes did not give consent to what he has started. Having completed the mosque, the group established a network that ran across the states in Northern Nigeria overtly and covertly, and started spreading antisocial sentiments in proxy *via* some religious and antigovernment activities, which earned them the name "Boko-Haram" roughly translated to "Western education is forbidden" (Walker, 2012; Start, 2014; NOREF, 2014). Due to the foundation of their ideology which lies on the hatred against normal social life and perceived derailment from sharia law, Boko-Haram started causing mayhem here and there, using the killing of their members by the security operatives as the justification for their action.

Although the general public in Nigeria and the international scene openly denounced Boko-Haram and their activities, we cannot deny the fact that no such group has existed anywhere in the world without staunch allies at home and abroad. By implication, Boko-Haram was nurtured, sustained and continue to be sustained by individuals and groups domestically and internationally. First and foremost, the salafist group which is part and parcel of Sunni Islam is believed to have provided ideological springboard for Boko-Haram by virtue of their principles and chatters. This group is perfectly accepted and even sponsored in proxy in Saudi Arabia from where they spread to develop extremists across the globe (Chattam House, 2014). Among the four components of salafism, such as authority, institutional, revolutionary and scholarly salafists, the revolutionary salafists encourages and are encouraged by the Islamic community to go out and raise supporters for the propagation of jihad ostensibly to protect Islam from *Bida'a* (religious innovation), and to get rid of the infidels and the perceived heretics such as the shi'a and the derailing Muslim leaders. Salafism which originated from the belief in following the ways of the ancestors in Islam had its foundation of violence on the interpretation and misinterpretation of the concept of jihad by the emerging group after the death of Muhammad.

Although Mohammed Ali (the originator of what later became Boko-Haram) was thought to be acting alone when he started his extremist teaching and withdrawal from the mainstream Muslims, evidences emerged that his inspiration and madness was the germinated seed of Osama Bin Laden's visit to the Northern Nigeria in the early 90s. This time, Bin Laden was said to have invested more than 3 million U.S. Dollars in his effort to encourage salafism in the Northern Nigeria (The Clarion Project, 2014). Again, Bin Laden's visit was the outcome of the meeting in Khartoum in which the Islamic nations mostly the Sunni Islamic nations met to discuss a strategy to take over the world. Here, Bin Laden had opportunity to meet with Muslims from more than 120 countries from which he later recruited people into Al-Qaeda (Andrey, 2006; Mockaitis, 2007). Apart from the fact that Bin Laden built foundation for Boko-Haram through salafism, Mohammed Yusuf who later expanded the foundation of Ali received huge sums of money from the Islamic community in Saudi Arabia during a number of hajj, which enabled his building of his own mosque and other logistics.

All the above-mentioned issues pointed to the fact that Boko-Haram received individual and collective support from some Muslim countries especially the ones that had been on the watch list of FBI & CIA for sponsoring terrorism such as Saudi Arabia (U.S. Department for states, 2010). At some point, some of the hilux trucks used by Boko Haram in their operations were suspected to have entered through Qatar while some of the material and logistic supports to Boko-Haram have been traced to Sudan, Somalia, Central African Republic, Mali, Libya etc. Boko-Haram have received training and assistance from Al-Shabaab, Al-Qaida in the Islamic Maghreb, Ansar Al-Dine, Al-Qaida, Taliban, etc (Start, 2014; Clarion Project, 2014).

At the domestic scene, Boko-Haram received donations and material support from the wealthy Muslims and politicians who saw their activities as a potential opportunity for Muslims against the infidels. Some even saw it as a way of Sunni Muslims to take upper hand against the shi'a in Nigeria. Among the Nigeria military, Boko-Haram received support from the members of Islam in military in the army who prefer to serve the interest of religion other than that of their nation. At some point this category of personnel decided to deliberately expose their colleagues to massive destruction in the battle field with Boko Haram by sabotaging the movement of their colleagues and even forcing them to embark on a mission they knew will end in the destruction of the security personnels involved (Maingwa and Uzodike, 2012; Oriyommi, 2011; U.S. Department of States, 2014; Campbell, 2014; Counter Terrorism Calendar, 2014). Some astonishing examples of domestic support for Boko-Haram included the open confession by a group of children indoctrinated into Boko-Haram in Maiduguri, that they were sent to Al-Qaida camp in Mauritania by a known wealthy business Muslim, to receive training on jihad (Walker, 2012; Paden, 2005). Again, the young man (Kabiru), who bombed the Catholic Church in Mandala, Abuja was found hiding in one of the Northern Nigerian senators' apartment in Abuja, where he was being prepared to be smuggled out of the country. While Boko-Haram was busy shedding the blood of the innocent citizens, the Northern Cabal made up of mostly Sunni muslims were busy distracting the federal government with the argument that instead of criminalizing Boko-Haram, they should be given amnesty like the Niger Delta youth who were struggling for their environment that were being destroyed by oil exploration (Paden, 2008; Campbell, 2014). This group of canker worms was fully aware of the fact that the money that was given to the family of Yusuf as compensation ended up in the hand of Boko-Haram for weapons and further destructions to reinforce the Boko-Haram mission. Indeed there were indications that Boko-Haram was bent to use any resources that come her way for the reinforcement of their mission other than accepting the laying down of arms (Human Right Watch, 2012, Counter Terrorism Calendar, 2014; Campbell, 2014; Start, 2014). More recently, a serving member of the national house of assembly summoned courage to request that the Boko-Haram be given Islamic republic. Boko-Haram was not operating in isolation even though on the surface no one accepted what they were doing. However, they were acting first, for the propagation of jihad in the interest of Islam as a whole which warrant sympathy from the fellow Muslims in all directions. Secondly, they were representing the interest of the salafists as well as Sunni Islam. Thirdly they were clearing the ground for the neocolonialism and imperialism agenda of the top Islamic nations who find it rewarding to surface when the ground has been cleared ostensibly for religious domination. Fourthly, they became the instrument for the Northern Nigerian politicians to frustrate the southern led government. Thus, Boko-Haram was a representative group and not an isolated group.

BOKO-HARAM, UNDERDEVELOPMENT AND FAULTY FOUNDATION OF FUTURE NIGERIA

According to Nnoli (1981:32) "Development is first and foremost, a phenomenon associated with changes in man's humanity and creative energies, not in things. It is the unending improvement in the capacity of the individual and society to control and manipulate the forces of nature, as well as themselves and other individuals and societies for their own benefit and that of humanity at large". Development aims to move human society forward for the good of individuals and groups in it. Under-development in itself which is relatively the opposite of development, has been approached through different dimensions however clarifications are needed in whichever way any one may define it. This is due to the circumstances surrounding the concepts of development and underdevelopment in the relationship between the developed nations and developing nations. For the interest of the issue at hand, underdevelopment is taking to be backwardness in human capacity and physical infrastructural improvement, which is bound to lead to the situation of stagnancy in political, economic and technological advancement among the group concerned.

Underdevelopment is the function of many other social factors such as disruption of formal education which is the frontline for human capacity development; disruption of peace which provides favourable environment for economic investment; disruption of domestic and daily socio-economic activities; threatening and discouragement of foreign investment into the domestic economy etc.

Boko-Haram since its inception for more than a decade now has created a chaos in all fronts against development and has prepared the ground for backwardness in the areas affected in particular and Nigeria as a whole. Boko Haram has disrupted education in most of the areas it operated, causing many children and youth to be out of school (Clarion Project, 2014). Between 2009 and 2014 alone, more than 20,000 youth and children were temporarily forced out of school both primary and secondary, while thousands more are feared to have been permanently forced out of school due to the death of their parents and other unforeseen circumstances (Start, 2014; Clarion Project, 2014). Many private investments in terms of companies have closed down in most of the areas within the ambit of Boko-Haram operation, forcing many to lose their jobs and means of livelihood. As at 2014, Boko-Haram activities have resulted to the death of more than 30,000 Nigerians both on the side of ordinary civilians and the Boko-Haram fighters with government security personnel. More than two million

Nigerians have been displaced by Boko-Haram activities. Agricultural and socio-economic activities have been interrupted in these areas affected. Furthermore, regional trade between Nigeria, Cameroun and Chad had been interrupted by Boko-Haram activities with some level of suspicion among these countries.

Many foreign investments which have direct connection with the areas affected by Boko-Haram activities have been disrupted with grave threat to future foreign investors to Nigeria. Boko-Haram activities have created more and more ripples which have translated to present and future underdevelopment specifically to the areas affected and generally to Nigeria as a nation.

Underdevelopment more than physical infrastructures, surfaces in a multiple fold mostly immaterially. For example, apart from the infrastructures destroyed by the Boko-Haram activities, the humanitarian aspect of it such as the decimated population, the interrupted education, the displaced, the recruited youth by the Boko-Haram, etc, will all translate into a huge gap in development in the nearest future, with other accompanying challenges such as socio-psychological rehabilitation, delay in population replacement, gap in human capacity development and redirecting of the available resources to the socio-economic rehabilitation instead of investment for continuous advancement of development.

Meanwhile, the insincerity of the Nigerian government towards resolving the issue of Boko-Haram has led a foundation of mistrust among Nigerians and continuous reinforcement by the group despite what the government claim to be doing so far. This by implication is making the group stronger by day and a potential map charting agent for mega global jihadists in Africa. As the Islamic State and other dangerous jihadists from the Middle East and Asia are being disturbed in their safe havens, they are looking for a new ground to conquer and establish themselves; this can be easy for them in a place like Nigeria and sub-Saharan Africa with the continued presence of Boko-Haram.

Nigeria is struggling to build powerful economy, this is vulnerable to jihadism as the jihadists are anti economic development. The only economic development among the countries covertly sponsoring jihads is to build ultra-modern nuclear weapons and to cause destabilization anywhere in the world; economic development is western oriented and does not tally with their philosophy and belief hence the youth are encouraged to work against economic oriented program anywhere among them. Again, Nigeria is struggling to maintain her unity, this will soon worsen as jihadists are intolerant of anything less than Islam and find every infidel unacceptable in their system. While other groups in Nigeria will be forced to feel threatened by the political class jihadists who are using the political apparatus to advance Islamism, the Boko Haram cam will escalate the situation as their allies from the global scene will start appreciating the potentials of their existence in Nigeria. There are countless threat which Boko-Haram pose to the Nigerian existence as far as it continues to receive the unalloyed support of the merchants of deaths who hide under the cloak of religion and ethnicity to perpetuate their unwholesome agenda.

CONCLUSION

Religion as a social phenomenon is vulnerable to human manipulation ideologically and otherwise; creating loophole for social miscreants and opportunists, who turn it into socio-economic agony among the human population. Among other things, jihadism is one of the concepts in Islamic religion, which its interpretations by various individual preachers and ideologists have translated into terrorism and other antisocial behaviours. To make maters worst, the hypocrisy among the stakeholders in Islam across the globe and the neocolonial/imperialistic agenda of the top Islamic countries, continue to fan the ambers of the vulnerability of Islam to individual/group ideologies. While the riddles about jihad among the Muslims has kept a fertile ground for Islamic militancy and terrorism, imperialistic and neocolonial agenda of the wealthier

Islamic nations continue to create fertile ground for the mutation of ideology and spread of terror across the globe. Boko-Haram, which is a representative group to both Islamic world in proxy and sub groups internationally and domestically, is one of the outcomes of vulnerability of Islam to ideology and, has devastated the Nigerian nation from all directions. Their activities have created both short term and long term economic setbacks resulting to present and future underdevelopment of the areas affected and the nation at large.

RECOMMENDATIONS

Based on the evidences on ground as the paper has revealed, the following recommendations were made:

- Nigerian government should choose a stand as a sovereign nation in their relationship with the Islamic nations of all categories to avoid being used as a religious dope for hidden agenda by these nations.
- The Islamic world should checkmate the tendencies of proliferation of illicit ideologies in their domain in order to save the image of the religion and save the world peace.
- The Nigerian Muslims should leave the shackles of religion and consider the interest of black man in their judgment of unwholesome activities under the umbrella of religion in order not to be building the ground for future imperialists and racists who are bound to dominate the world *via* religion.
- Northern Nigerian political elites should consider the collective effort in building the future of the nation other than segregation arguments which are giving foothold for sentiments and terror activities by the Islamic militancy.
- The federal government of Nigeria should enforce compulsory formal education among the youths at least to secondary school level in all the states in Northern region.

- Granting Boko-Haram amnesty may be a temporary relief but cannot guarantee the future of the region they have dominated as there is likelihood the group will resurface in other multiple dimensions, in the best interest of all and sundry, the root of the problem should be considered before we end up with wrong approach to the situation which will backfire latter.

REFERENCES

Abdallâh ´Abd as-Salâm (2005). *Kalâm 'irhâbî (Terrorist Words),In*: Al-Ahram.

Abu-Amr, Z. (1993). Hamas: A historical and political background. *Journal of Palestine Studies,* 22:5–19.

Alexander, Jeffrey C. (2004). From the Depths of Despair: Performance, Counterperformance, and "September 11. " *Sociological Theory,* 22(1): 88–105.

Anderson, Sean K. and Sloan, Stephen (2003). *Terrorism: Assassins to Zealots*. Lanham: Scarecrow Press.

Andoni, L. (1997). *Searching for Answers: Gaza's Suicide Bombers. Journal of Palestine Studies,*(26):33–45.

Audrey Kurth Cronin(2006). *How al-Qaida Ends: The Decline and Demise of Terrorist Groups*. International Security.

Ansari, Hamied (1984). The Islamic Militants in Egyptian Politics. *International Journal of Middle East Studies,* 16: 136–140.

Bakker, Edwin (2007). *Jihadi Terrorists in Europe*. The Hague: Netherlands Institute of International Relations.

Bangstad, S. (2002). *Palestinian Islamist Movements: An Annotated Bibliography*. Bergen: Chr. Michelsen Institute, CMI Report R 2002-21 Available: HTTP://WWW. CMI. NO/PDF/2002/REPORTS/R%202002-21. PDF.

Barak, O. (2002). Intra-communal and inter-communal dimensions of conflict and peace. *In:* Boer, H. R. (1969). *A brief history of Islam: A Christian interpretation*, Ibadan: Daystar press.

Campbell, J. (2014). *Boko-Haram: Origins, challenges and response:NOREF Policy Brief.* Norwegian Peace building Resource Center.

Carapico, S. (2002). Foreign aid for promoting democracy in the Arab world. *Middle East Journal,*(56):379–395.

Chaliand, Gérard andBlin, Arnaud (2007). *The History of Terrorism, from Antiquity to Al Qaeda*. Berkeley: University of California Press.

Chatham House (2015). *Islamism and its Alternatives in the GCC: Meeting Summary Middle East and North Africa Programme | 13–14 December 2014.* United Kingdom: The Royal Institute of International Affairs, 2015. WWW. CHATHAMHOUSE. ORG/MENA

Counter Terrorism Calander (2014). Boko Haram HTTP://WWW. NCTC. GOV /SITE/GROUPS/BOKO_HARAM. HTML

Craig, J. (2001). A life with the Arabs. British *Journal of Middle Eastern Studies,* (28):141–150.

RashwanDiaa (2001). *A war over resources,In*: Al-Ahram,*Weekly*, 552.

RashwanDiaa (2003). *Qualifying al-Qa´eda, In*: Al-Ahram *Weekly*, 639.

Ebrahim, S. E. (1980). Anatomy of Egypt's militant Islamic groups: Methodological notes and preliminary findings. *International Journal of Middle East Studies,* p. 12.

Edelman, M. (2001). Social movements: Changing paradigms and forms of politics. *Annual Review of Anthropology,* 30:285–317.

Said Edward (2001). *Collectivepassion, In*: Al-Ahram,*Weekly*, 552.

EFRAIM, K. (2006). *ISLAMIC IMPERIALISM: A HISTORY. NEW HAVEN:* YALE UNIVERSITY PRESS.

Eickelman, D. F. (1998). *The Middle East and Central Asia: An Anthropological Approach.*

Upper Saddle River, N. J. : Prentice Hall.

HowaydîFahmi (2001). *Daw´a li-tahâluf ad-duwalî did al-Kirâhiyâ (Call for an international alliance against hatred). In*: Ash-Sharq, Al-Awsat.

Faqir, F. (2001). Engendering democracy and Islam in the Arab world. *Third World Quarterly,*(18):165–174.

Fuller, G. (2002). The future of political Islam. *Foreign Affairs,*81:48–60.

Gall, C. (2016). Pakistan's Hand in the Rise of International Jihad: Sunday Review,News Analysis. Shah Marai/Agence France- Presse.

Ganor, Boaz (2002). Defining Terrorism: Is One Man's Terrorist another Man's Freedom Fighter? *Police Practice and Research,* 3(4): 287–304.

Gerges, Fawaz (2005). *The Far Enemy: Why Jihad Went Global*. New York: Cambridge University Press.

Gilsenan, M. (1996). *Lords of the Lebanese Marches: Violence and Narrative in an Arab Society*. London: I. B. Tauris.

Glubb, J. B. (1971). *The life and time of Mohammad*. New York: Stein and Day.

Gunaratna, Rohan (2002). *Inside Al Qaeda. Global Network of Terror*. London: Hurst; Spencer.

Gunaratna, Rohan (2007). Ideology in Terrorism and Counter Terrorism: Lessons from Combating al Qaeda and al Jemaah Islamiyah in Southeast Asia. *In*: Aldis Anne and Graeme Herd (*eds.*), *The Ideological War on Terror: Worldwide Strategies for Counter terrorism* New York: Routledge, pp. 21–34.

Hafez, Mohammed M. (2007). Martyrdom Mythology in Iraq: How Jihadists Frame Suicide Terrorism in Videos and Biographies. *Terrorism and Political Violence,* 19(1): 95–115.

Hamzeh, A. N. (2000). Lebanon's Islamists and local politics: A new reality. *Third World Quarterly,*21: 739–759.

Human Rights Watch (2012). Boko Haram Attacks and Security Force Abuses in Nigeria. *HTTP://WWW. HRW. ORG/NODE/110632/SECTION/7.*

IbrahîmHigâzi (2001). *Rahmatullâhalâdahâyâirhâb 11 sibtimbir al-amrikîyîn (May God take pity on the American victims of terrorism),In*: Al-Ahram.

ImreRobert, Brian,Mooney T. and Clarke, Benjamin (2008). *Responding to Terrorism*. Farnham, England: Ashgate.

Islam, Muhammad Q. and Shahin, Wassim N. (2001). Applying economic methodology to the war on terrorism. *Forum for Social Economics,* 31(1): 7–26.

Ismail, S. (2000). The popular movement dimensions of contemporary militant Islamism: Socio-spatial determinants in the Cairo urban setting. *Comparative Studies in Society and History,*(42):363–393.

Jackson, Richard (2005). *Writing the War on Terrorism: Language, Politics and Counter-Terrorism*. Manchester, England: Manchester University Press.

Jaffar (2000). Interview with Jamil Hamad: First Person: I Shot an Israeli. *Time*.

Jenkins, Brian M. (1985). Terrorism Prone Countries and Conditions. *In*: Merari, Ariel (*ed.*), *On Terrorism and Combating Terrorism.* Frederick, MD: University Publications of America, pp. 25–40.

KarîmBaqr 'Adwânî (2001). *As-Sadmawa-l-masdûmwa-murâja'al-mawgi'a (The Push and the Pushed and the painful revision). In*: Ash-Sharq al-Awsat.

Kepel, G. (2002). *Jihad: The Trail of Political Islam*. London: I. B. Tauris.

Khan, M. A. M. (2001). The political philosophy of Islamic resurgence. *Cultural Dynamics,*(13):211–229.

Khouri, R. G. (2008). Apples and oranges: Identity, ideology and state in the Arab world. *In*: Pandya, A. and Laipson, E. (*eds.*), *Transnational Trends:* Middle Eastern and Asian Views. Washington D. C.: The Henry L. Stimson Center.

Khutûratul-Kalâm (2001). *fî l-'Ayyâmil-Harija (The importance of words in critical days). In*: Ash-Sharq al-Awsat.

Leonid, K. and Andrey, K. S. (1997). *Epigraphic South Arabian: Semitic Languages*. London: Routledge.

Li, Quan and Schaub, Drew (2004). Economic globalization and transnational terrorist incidents: A pooled time series analysis. *Journal of Conflict Resolution,* 48(2): 230–258.

MâdâJarâ (2001). *fî l-Wilayât al-Muntahida? (What happened in the United States?). In*: Al-Ahram.

Maingwa, B. and Uzodike, U. O. (2012). *The Changing Dynamics of Boko Haram Terrorism*, Al-Jazeera Center for Studies. http://studies. aljazeera.net/ResourceGallery/media/Documents/2012/7/31/201273168 43815734The%20Changing%20Dynamics%20of%20Boko%20Haram %20Terrorism. pdf.

Martin, Gus (2010). *Understanding Terrorism: Challenges, Perspectives and Issues*. Thousand Oaks, CA: Sage.

MatusitzJonathan (2008). Similarities between Terrorist Networks in Antiquity and Present-Day Cyberterrorist Networks. *Trends in Organized Crime,* 11(2): 183–199.

Mauro, R. (2014). *Special Report: Boko-Haram Nigerian Islamist Group*. The Clarion Project WEBSITE: WWW. CLARIONPROJECT. ORG.

Mawdudi, A. A. (1981). *Towards understanding Islam*. Leicester: Islamic Foundation.

Milton-Edwards, B. (2000). *Contemporary Politics in the Middle East*. Cambridge: Polity Press.

Mockaitis, T. R. (2007). *The New Terrorism: Myths and Reality*. Westport, London: Praeger Security International.

Morgan, Matthew J. (2004). The Origin of the New Terrorism. *Parameters*, XXXIV(1): 30–31.

Moustafa, T. (2000). Conflict and cooperation between the state and religious institutions in Socio-spatial determinants in the Cairo urban setting. *Comparative Studies in Society and History,*(42):363–393.

Nnoli, O. (1981). *Path to Nigerian development.* Dahkar: CODESRIA.

Omeire, N. E. (2006). *History of Islam in West Africa*. Owerri: Omega Communication Press.

Onyeidu, S. O. (2001). *Introduction to the study of religion.* Nsukka: Fulladu Publishing Company.

Oriyommi, R. (2011). *Nigeria's Boko Haram: On Islam*. HTTP://WWW. ONISLAM. NET/ENGLISH/NEWS/AFRICA/455146-NIGERIAS-BOKO-HARAM-PROFILE. HTML

Paden, J. (2005). *Muslim, Civic Cultures and Conflict Resolution: The Challenge of Democratic Federalism in Nigeria*. Washington, DC: Brookings Institution Press.

Paden, John (2008). *Faith and Politics in Nigeria: Nigeria as a Pivotal State in the Muslim World*. Washington, DC: U. S. Institute of Peace Press.

Pellot, B. (2014). *The Worst Countries for Religious Freedom. X Index. The Voice of Freedom of Expression.*

Pew Research Center (2007). *Muslim Americans: Middle Class and Mostly Mainstream*. Washington, D. C. : Pew Research Center. Available at HTTP://PEWRESEARCH. ORG/ASSETS/PDF/MUSLIM AMERICANS. PDF

Pew Research Center (2009). *Mapping the Global Muslim Population*. Washington, D. C. : Pew Research Center. Available at http://pewforum. org/newassets/images/reports /Muslim population /Muslimpopulation. pdf

Rand (2011). *RAND Database of Worldwide Terrorism Incidents*. Santa Monica: RAND Corporation. From http://www. rand. org/nsrd/projects/ terrorism-incidents. html

Renold, D. F. (2015). *Cambridge Companion to Modern Arab Culture. Cambridge:* University Press.

Risks International (1985). *Major Incidents of Terrorism:* 1970–1984. Alexandria, VA: Risks International.

Roy, O. (1994). *The Failure of Political Islam.* London: I. B. Tauris.

Roy, O. (2003). *Globalised Islam: Fundamentalism, De-territorialisation and the Search for the New 'Ummah'.* London: Hurst.

Sa´îd ´Abd al-Hâliq (2001). *Awlamat al-Irhâb (The Globalization of Terrorism), In*: Al-Ahram.

Salama Ahmed Salama (2001). *Sore Spots, In*: Al-Ahram, *Weekly*, 553.

MuntasirSalih (2001). *Mahâm Bush (Bush's Missions),In*: Al-Ahram.

Lone Salim(2005). *Iraq: Withdrawal is the Only Way to Curb Terrorism, In*: Arab News.

Schmid Alex and Jongman Albert (1988). *Political Terrorism: A New Guide to Actors, Authors, Concepts, Data Bases, Theories and Literature.* Amsterdam: North Holland, Transaction Books.

Stakelbeck, Erick (2011). *The Terrorist Next Door: How the Government is deceiving you about the Islamist Threat.* New York: Regnery Publishing.

START (2014). Boko-Haram Recent Attacks: Background Report. *National Consortium for the study of terrorism and response to terrorism, visit* WWW. START. UMD. EDU/GTD.

U. S. Department of State (2014). *Country Report on Terrorism2013.* HTTP:/ /WWW. STATE. GOV/DOCUMENTS/ORGANIZATION/225886. PDF

WALKER(2012). What is Boko Haram? Special report 308. *The United States Institute of Peace. An online edition of this and related reports can be found on our Web site (www. usip. org), together with additional information on the subject. www. usip. org*

Walker, A. (2012). *What is Boko Haram*? United States Institute of Peace. HTTP://WWW. USIP. ORG/PUBLICATIONS/WHAT-BOKO-HARAM

Winer, J. M. and Roule,T. J. (2002). Fighting terrorist finance. *Third World Quarterly,* 44:87–104.

Yoel, N. (2004). 164 *Jihad Verses in the Koran.* www. Answering-Islam. org/ Bailey/jihad. html.

Zeghal, M. (1999). Religion and politics in Egypt: The ulama of al-Azahar, radical Islam and the state (1952–94). *International Journal of Middle East Studies,* 31:371–399.

9

Approach of Religious Intellectuals Regarding to Religion Function Before and After Islamic Revolution in Iran

HAMID SARMADI[1*], MORTEZA BADRI[1],
SIROUS SAADATI[1] AND JAFAR GHANEI[2]

ABSTRACT

Religious intellectual in Iran is dynamic process that has been began within one hundred years ago and those intellectuals that don't enough traditional reads reasons to resolve theoretical issues and try to rely on modern science adapt religion presence in modern world. As far as effect to this process has been three elements: theoretical questions of term, scientific problems, and knowledge and people age cognizance. Words like that revival, reform, pluralism, hermeneutic and... is western received concepts that Iranian intellectuals sue adaptation with doctrines of traditional religion.

Generally religious intellectual in Iran pass from three period: 1. before constitutional age 2. age 1941-1960 that strong point is

[1] Department of Politics and Law, Science and Research Branch Islamic Azad University, Tehran, Iran.

[2] International at Bonb Azad University, Iran

**Corresponding E-mail*: hamedsarmadi2000@gmail.com

coup 3. divide in two period: number one is Islamic revolution intellectuals and secondary after revolution intellectuals this periods including are sequence of three general readings: ideologically- scientifically-epistemologically. Before Islamic revolution religious intellectuals have outlook of external about religion and regarding concepts of absolutism, idealism, religion presence in public and privacy domain and sue consistency of religion and politics and putative this agent in eradicate of oppression. Whereas post-revolution religion intellectuals sue ponder in modernism concepts and express self imagination in concepts of justice and freedom compatible this base and have outlook of impressionistic between religion, age and position and those subjects. Abdolkarim Soroush believe rely to intra-religion resources is not enough, instead regarding to discuss and rationality and endeavors indicates religious sensitive in adaptation of pluralistic and democratic properties.

Key words: Ideology, Pluralism, Intra-religious attitude, Extra-religious attitude, Hermeneutic.

THEORETICAL BASIS

Kinds of Religious Intellectual

More than formal religion researchers in history intellectual religious in recent century, had exist in most of secular intellectuals expediency, instrumental, vulgar and conservative outlook to religion and clericals. Mirza malkam khan recommended to friends, after presenting of western socio-philosophical principals told that Islam is resource of this principals. Too Yousof Khan Mostashar-Aldoleh explain western and French rules with blond of Islamic rules. So they try presenting modernization idea to society in wrapper packet of religion because of themselves thoughts don't effect contrast of Islam and religion (Broujerdi).

Generally religious intellectual in Iran from beginning passed three period:

1. Period of before constitutional, constitution and Reza Shah period that was main characters Seyyed Jamal-Aldin Asadabadi, Ayatollah Naeeni, Ayatollah Tabatabaee and Behbahani. Religious intellectuals in this period was reaction against enter of modern thoughts and process of western modernization and formed from modulation of this thoughts with religion principals.
2. Period of empirical intellectual that is from August of 1941 to end of 1950 decade. Turning point of this point Coup of 19 August 1953 and main character is Ayatollah Kashani.
3. Third period divide to two period: first beginning from 1961 and turning point is Islamic revolution in 1979 and main character is Shariati and Bazargan. Second are post revolution religious intellectuals such as Soroush, Shabestari, Malekian , Naraghi and etc. this three period in format of theories adapted to three general descriptions:

***Ideological statement*:** Meaning that interpretation of religion alike action index and mundane platform. In other word use of religious elements in rehabilitate of an ideology for social change. Indexes of this reading are:

a) change of current position

b) emphasis to political and practical project

c) stockade between self and others

d) create of expectancy basis of religion doctrines

***Scientific statement*:** Principal scientific reading on adaptation of religion and science. Based on religious intellectuals by means of adaptive independent judgment try to prove that first religious propositional are logical-rational so not only adapted to neo-science but also neo-science can explain religious propositions. On the other hand scientific propositions have religious origins.

***Secularization statement*:** This reading began and growth after Islamic revolution in Iran. Main characteristics is stressed to researches program, gradual reform of traditional religion, separation of religion realization from religion and humanization of religious knowledge that open window to critic of religious realization, reduction of expectation of religion and historical attitude to religion that cause conceptual of religion be critics. This reading believe categories like that freedom, democracy, human rights and wisdom have forms of extra-religion and Islam should be adapt them and religionization of society don't inclusion of every things.

Period of second Pahlavi and Islamic republic was turning point governmentally structure in religious intellectual. This process became resultant synthesis of western leftist and religion center with scientism and rationalism that in result create two kind of intellectuals: 1. Leftist and revolutionist religious intellectual and 2. Liberal religious intellectual. Critical and revolutionist Islam belong to Ali Shariati that followed restitute of individuals and society to values and primary Islam traditions and too Alavi Shiite and then add with dimensions of positive and requirements of modern civilization like that justice and freedom to change of Islam to combat of colonial, arrogant and dictatorship. In other hand scientific and liberal religious intellectual that was first descendant in Iran that acknowledge Islam with scientific results and present type of Islam that follow after 60 years. New religion center process not accept titles such as religious intellectual or Muslim and scientific and religion contrast and modern achievements. This current not recognize religion as lag agent, stereotype and nor able not response for modern demands and on the contrary believe that revert to pure religion and reject of tradition superstitions can adjustment of Islam according to new requirements and scientific and change those to propulsion of society. Mission of this current is values and Islamic rules redefinition, critic of traditional Islam and advocators and commensurate with current thoughts and synthesis together. Mainspring of this current that believe to Islamic rules is contrast and confrontation to masses and material and secular groups that prior like introduce religion contrast to science.

Both of left and right currents has been knowledge of religion effects in create of motivation and evolution in society and those potential abilities in stimulation of individuals. Other similarity is that both currents believe tradition religion and tradition custodians cannot realize religion dynamics and modern aspects consistent with modern world. On this reason they want and wanted with refuse of traditions, superstitions and religion bring out of tradition clerical hands, unbrace of creation, innovation and progress methods

Past-Revolution Dominant Current

Religious intellectuals in Iran before 1979 revolution follow connection of religion and politics and applicant religion as effect element in eradicate of corruption and downtrodden. So sue Islamize of politics and influence of religion in socials and politics and try use of holy texts for social interests that inclusion of three currents: 1. Current base of religious thoughts that Bazargan was predominantly in this axis. 2. Current of leftist Muslim that intellectually was in Ali Shariati. 3. Current part of religious special that was concentrate on Fatwa, religious characters and religious jurisprudence that including in thoughts of ayatollah Tabatabaee and Motahari. First and second currents is main argument of this article before victory of Islamic revolution attempt along with other revolutionist currents for overthrow of Pahlavi regime. So take themselves ideologue and indication, thoughts persons like Shariati as intellectual current indication and too ayatollah Khomeini from religion and tradition arena and others and totally defense thesis integration of religion, politics and Government. Shariati present new interpretation from revolution movement direct to Islamic doctrines with connection main elements of tradition and modernity by revolutionist ideology (Pedram, 76). So in past period of revolution prevalent concepts such as revolution, factionalism, classless society, socialism and etc and religious thinkers like that Ali Shariati and Mahmud Talegani proceed to theorize in finite dimension. Too most of religious intellectuals sue compilation positive aspects of religious tradition and modern ideas and modern institutions achieve to Islamic society. Most of this intellectuals pertain warranted Shariati and others intellectual endeavors for construe concepts such as justice, freedom and genuine democracy and socialism under reconstructed Islam about refer to genuine society culture and his desires for overcoming to alienation by ideologic model on absolute Islamic renaissance. In this period religious intellectuals accept or reject concepts of tradition and modernity without discovery those aftermath and consider those as appropriate or inappropriate option for attain to ideal political and social system (Shariati Ali, 77–78). Between of tradition Islam representatives that take it this concepts such as ayatollah Motahari and Khomeini but proceed gradually critic of some religious intellectual thoughts and Marxists.

More than Shariati, Bazargan presented pattern of Islam that to be consistent with science and society in modern era. This pattern be based on Islam compatible with modern world requirements with emphasis of axis role of labor, responsibility, work consciousness, Islam impressive role in prosperity and those capability for compete with competitions (spatial Marxism). In his believe "a virtual civilized person wholly is a social person that overpass individual interests instead social responsibilities". In this base believe that Islam is influential generate program for mundane and otherworld life. He considered freedom in mean of liberal and take political act based on liberal democracy ideas and compatible them but don't consider during of revolution period transformations according to revolutionist exigencies in latest decade of 70 and then suppressed by grow of Islamic radicalism. With establish of Islamic system and Islamize of sovereignty, religion exposure *versus* big historical examination and during of post-revolution period, Bazargan amendment his outlook about Islam interference in politics. This reform based on government experience by clericals in period of post revolution. In outlook of Bazargan affairs such as politics and society management assignation to humans and like of other affairs can arrange by experiment and rationality.

Post-Revolution Intellectual Religious

Last confrontation of religious intellectuals with modernity accompany with difference and sometime contrast approaches to Islam. This approaches religiously divide to three category including deny, accept and modernity selection. This Islamic ideas indicate to defect of orientalism outlooks in analysis of religious intellectual in society like that Iran, because orientalism entail refuse interfering of Islam and modernity horizons and so entail refuse of Islam fulfilment positive role and even different role in creation of political and social theories. In period of post-revolution, accept and rejection of institutions and modern ideas, joint predominantly with cogitate in concept of modernity and pillars. In this period religious intellectuals ponder in concepts such as rationality, modern science, progress and promotion and secularization process and eventually try express themselves imagine of justice and freedom on this base. In past-revolution period most of religious intellectuals defense of modernity with consideration of advance technical instrument and some of modern ideas and institutions like that democracy, human rights, representative and administrative system but in post-revolution period all of this issues has been and gets analysis in theory and practical with consideration of insightful fundaments, manner and modernity results. Ideology issue and those critic presented liberally by Abdolkarim Soroush with analysis of ideology position in an Islamic government and religion interference with government (Pedram, 83). His challenge to an ideological government entice attention many of religious intellectuals of political system that establishment by clericals.

Soroush explain and justify concepts of rationality, modern science and progress in form of secularized religion and presented epistemology in base of analytical philosophy to express axis of experiment and human knowledge in realize of phenomenon. In this base, in level of political and social theory, he indicate results of liberalism in religious societies. Then explain justice and freedom haven't applicable prove from religious propositions and should be consider them as general human values that evaluate out of religion arena. Soroush stressed on humanize of religious knowledge and those evolution supplement in effect of other human knowledge. He argue that religious knowledge become constrict and expand in any person and any era by constrict and expand sum of knowledgements. This epistemology categorize in seven parameters:

1. Sharia is invariant and what changing is perception.
2. Any new perception of sharia is based of internal and external pillars.
3. Perception of sharia changing constantly.
4. Changing of perceptions depend on internal pillar, meaning that religious scholars knowledgement.
5. Secularize of religion not only meaning resolve of new problems but also meaning compatible of religion knowledge with other knowledgements.
6. New of perceptions don't meaning religion evasion.
7. Sharia perception depended on external basis of sharia.

Too religious knowledge like that any other knowledge is result of human discovery and contemplate and is synthesis of suppositions, certainties, rights and voids and change and evolution of this class (Soroush, constrict and expand _22; 269-270).

Between of religious intellectuals in Iran happen endeavors to explain of Islam and democracy connection. Shariati synthesis engaged democracy as native western democracy with religious doctrines. His reconstruct of Islamic concepts such as Imamah, administration, council, blasphemy, gnostic, theism and ... under sum of modern ideas such as freedom, intellectual, justice, social rights and democracy be powerful motive force in mobilization of intellectuals despite dominant of leftist thoughts not allow to provide perusing in actual content of this concepts (Broujerdi, 39–40).

Religious intellectuals call formal of religion arenas confrontation to modern world questions. Soroush consider to critic of religious ideological narrative and analysis critically Shariati theory of Imamah and Emmett and eventually present of religious democratic government try reconcile religion with democracy. He present two kinds of religious insight:

First, maximalist insight or maximalist anticipation that believe all of information, measures, enough and necessary rules for economy, government, commercial, law, ethic theology and etc for any mind including simple and complex entered in Sharia and so believers don't need any resource.

Second, minimalist insight that believe sharia learn us necessary minimum and no more. So intellectual religious should be with minimal outlook emancipate religion from control of Fiqh, government and political power too can assist to Muslim spiritual affluence.

Malekian is one of the religious intellectuals that have methodological thoughts in approach of quotidian issues. He has three impressions on Islam word: first Islam is some of Muslims holy texts like that Quran and tradition that upper than dispute. Second Islam is practical Islam. Third Islam sum of descriptions, interpretations and analysis that provided along of Islam history by Quran interpretations, narrative descripts, philosophies, mystics, theologians, ethic scholars and jurisprudents. In his believe variety Islam having different answer to questions.

Democracy partials in religious framework in Iran divide two main groups: 1. Those contemplate to reform of Islam for reconcile to democracy (religious democracy) and 2. Those contemplate to amendment of constitution for secularization and create of secular democracy (liberal democracy). Basic assume of this thoughts is on basic differences between two political and intellectual system about ontological, epistemological, anthropological and political system functions (Tagavi, 98).

TURNS OF THEORY BASIS

Past-revolution branch of religious intellectual is synthesis of Islam, nationalism and socialism that have two common bases: (A) westernization (B) religious modernization or religion reform. This currents have two parameters:

- Believe to Islam except clericals
- Believe to supremacy of empirical science and interpretation of Quran and religious concepts base on positivism and hermeneutics.

After Islamic revolution, religious intellectual create basic transform in literacy and religion centric and connection with religion because of revolutionary and religious sovereignty discourse supremacy to other current discourses under clerical's current, special ayatollah Khomeini thought line. Claim of religious intellectual current after revolution is that traditional religion haven't consistent with new civilization achievements and clericals aren't only religion interpretations. Those outlooks haven't different with religious and secular intellectuals and alike of modern world intellectual currents cannot ignoring religious discoveries and achievements in variety dimensions. Tradition in those outlooks has been catch to obscurity, inability and insufficient in new world and modernity and modernization haven't able to institutionalize in individuals mental structure, because is imported, superficiality and would be unlike with accepted society traditions. Solution of this current is that should be create synthesis and coordination between this achievements and religion. So more than critic of society and Islamic republic system, in reform dimension take to comply of religion with modernity in rational meaning and receive in coordinate of variety rational readings and religion epistemological. Too Thought and politically trend take to critic of Islamic republic system and religion sovereignty discourse (Forough, 130–145).

Generally can mention contently religious intellectual move frankly to liberal intellectual aims and approximately defense alike to laic and secular intellectuals from alike non-religious government structure although not necessarily non-religious. Despite of this content changes, religious intellectuals express his claims under religious reasons and strictly abide against those that call liberal, secular and non-religious and statement many argumentations in exigency religious of intellectual in Iran society. So any change and reform should be pass by religion and should consideration to social dimension of religious life and don't consider only to individual and rational dimensions of modern human. On base of this attitude, mentioned confrontations attain to any result and reduction to quasi-modern in society alike of past periods (Hashemi, 142–143).

Moreover religious intellectuals consider district of religion arenas and rely on self-founded wisdom as main mission for attain to ideal society and pass from tradition to modernity and set up of modern society. In this society religion cannot be in political and social arenas that call as general arena that take delimitation between religion and government and so restrict of religion and reduction to individual-obligate affairs and not social. This endeavors leading scientific and concrete differentiation between religion and politics and sometime debris in theoretic level. Actually thought evolvement from Islamization to secular Islam. Soroush believe that religion is corpulently from ideology and basically ideologies are anti-rationality and wisdom and are hostile of human and systematic wrong of wisdom.

Despite of ideological outlook, enter of secular thoughts, knowledge sociology, pluralism, epistemology, scientific religion and etc., open manner to equality between science and religion. Human as rational person can recognize welfare and evil, by this recognize inconvincible against antecedent traditions because recognize incompatible of current requirements. This important result enter of positivism and empirical sciences in modern era (Kazemi, 65).

One of the intellectuals religious is Mojtahed Shabestari. He applicant of hermeneutic methodology critic formal recitation of religion and believe public information, admissions, jurisprudent anticipations and interests whether political and social issues and whether worldview conducted his for inferred. Too believe that in modern era, modern human too enhancement possible of quality choice for human and too have been raise non-religious quantity measures. He consider government as exterreligious affair. So applicant of religion as governmental manner is detriment of both because government and politics is rational and rationality that carried commensurate with policymaking exigencies and not invariable principals. Moreover religion language is prayer and obligate center ethic and rules language and not ideology language and rational philosophy and when religion evolve into ideology, both lose its language and gain one ideological language and so become absurd from its identification (Shabestari, 236–237).

ERA KNOWLEDGE AND SECULARIZATION OF RELIGION

Era knowledge of religion should be include as part of secularization sub discourse that religious intellectual in decade of 90 are those represents. In secularization discourse, instead change of political and social situate that is base on invariable perception on religious rules, religion change base on civil status, meant contents such as democracy, human rights, equality and rule situating based on religious realize and religious knowledgement that inherently are secular contents. Modernization of religious knowledge providing new possible for advent of secular perceptions that can has been themselves unique position. Soroush theory of constrict and expand of sharia presented in sub discourse of religion secularize and sue creation of minimal religion to challenge classic religion knowledge authority. Base of this theory is on dissociate between nature of religion or what realize by prophet and perception of religion or what realize by Muslims. Moreover, his critic from ideology including Marxism ideology and ideological Islam as cited in Shariati thoughts assist religious pluralism to be advance. He emphasis to pluralism in social theory arena as liberalism principal and led epistemological pluralism basis of social pluralism. Soroush in defense of rationality presented justice content and reject idea that express justice and freedom are two contrast categories and then explain if this categories (entitled contrast of socialism and democracy) being separate, is imaginary contrast. In his believe if consider justice as realize all of humanity rights, in this case freedom is one of this rights and indeed freedom is one of the justice components and so justice without freedom isn't perfect (Pedram, 16). Soroush believe justice is include of comprehensive humanity means and cannot restrict to religious rules and religious justice based on sharia rules that directly construe from Quran. Actually nature of Soroush religious government no different with other humanity governments and religious aspect is only to exigency of humanity society and not base of government nature and manner of governors. So Soroush explain that religious government is essentially humanity government and not less and not more and should be alike of other governments. He differentiated between religious revelational nature and humanity knowledgement. Revelational religion is surd and immune from revision, inverse humanity knowledgement in religion is interpretation from religion that is relative, related to era and incomplete human discovery. So in this category, human kind confront to religion humanity knowledgment and fact of religion is far-reaching and realize of new knowledgement, merely don't enhance prior knowledgements but impressing all of process (Soroush, constrict and expand theory, 307; 361–365).

CONCLUSION

Religious intellectual thought began after twenty century and in last decade of 50 and 60 enter to political campaign aspects and vast its attempts. After 60 decades and among of political campaigns, formed philosophical basis that be synthesis of religious thoughts and principals of western thoughts such as liberalism and Marxism. Before of Islamic revolution in Iran, religious intellectuals sue compatible of religion with modern ideologies special socialism and essentially religion interpretation be for transform to revolutionary ideology. After Islamic revolution, intellectuals attempt with reinterpretation of religion, unshackled it from politics, revolution, ideology and intra-religion attitude. Stress of dominant current in past-revolution on capitalism, imperialism, justice, freedom and return to essential traditions but after 80 decade, intellectual religion with emphasis to liberalism and secularism confront against Islamic radicalism and provide manner for resolution in modernity. So tradition discourse led contents such as absolutism, religion presence in public and private fields, idealism, originality of sharia rules, motivation of religious sensibilities, clericals authority and adversary to west as whole and revision of tradition but post-revolution current have impressionistic outlook to religion, time, position and those subject. This class have scientific perception to religious issues and with advocate of positivism, empiricism and hermeneutic reading, consideration to religious contents analysis and don't believe to Ijtihad of tradition Fiqh. Those base in politics, separate of religion and politics and since are engage to sharia, haven't metaphysical understanding from religion and in his believe would abide religion in holy aspect and presented only mundane politics to society. Too believe everybody base of his knowledge use and apply religion texts. So intended democratic government concomitance with Islamic values and religious attitude to democracy rely on self-founded rationality. They endeavor by present of minimal Islam and exception of Fiqh and extra-religion and multidimensional approach sue reconcile between Islam and democracy. Generally intellectual base of last generation instead empirical finality mean what considered by revolutionary religious intellectuals, is critic wisdom that don't alleged definite recognize of world, and always considerate to doubt, critic, new detection and ontological hermeneutic.

SOURCES

Borujerdi, Mehrzad (2005). *Iranian intellectuals and west*; Translated by Majid shirazi; Tehran: Foruzan press.

Farasatkhah, Maghsoud (1995). *Began of religion and non-religion intellectual*; Tehran: Enteshar cooperation company.

Hashemi, Mohammadmansour (2006). *Modern religious intellectuals from Shariati to Malekian*; Tehran: Kavir press.

Hermeneutic, Quran and tradition; Tehran, Tarhe now press (1996).

Jahanbakhsh, Forough *Islam* (2004*). Democracy and religious modernism in Iran from Bazargan to Soroush*; translated by Jalil Parvin; Tehran: Game now press.

Kazemi, Abbas (2004). *Sociology of religious intellectual in Iran*; Tehran: culture ministry publications.

Mistery, intellectual and faithful; Serat cultural institute (1998).

Mohammadrezaee, Mohammad (2002). *Provenance of religious intellectual*; Tehran, Zolale kosar press.

Mojtahede Shabestari Mohammad (2001). *Critical to religious formal citation*; Tehran: Aban press.

Pedram, Masoud (2003). *Religious intellectuals and modernity in Iran after revolution*; Tehran: Game now press.

Shariati, Ali (1983). *Sets of works*; Tehran: Elham press.

Soroush, Abdolkarim (1991). *Constrict and expand of sharia theorize*; Tehran: Serat press.

Taghavi, Seyyed Mohammadnaser (2006). *Religion and democratic fundaments*; Tehran: Culture Research and Islamic thoughts Publications.

Tradition and secularism, speeches from Soroush and others; Tehran: Serat press (2002).

10

The "Fallen Woman" in Selected Nineteenth-Century British Fiction

Majid Salem Mgamis[1]*

ABSTRACT

This study aims at investigating the image of the fallen woman in Victorian literature. It tackles selected works by male and female Victorian authors with view at showing how the depiction of fallen women enhances the feminist premise of their works. Each work deals with a particular anifestation of the fallen women to highlight her struggle. Ultimately, the study aims to prove that the fallen women, though socially repulsed, proved to be a woman who strongly seeks freedom out of the shackles of the patriarchal society.

Key words: Fallen woman, Victorian literature, Feminism, Patriarchy, Emancipation.

The image of the fallen woman permeates Victorian literature. As such, it reveals a lot about the nature of Victorian literature in terms of its principles, values and its view of women. Evidently, the figure of the fallen woman carries feminist innuendoes. Not only does it provide a critique of the Victorian man-made society

[1] English Department, Tafila Technical University, P.O Box 179 – Tafila, 66110 – Jordan.

**Corresponding E-mail*: esotericities@yahoo.co.uk

and shows the plight of the fallen woman and criticize the label, but it also gives writers the freedom of writing. In this regard, Angela Leighton's feminist reading of the figure of the fallen woman is confirmed in the Victorian novel. Leighton pinpoints that:

"the vivid emblem of a social and sexual secrecy which is still clamorous with self-discovery. The figure of the fallen woman is also, however, a sign for women of the power of writing. Her wandering, outcast state seductively expresses the [writer's] restlessness and desire. To summon her is not only to assert a political purpose which breaks the moral law, but also to claim the power of writing as necessarily free of control, of rule (125).

Victorian writers demonstrate the debilitating situation of the fallen woman on their identities as it gave them no space or time to realize their dreams. In nineteenth-century Victorian society, the image of the fallen woman was highly incompatible with her search for self-actualization. The gender roles that characterized the patriarchal mentality limited the options available to those women and deprived them from achieving their ambitions. This situation was depicted in the literature of that period. This view can be substantiated with view at some Victoria novels.

It should be noted that the religious institution played an important role in fostering the Victorian rules which relegated the fallen woman into a miserable situation. The religious domain in nineteenth-century England gave the patriarchal hegemony a divine backing substantiating its claims and proving its prevalence. Hence, the literature of the Victorian period exhibited a critique of the religious institution which contributed to the oppression of women. Both men and women writers of that period showed the fallen woman as part of women who were oppressed by the religious instructions and sometimes tried to rebel against it as well as women who viewed religion as a source of support that may contribute to their search for self-realization.

Exploring the religious institution which "severely restricted, even denied, (women) a voice in the dialogues that shaped theological doctrines" (Jenkins, 16) appears in the works of many writers. Examples on these works include Elizabeth Gaskell's *Ruth*, George Elliot's *Adam Bede,* Mary Braddon's *Lady Audley's Secret*, and Thomas Hardy's *Jude the Obscure*. These authors highlight examples on fallen women who suffered from the conventionality and double standards of the Victorian society.

Gaskell's Ruth is a prime example on this idea. Through employing the figure of the fallen woman represented in Ruth, Gaskell freely criticizes religion for its role in fostering the gender roles perpetuated by the patriarchal society through establishing a penal system that targets women as its victims rather than men. Joana Mink observes that the nineteenth century witnessed a strong tendency to punish women who were regarded fallen. *Ruth* is Gaskell's commentary on this issue. The novel highlights the hardships through which the heroine goes and the callousness of the patriarchal system which condones men for their sins and imposes its punishment only on women.

The major critique on the patriarchal religion is targeted towards the double standards it employs in examining moral and ethical issues. It is Ruth only who faces the negative attitude and punishment of society. Bellingham, on the other hand, is not even questioned. Ironically, the punishment is imposed only on Ruth, though the "crime" that she committed necessarily entails the existence of a partner. What adds to the severity of this double standard is the fact that Ruth was a naive girl who had her sexual relationship with Bellingham not recognizing its consequence. She says, "I was very young; I did not know how such a life was against God's pure and holy will - at least not as I know it now" (Gaskell, *Ruth* 238).

Additionally, within the patriarchal religious parameters, women had to bear more responsibility when it comes to issues of religious morality and conduct. That is why Ruth is immediately fired by her boss when she is seen walking with Bellingham. This shows the great emphasis on female piety and the instant condemnation of women when transgressing the religious barriers.

Ironically, Ruth is more religious than the majority of those who pretend to be so. Her ambition was to bring up the child in a religious manner and do well for the rest of her life.

This opens up avenues for critique of the religious principle of mercy. Ruth ultimately realizes her sin and intends to lead a pious life; still the society does not forgive. Ruth gets no sign of mercy or understanding from society. She was not only seduced and deserted by the same man, but she is also rejected by society and has to face its harsh condemnation and punishment. In brief, the image of Ruth as a fallen woman gave Gaskell the freedom to enunciate her belief that "(the female) sex is badly enough used and legislated against" (qtd. in Beer, 35).

Like Gaskell, George Eliot uses the figure of the fallen woman as major tool for a larger social criticism. *Adam Bede* is a prime example on fiction that highlights women writers' critique of the image of the fallen woman. The novel is viewed as a fitting example on expounding the issue of the identity of the fallen woman in the Victorian society and how the condemnation of that woman hinders her search for self-actualization. In this regard, Hetty Sorrel sets a model for the destiny of a woman who does not abide by the patriarchal prescriptions regarding motherhood.

Hetty represents the type of Eliot's female characters whose oppressive life "leads her to renunciation in an unrealistic and almost pleasurable way" (Beer, 180)." Hetty buries her son; perhaps a sign of rejection for an imposed role. Ultimately, in contrast to Dinah who is "rewarded" with consent and approval for her ultimate surrender to the man-made world, Hetty is rebuked and punished for rejecting her maternal duties. Patricia Beer comments on the brutality of the patriarchal judgment regarding Hetty and declares that "to hang Hetty as a murderess seems as inappropriate as executing a cat for killing its kitten" (205).

Eliot's criticism of the crushing punishment of the fallen woman comes through depicting other female characters who lead a better life just because, unlike the fallen woman, they conform to the social expectations. For example, Dinah Morris is an intelligent and wise lady who has actualized a certain level of autonomy through which she participated in one of the most important institutions supporting patriarchy; namely the religious institution. She has a voice in the public sphere through which she preaches; something considered unordinary for women taking the limitations imposed on women regarding expression of religiosity. Not only has Dinah achieved a profession, but her profession is far away from those allowed for women. She is a Methodist preacher who assists and advises others. Until this point, Dinah sets an example of a woman who not only rejects the patriarchal image of Woman, but turns the table on it and instead of being preached upon, she becomes a preacher. She uses one of the tools used to suppress women for her own emancipatory goals.

However, although Dinah is fully aware that marriage would make an end for her career as a Methodist preacher and ultimately hinder the process of her self-attainment, she ultimately embraces the domestic role assigned for women and gets married to Bede. It is really significant that Dinah's final consent to marry Bede comes as a result of her conviction that it is God's will. This is an indirect attack on the side of Eliot on the institution of religion showing how it may manipulate people into following the traditional system. Ultimately, the institution through which Dinah used to substantiate her identity came to eradicate the very essence of this identity.

In addition, it is the Methodist church that mainly puts and ends to her career as the church banns preaching by women. Adam ratifies this decision by declaring that preaching is not a beneficial career for women. Ultimately, Dinah is confined to domesticity and her career eventually comes to an end. Thus, within marriage, Dinah starts a new form of identity. But for this time, it is a totally different identity that is dictated by the patriarchal ideology. Dinah moves from the position of preacher who had a voice to help others to the position of a woman who is dependent upon her man and looks forward to fulfilling her role as a submissive wife. In other words, by marrying Adam, Dinah completely compromises her identity and gives up her search for freedom.

In a similar fashion, Braddon, in *Lady Audley's Secret*, employs the image of the fallen woman to comment on the atrocities of their situation. What is more, through the figure of the fallen woman, Braddon freely comments on the debilitating situation of women as imprisoned either by fathers or husbands. For example, in the novel, Clara is repressed by a callous father and not allowed to express her feminine desires. She sums up the stifling situation she lives in as she declares that she is living in an "atmosphere of suppression" (Braddon, *Audley* 222). Similarly, Alicia Audley attends to her domestic duties and should obey her father. Phoebe also loses her independence in marriage to a husband who clearly shows his hegemonic nature as he states, "When you're my wife, you won't have over-much time for gentility" (Braddon, *Audley* 66).

Lady Audley's situation proves to be double jeopardy. She is the victim of both, a drunken father and a husband who deserts for purely materialistic purposes. However, unlike the other female characters, Lady Audley does not succumb to the dictated role of the wife. She repudiates her miserable situation and embarks on her journey for independence from the patriarchal oppression. Ultimately, as a disobedient (fallen) woman, she faces condemnation and rejection by the man-made society.

Lady Audley is diagnosed as a mad woman. Just like other women who reject the domestic sphere and the socially-constructed image of women, Lady Audley is relegated to the position of a madwoman as she revolts against the restrictions imposed on her identity. The patriarchal message is clear; within the masculine society atmosphere, a woman has to be obedient to the masculine ideology and fulfill the societal expectations of the docile wife; otherwise, she will face rejection and expulsion from the socially-prescribed model of normality.

Through the character of Lady Audley, Braddon subverts the traditional image of woman, which labels them either angels on the one hand or fallen women or mad women on the other. Thus, Braddon critiques the image of the angel in the house' that is a motif in Victorian novels. Lady Audley repudiates the angel's image and adopt the fallen woman role. Braddon thus shows how madness is a label that is given to a woman who rejects the social norms. Through this critique, Braddon's novel stands as a trenchant attack on the Victorian ideals of femininity, which forces women to become fallen and punishes them for becoming so.

The figure of the fallen women gave the freedom of critique not only to female writers, but to male writers as well. For example, in *Jude the Obscure*, Hardy uses the figure of Sue (labeled as fallen woman) to promulgates a wholesale rejection of the religious patriarchal constraints that restrict women's freedom. He launches a trenchant attack on the Victorian religious conventionality that goes against women's search for freedom, independence and happiness. Hardy's views on religion are articulated through Sue. Sue is portrayed as a woman who aspires to break away form of religious dictates and questions the basic orthodox religious principles regarding morality and marriage.

Right from the outset, Sue is described as "a woman clipped and pruned by severe discipline" (Hardy, *Jude* 136). Sue exhibits a rejection of this discipline. Her attitude and behavior rejects all conventional Victorian morality and ethics. She emerges as a woman who weighs matters by reason, subverting the idea that women are governed by their emotions. In her dissenting conversations, Sue puts into question rigid religious and conventional ideas regarding marriage and morality.

Sue does not keep her liberal ideology in a theoretical frame; rather, her behavior substantiates her stand regarding religion. Sue rejects all forms of religious prayer as a manifestation of hypocrisy. Her repudiation of the religious institution is best represented in her negative view of Christminster describing it as characterized by "timid obsequiousness to tradition" (Hardy, *Jude* 329). Most importantly, the fact that she leaves her lawful husband to live with someone to whom she is not married is a blunt rejection of religious dictates.

Sue shows her extreme disregard for the confinements of marriage sanctioned by religion. For her, such institution, with its religious foundations, is the antithesis of freedom. She lambasts the extreme conventionality of society which relegates marriage into a mere obligation that has to be fulfilled. She views marriage as a "vulgar institution" that issues 'sordid contract" in which the woman's affection should be given to the man "appointed by the bishop's license to receive it" (Hardy, *Jude* 256). Sue mainly criticizes the obligatory nature of marriage as she cannot accept the view of marriage as an institution where one "*must* and *shall* be a person's lover" (Hardy, *Jude* 267). (Italics mine).

Like most women in nineteenth-century society and literature, Sue is trapped in the conflict between satisfying her emancipatory impulse and conforming to social norms that are substantiated by religion. She ultimately chooses the latter. Still, Sue's return to Phillotson is not a manifestation of defeat of her revolutionary nature; rather it comes as a final choice; a representation of a fear of some supernatural power that she may not be aware of. Her retreat into the religious domain is a protective strategy. She regards her marriage to someone whom she does not love as a sort of punishment and a source for redemption and shelter from further tragedies that may come if she keeps on her transgression. Here, Sue never contradicts herself and never abandons her repudiation of conventionality. She has always been a believer; however, like Hardy, she has been critical of the religious institution that embraces conventionality and inhibits women's freedom.

To conclude, the above argument aims at showing shows that depicting fallen women like Sue and others mentioned above empowered female (and male) writers to launch trenchant attack against this oppressive label and the way society deals with such women. On a broader term, this gave writers the opportunity to widen their criticism to touch upon other feminist concern, most importantly the critique of the religious institution in its contribution to the oppression of women.

In the Victorian period, women had to face the oppressiveness of the religious system which provided unquestionable authority to the patriarchal system under which they suffer. For the male society, men's dominance over women was religiously ordained, and women had no choice but to show complete submissiveness and acceptance to the repressive system. Religion constituted the mechanism by which male hegemony authenticated its power over women and instilled its repressive agenda.

Within this context, women who expressed their rejection of the religious dictates, such as the case with Sue, faced the thrilling power of patriarchy. Ruth's story also emblematizes the double standard that is at the core of the masculine religion. On the other hand, some other women managed to find a way out of this labyrinth, gain an informal voice within the religious institution and use it to serve their purpose.

WORKS CITED

Beer, Patricia (1975). Reader, I Married Him: A Study of the Women Characters of Jane Austen, Charlotte Bronte, Elizabeth Gaskell and George Eliot. London and Basingstoke: Macmillan.

Braddon, Mary (2003). *Lady Audley's Secret*. 1862. Huston, Natalie (*ed.*), Canada, Broadview Press Ltd. Great Britain: Oxford Press, Print.

Eliot, George (1985). *Adam Bede*. 1859. Ed. Stephen Gill. London: Penguin, Print.

Gaskell, Elizabeth Ruth (2011). Edited with a New Introduction and Notes by Tim Dolin, 1853. Oxford World's Classics, Oxford and New York, Oxford University Press, Print.

Hardy, Thomas (1985). *Jude the Obscure*. 1895. Ed. & Intro. Patricia Ingham. Oxford: Oxford UP.

Jenkins, Ruth Y. (1995). *Reclaiming Myths of Power: Women Writers and the Victorian Spiritual Crisis*. Lewisburg: Bucknell UP, Print.

Leighton, Angela (1989). "'Because men made the laws': The Fallen Woman and the Woman Poet". *Victorian Poetry*, 27: 109–127.

Mink, JoAnna Stephens (1987). "The Emergence of Woman as Heroine in the Nineteenth Century". *Heroines of Popular Culture*, Browne Pat (*ed.*), Bowling Green, OH: BGSU Popular, p. 66.

11

Carnap's Internal-External Questions: It's Implication for Language

FELIX AGBO OKWA[1]*

ABSTRACT

Contemporary Analytic Philosophy is conceived as a style of philosophizing characterized by serious emphasis on clarity of language and arguments through the use of formal logic and rigorous analysis of concepts. This was said to be the hallmark of the members of Vienna Circle, of which Rudolf Carnap was a frontline member. Carnap argued for a sincere organization of our language in a pragmatic manner that eliminates concepts that have little or nothing to do with empirical realities and strict scientific reasoning. In the light of this, Carnap presented a pragmatic verification principle that for any statement to be meaningful, it must either be analytic or synthetic. Propositions outside the analytic / synthetic framework are considered pseudo-statements. Such as the statements and propositions found in Metaphysics. But can this theory verify itself? What is the implication of this for language?

Keywords: Language, Linguistic framework, Verification, Verifiability, Meaning.

[1] Augustinian Institute, Otukpo Road, P.o Box 584, Makurdi, Benue State, Nigeria

**Corresponding E-mail*: Okwafa@yahoo.com

INTRODUCTION

Philosophy of language, the most vital and indeed the key of any philosophical endeavour is traceable to the very beginning of philosophy. This branch of philosophy, viewed as an aspect of epistemology brings to the fore the very fact that there can be no meaningful discuss of knowledge without being able to communicate it and communicate it efficiently. Put differently, one cannot claim to know anything without the use of language to communicate this knowledge to others, hence, we can say, there is no real knowledge without knowing the means of communicating it.

In this work, we set out to critically examine the salient contributions of Rudolf Carnap to this branch of philosophy that has proved to be key to any philosophical endeavour. Carnap as we know, is one of the most influential member of the Vienna Circle. To be able to carry out our task efficiently, we shall first and foremost take a look at the personality of Carnap. This is because, a person's background goes a long way to shape a person's conception of reality as well as his/her world view. In doing this, we shall put in mind the major tenets of the Logical Positivists, this would in no little way aid us in the discuss that ensues. As a follow up to this, we shall delve into Rudolf Carnap's analysis of linguistic framework, bringing to bare the two vital questions: Internal and External Questions. This shall invariable lead us to the discuss of Meaning and Verifiability Principle as well as Rudolf Carnap's Elimination of metaphysics. We shall then engage in the objections or criticisms of the verifiability principle and saliently bring to the fore its implication to language.

CARNAP AND LOGICAL POSITIVISM

Carnap as we must acknowledge, was a dominant figure in the development of post war philosophy in the USA. He was a German positivist philosopher as well as one of the most influential member of the Vienna circle[1]. He was a student of Frege and was greatly influenced by the works of Russell and Wittgenstein. Carnap was a strong proponent of the verification principle, a principle that states that for anything to count as contribution to human knowledge it must either be justified by observation and experience or is merely formal and thus expressed in tautological proposition[2].

Logical positivism was borne in Austria and Germany during the 1920s and was primarily concerned with the logical analysis of scientific knowledge. Logical positivists include notable scholars like Moritz Schlick, C.G Hempel, A.J Ayer, Victor Kraft and others. They vehemently rejected metaphysics and traditional philosophy, claiming that many philosophical problems are indeed meaningless. The main philosophical tenets of logical positivism include the verifiability principle. A principle that states that there are only two sources of knowledge which are, logical reasoning and empirical experience. In this sense, logical-reasoning is taken to be an *a priori* form of knowledge which is also regarded as analytic, while empirical experience is taken to be the synthetic *a posteriori*.

A second tenet of logical positivism is the elimination of metaphysics. They held that metaphysical statements do not fall under the purview of experience and so are regarded as meaningless. Another important tenet of logical positivism include the language of science. According to logical positivism, a scientific theory is an axiomatic system that acquires an empirical interpretation only by means of appropriate statements called rules of correspondence, which establishes a correlation between real objects and the abstract concepts of the theory. Without such types of statements a theory lacks physical interpretation and is not verifiable. We now move further to examine the contributions of Rudolf Carnap on Linguistic Framework: Internal and External Questions.

---

[1] Miller, A. (2007). *Philosophy of Language.* London and New York: Routledge Publishers, p. 115.

[2] Stokes, P. (2006). *Philosophy*-100 *Essential Thinkers.* New York: Enchanted Lion Books, p. 173.

CARNAP'S LINGUISTIC FRAMEWORK: INTERNAL AND EXTERNAL QUESTIONS

Rudolf Carnap's article "Empiricism, Semantics and Ontology" sets out to deal with the implications of accepting language which refers to abstract entities. First and foremost, it is noteworthy to state here that ontology as we know it, is charged with the responsibility of defining contents of our universe, which invariable implies that such endeavor should be the first project of any incipient philosophical system. For Carnap, discussing new forms or kinds of entities requires the construction of what he calls – Linguistic Framework. Put differently, constructing a novel linguistic framework was necessary to be able to discuss adequately new kinds of ideas. This project of Carnap we must say, is both pragmatic and straightforwardly empirical[3]. The question however is, what is a linguistic framework? Linguistic Framework is viewed as a "new set of rules governing the ways in which these entities are described and referenced"[4]. From this definition, we therefore understand that a linguistic framework is thus a human conscious thrive to organize her language, by implication, straighten her modes of communication of certain experiences and or observations.

Empiricism on the other hand, is a veritable school of thought in philosophy that is very suspicious of abstract entities, claiming that metaphysical language and ideas do not exist, and even if they exist, they cannot be known, simply because there is nothing that can be known except through experience, through the senses. Empiricists therefore stick to the use of nominalistic language. With this in mind, the empiricist may be moved to declare part of the language of physics as uninterrupted and uninterpretable- such as that which refers to real numbers as space-time coordinates or as values of physical magnitudes. Within the spheres of semantics and particularly in the aspect of theory of meaning, empiricists

[3] Stafford, K. (2005). *The Structure of Carnap's Linguistic Frameworks.* Unpublished work, p. 1.

[4] Ibid, p. 1.

declare that certain expressions designate certain entities: abstract, and this ought not to be the case since there cannot be a valid principle to ascertain these claims. Carnap thus sets out to show how such language could be put in a new set of linguistic framework which would make this compactible with empiricism and strict scientific thinking. For every linguistic framework, two types of questions abound: Internal questions and External questions.

Internal Questions

Simply defined, internal questions are those questions asked and answered within the framework. Graham notes that, the various misinterpretations of Carnap's view is that there exists "four-fold" distinction, contrary to the simple dual contrast usually put forward by different scholars. Hence, under the internal question, we have two-fold distinctions: the particular and the general questions. For Graham, the rules, syntax, vocabularies and or test procedures of a linguistic framework are capable of settling particular internal questions[5]. The questions that fall under this variant of internal questions invariably include claims of some sort of empirical kind and thus would form an empirical system[6]. On the other hand, Carnap distinguishes what he calls the 'thing' language as a variant of internal questions. The thing language suffices for physical objects as well as number languages "dealing with basic arithmetical operations on natural numbers"[7]. This consequently forms a logical system or a non-empirical system. It is important to state that these internal questions may altogether concern themselves with definitions and or facts, hence, they may be analytic or synthetic. For example, "is there any books on the

[5] Bird, G. (2003)."Carnap: Internal and External Questions Part 1, Quines Criticisms". *In*: Thomas, B. (*ed.*). *Language, Truth and Knowledge, Contributions to the Philosophy of Rudolf Carnap*. Kluwer Academic Publishers, p. 97.

[6] Ibid, p. 98.

[7] Ibid, p. 98.

shelve?" who is the Governor of Oyo State? All these are internal questions, and so to answer these questions, one simply needs to fit their answers into a consistent thing-system that obeys the laws of the framework. Simply put, internal questions are questions asked within a particular linguistic framework, and the answers and also found within the same framework.

External Questions

External questions on the other hand are questions asked of the larger system within which entities are supposed to exist[8]. As stated above however, Carnap distinguishes the external questions into two folds according to Graham. The first distinction Graham calls practical and the second he calls theoretical questions. For example, questions such as 'what are things?" Are numbers real"? These are clearly external questions for they are sort of questions that concern the existence or reality of the system of entities as a whole. External questions for Carnap, are not just unanswerable, but fundamentally flawed in their formulation.

It is meaningless to ask what is "real" outside the context of the framework because it is the framework that contributes the cognitive content with which these questions are posed. To be real in the scientific sense means to be an element of the system; hence, this concept cannot be meaningfully applied to the system itself[9].

Thing language does not exist out there, so, there should be no talk about things outside a particular framework. Carnap believes this external questions are only asked by philosophers and they are not intended to question whether or not a set of entities exist, rather, they are practical questions asked by philosophers to simply check whether or not the linguistic framework introducing these entities is useful and worthy of adoption.

[8] Stafford, K. (2005). opcit, p. 1.
[9] Ibid, p. 2.

CARNAP ON MEANING AND VERIFICATION

Though often times we are not conscious of the exact meaning of our utterances, we seem to make statements easily, almost unconsciously, it remains an obvious fact however, 'each' expression of a language surely means something. The question now is, what does it mean? We live in a world of language. Whatever we do when we come together, be it play, quarrel, argue, make love, fight, we are talking. We talk to friends, wives, husbands, family members, pets and even sometimes to ourselves. According to G.O. Ozumba, language can be understood as the means of communicating ideas and thought[10]. Put differently, language could be understood as the ability and capacity to acquire and make use of systems and modalities of communication. Hence, when you know a language, you can speak and be understood by others who know that language. Language is however said to be much more than speech. Language is said to evolve and diversify over long period of time. For language to be meaningful, and for communication to be carried out, the laid down rules of that language, which is understood by the speakers of that language must be strictly respected because language has various dimensions ranging from semantics, syntactic, morphemic, phonetic and semiotic dimensions.

From our understanding of language, we discover that when you know a language, you can speak and be understood by others, for this to be, the words or signs used in such a language must be meaningful and the meaning must be shared by speakers of that language. The question that could be asked at this point therefore is, what is meaning? Meaning could be understood generally as the signification of a word or sign[11]. Hence, to mean is to be significant, possessing designated understanding worthy of existence as part of the linguistic repertoire. A theory of meaning is regarded as a theory that attributes to each experience in the

[10] Ozumba, G.O. (2004). *Introduction to Philosophy of Language.* Ibadan: Hope Publications, p. 18.

[11] Ibid. p. 19.

language its literal meaning that would be understood by the speakers of the language. We have various theories of meaning, psychological theory of meaning, truth-conditional semantic and others. For the purpose of this work however, we shall concentrate on the verifiability principle and by implication the verification theory of meaning as put forward by the logical positivists and Carnap in particular. What is the verification theory of meaning all about? According to John Skorupski,

> Verification is the view that understanding a sentence consists in grasping what information states would verify it. An information state verifies a sentence just if a person in the state is warranted in asserting it. All significant sentences have assertion conditions[12].

According to Skorupski, following this explication of verificationism, a sentence only has meaning if the information contained therein can be verified empirically. Before we move any further however, it is necessary to take us back to the formation of the verification principle. This verification theory of meaning has as its exponents the logical positivist, who believed that empiricism was all that is needed to acquire knowledge. Following this then, statements are divided into two analytic and synthetic. A synthetic statement is that statement whose validity is determined by the facts of experience while analytic statements are statements whose validity depends solely on the definitions of the symbols it contains. Owing from the above definition, we shall thus understand that synthetic statements qualify as meaningful statements in virtue of their being associated with a method of empirical verification while analytic statements qualify as meaningful statements without possessing factual meaning[13].

[12] Skorupski, J. (1998). "Meaning, Use, Verification". *In*: Bob, H. and Crispin, W. (*eds.*). *A Companion to the Philosophy of Language.*New York: Blackwell Publishers, p. 41.

[13] Miller, A. (2007). opcit, p. 95.

Analytic statements therefore are in no need of any form of verification since by their very definition they are considered to be meaningful, it therefore suffices to state that, we are concerned herein with only synthetic statements, because they possess the virtue of verification to be literally meaningful.

In providing a criterion of meaningfulness in synthetic statements, A. J Ayer states that

> *The criterion which we use to test the genuineness of apparent statements of fact is the criterion of verifiability. We say that a sentence is factually significant to any person if, and only if, he knows how to verify the proposition which it purports to express- that is, if he knows what observations would lead him, under certain conditions, to accept the propositions as being true, or reject the propositions*[14].

Sequel to this criteria of verification as espoused by Ayer, meaning can only be given to a posteriori sentences through its method of verification. For example, "Feux is a red cat". This a posteriori statement is meaningful if and only if one knows how to verify the proposition in a conclusive manner. It is important to state here that there exists however, many statements that would fail to have meaning in accordance with this formulation of principle. For example, how do we account for meaningfulness in statements that concern non-verifiable facts, such as statements in metaphysics, psychology, ethics and theology?

There has been a long lasting dispute between the Nominalists and the Platonists as regards the ontological status of abstract entities. For the Platonists, such arithmetic statements such as "5 is a prime number" to imply the existence of a range of abstract objects, which could be said to exist in space and time as well as completely connected concrete entities. On the other hand

[14] Ayer, A.J. (1946). *Language, Truth, and Logic*. New York: Dova Press, p. 34.

however, the Nominalist analyze statements such as "5 is a prime number' to not imply the existence of abstract entities. This idea is in total negation of the Platonist understanding of the ontological status of abstract entitles[15]. According to Rudolf Carnap, in his exposition of Linguistic framework, and particularly the Internal and external questions, trying to resolve the long lasting dispute between the Nominalists and the Platonists as regards the ontological status of abstract entities, distinguishes between Logical framework and factual framework. As a way of recap, logical framework is understood as that variant of Carnap's linguistic framework which is such that all the internal questions formed within it are regarded as analytic and so are meaningful without the necessary ingredient of verification. On the other hand, factual framework refers to that framework within which all the internal questions are formed, but in this light, all the questions formed are synthetic. Owing from our previous discussion on analytic and synthetic, it is almost explicitly glaring that the verification principle therein concerns itself with only the factual framework of Carnap's linguistic framework. To further understand Carnap's conception of meaning and verification, we now move to his discuss of the Elimination of metaphysics.

CARNAP ON ELIMINATION OF METAPHYSICS

Right from the outset, it is important to state that metaphysics has various opposition and objections. We can say categorically that the opponents of metaphysics can be traced to the Greek skeptics down to the empiricists of the 19th century. As the era varies, so too does their kinds of criticisms. Essentially however, their criticisms range from the fact that the doctrine of metaphysics contradicts our empirical knowledge, they critics say, knowledge of such is essentially of a false doctrine.

The development of applied logic is said to possess both a positive and a negative consequence. The positive consequence is

[15] Miller, A. (2007). opcit, p. 115.

said to be in the realm of the empirical sciences, various concepts of the various branches of science were clarified, leading to their formal-logical and epistemological connections been made explicit. The negative consequence however, which cannot be overlooked, sterns in the area of metaphysics and indeed the philosophy of normative and value theory which concludes that all statements in these domains are entirely meaningless[16]. It is in the light of this negative consequence of the development of applied logic that we wish to discuss Carnap's view as regards the radical elimination of metaphysics.

First and foremost, Carnap is of the view that statements of metaphysics are pseudo-statements. He holds that as discussed in his linguistic framework, language consists of set of words which have meaning and rules of sentence formation. Put differently, for Carnap, language ought to possess vocabulary and syntax. This vocabularies consequently informs the manner and methods of sentence formation. Pseudo-statements are of two kinds. Those formed through the use of words which are erroneously believed to be meaningful, and those been put together in a counter-syntactical form, so do not constitute meaning in the end. For Carnap, this two forms of pseudo-statement production occur in metaphysics[17].

The question however is, if words are said to be constructed in a particular language for the singular purpose of expressing something, and this particular word had meaning at some point, what then happens that a word loses its meaning to become utterly meaningless, so much so it comes a word erroneously believed to be meaningful? For Carnap, a word that becomes meaningless is referred to as pseudo-concept. This pseudo concept comes about possibly through the cause of historical development, through this,

[16] Carnap, R. (1996). "The Elimination of Metaphysics through Logical Analysis of Language". *In*: Sahotra, S. (*ed.*). *Logical Empiricism at its Peak: Schlick, Carnap and Newrath*. New York: Garland Publishers, p. 12.

[17] Ibid, p. 13.

a word may be said to change its meaning and then acquire a new meaning. With this, a word still has meaning; the new meaning. But when a word changes its meaning or its old sense without acquiring a new sense, it becomes a pseudo concept.-meaningless.

What then is the meaning of a word? For Carnap, to be able to determine the meaning of a word, we simply need to get the syntax explicitly spelt out. By syntax we mean the mode of its occurrence in the simplest sentence form in which it is capable of occurring. For example, for a word like "stone", we simply would say "x is a stone". If we wish to find the meaning of a word such as "diamond", we would simply say, replacing 'x' with 'diamond', "diamond is a stone". This then shows that diamond has all the qualities of a "stone". To know the meaning of stone, we need to pass through the process of deducibility. Furthermore, what we must know about a sentence in order for it to be meaningful is to ask, what sentences are deducible from the sentence? Under what conditions can we say the sentence is supposed to be true, and under what conditions false? How do we verify the sentence?

The question we can ask at this point is, how then do we account for some overwhelming words? For Carnap, we can simply specify their meaning through the method of reduction. And moves further to give an example,

> *"Arthropods are animals with segmented bodies and jointed legs" thereby the above mentioned question for the elementary sentence form of the word "arthropod", that is for the sentence form "the thing x is an arthropod" is answered: it has been stipulated that a sentence of this form is deducible from the premises of the form "x is an animal", "x has a segmented body", "x has jointed legs" and that conversely each of the sentences is a deducible form of the former sentence*[18].

[18] Ibid, p. 14.

From the above therefore, we can say that through this method of reduction, such words like 'arthropods' have meanings. Furthermore, we can say that for Carnap, the meaning of a word is determined by its criterion of application; by its truth conditions and by the method of verification. We see a shortfall from this conception of meaning, for if meaning is solely determined by its application, it therefore means that one's freedom to decide what one wishes to mean by a particular word is entirely far removed. Following this theory of meaning, it invariably suggest that for any word to be meaningful, it must be nothing less than the criteria, in the same vain, nothing more than the criteria can be ascribed to a particular word.

> *Let "a" be any word and "S (a)" the elementary sentence in which it occurs. Then the sufficient and necessary condition for "a" being meaningful may be given by each of the following formulations, which ultimately say the same thing in different ways*[19].

- The empirical criteria for 'a' to be known
- It has been stipulated from what protocol sentences "S (a)" is deducible.
- The truth conditions for "S (a)" are fixed
- The method of verification of "S (a)" is known.

Sequel to the above, we see clearly that many words in metaphysics fall short of this meaning criteria as put forward by Carnap. For this reason, Carnap advocates for the total elimination of metaphysics since its sentences or statements are only but pseudo-statements and thus have no meaning. For example, if we take the word "principle" in metaphysics and try to subject it to the criteria of meaning as put forward by Carnap, we would then be forced to ask the four cardinal questions for the determination of meaning and if the concept is able to scale through, then it can

[19] Ibid. p. 14.

be regarded as meaningful, otherwise, it is then regarded as a pseudo-concept.

First and foremost, we should know that principle in metaphysics herein refers to the principle of being. Metaphysicians understand this to be discuss about the highest stuff of existence. The question Carnap asks therefore is, can the metaphysician proffer answer to the criteria of application of principle?[20] Under what conditions then can the statement of the form "x is the principle of y", would be said to be true and under what condition would it be said to be false? Put differently, what is the empirical criteria for x to be known? Is the truth condition for "S (a)" fixed? If yes, what is the truth condition? What would be the verification method of "S (a)"? Obviously, metaphysics cannot be said to proffer these sorts of question simply because these questions deal with empirical realities while metaphysicians tend to deal with abstract and non-empirical realities. The question we can ask at this point is, does everything end with the empirical realities? Are we saying there are no realities outside of the sensible? If no, how then do we account for their existence and meaningfulness of sentences used to acquire and transmit their existence?

AGAINST VERIFICATION THEORY OF MEANING AND ITS IMPLICATION FOR LANGUAGE

As explicitly discussed above, we understand that the verification theory of meaning is indeed an epistemic account of meaning, by implication, this theory of meaning tends to find or adjudicate meaning in our ways of coming to know things. As a way of recap, verificationists such as Carnap make clear distinction between analytic and synthetic statements. Analytic statements are allowed to possess meaning even though they do not have empirical content. By implication, such statements are by their definition, true. True solely in virtue of the meanings of the terms they are composed

[20] Ibid. p. 14.

therein[21]. For example, six shirts are more shirts than three shirts. No bachelor is married. If it is raining, then it is raining. These statements or sentences are considered as meaningful by the verificationists, they are true statements and thus require no form of verification or empirical predictions. Conclusively therefore, no matter how trivial they may appear or sound, the meaning is guaranteed by the collective meaning of the words that recur in them[22].It is therefore the synthetic sort of sentences that necessarily need verification to provide it with meaning.

Like any other theory, verification theory also has some flaws or objections as the case may be. For the purpose of this work however, we shall identify and discuss two basic objections to the verifiability principle. The first major objection to the verificationist theory of meaning sterns from the fact that this theory leads to a highly controversial metaphysics. By controversial we mean that, owing from the principle of verification, we see that the primary condition for verification is experience. This theory subscribes to the theorem that any statement that cannot be verified is ipso facto termed meaningless. From this theory, when we put to consideration metaphysical, ethical and psychological statements, they would only constitute meaningless statements for they are neither empirical nor factual and thus cannot be verified.

For William Lycan,

> *When we turn to questions about the human mind, we find that a very strong version of behaviorism falls right out; statements about people's mind are mental abbreviations of statements about those people's overt behavior. For the only sort of observational evidence I ever have regarding your innermost thoughts and feelings is the behavior I see and hear you engaging in. If one is a verificationist, philosophy of mind is over and done with*[23].

---

[21] William, G.L. (2008). *Philosophy of language, A Contemporary Introduction.* New York: Routledge Publications, p. 100.

[22] Ibid, p. 100.

[23] Ibid, p. 103.

Lycan therefore makes clear that the verification theory of meaning which limits meaning to the possibility of being verified conclusively does not proffer or give room for those other statements that are considered as meaningful but cannot be verified because they are not overt in nature. If verificationism is to be followed radically to the logical conclusion. It implies that disciplines such as metaphysics, psychology, philosophy of mind and ethics would invariably become things or disciplines for the abyss.

A second and very significant objection to the verificationist theory of language is the fact that the theory applies only to what the positivists themselves call descriptive, fact-stating language. By implication, only statements that are descriptive in nature as well as purely states facts can be verified. The question then is, is descriptive and fact-stating language the only kind of language we have? Obviously, the answer is in the negative for we also ask questions, give orders, tell jokes and the rest. How then do we verify these sorts of statements in the light of verificationist theory of meaning? Since all these are uses of language, one would expect that a theory of meaning should put to consideration all these uses of meaning for they are also part of language.

CONCLUSION

In this work, we have been able to critically examine the salient contributions of Rudolf Carnap to Philosophy of Language and in particular, his conception of meaning and verification. Carnap as we know, is one of the most influential member of the Vienna Circle. In this endeavor, we first and foremost started with some insights about the personality of Carnap as well as Logical Positivism, concentrating on the major nets of the Logical Positivists. As a follow up to this, we engaged on Rudolf Carnap's analysis of the linguistic framework, stating the major differences between the two vital questions: Internal and External Questions. This consequently led us to the discuss of Meaning and Verifiability Principle as well as Rudolf Carnap's Elimination of metaphysics.

As a way of evaluation, we engaged in some of the major objections or criticisms of the verifiability principle.

In conclusion, we therefore state that, even though the verification theory has been significant in the area of the empirical sciences, wherein concepts of the various branches of science are empirically clarified, making their formal-logical and epistemological connections clear and explicit. It has judiciously failed as a theory to proffer holistic conception of meaning to all aspects of language. Verifiable principle limits itself to only descriptive and fact-stating aspect of language and neglects other aspects like questions, jokes, query, command and others.

REFERENCES

[1] Ayer, A.J. (1946). *Language, Truth and Logic*. New York: Dova Press.
[2] Bird, G. (2003). "Carnap: Internal and External Questions Part 1, Quines Criticisms". *In*: Thomas, B.(*ed.*), *Language, Truth and Knowledge, Contributions to the Philosophy of RudolfCarnap*. Kluwer Academic Publishers.
[3] Carnap, R. (1996). "The Elimination of Metaphysics through Logical Analysis of Language". *In:* Sahotra, S. (*ed.*), *Logical Empiricism at its Peak: Schlick, Carnap and Newrath*. New York: Garland Publishers.
[4] Miller, A. (2007). *Philosophy of Language*. London and New York: Routledge Publishers.
[5] Ozumba, G.O. (2004). *Introduction to Philosophy of Language.* Ibadan: Hope Publications.
[6] Skorupski, J. (1998). "Meaning, Use, Verification". *In*: Bob, H. and Crispin, W. (*eds.*). *A Companion to the Philosophy of Language.* New York: Blackwell Publishers.
[7] Stafford, K. (2005). *The Structure of Carnap's Linguistic Frameworks.* Unpublished work.
[8] Stokes, P. (2006). *Philosophy*-100 *Essential Thinkers*. New York: Enchanted Lion Books.
[9] William, G.L. (2008). *Philosophy of language, A Contemporary Introduction*. New York: Routledge Publications.

12

The Fight

Ousman Bajinka[1*], Pa Modou Drammeh[1],
Cansu Aydin[1] and Momodou Lamin Janneh[2]

ABSTRACT

The fights in life are enormous and infinite, thus we strive to be the best we can and wanting to see the best others can see in us. This article meanders through the fear in failing we encounter in life; if there is anything like fear of failure. The fear to fail is the failing we desired. There is no point in failing instead the conflict of interest that we occasionally try to escape. The survival of the fittest is real and we should be ready to face it. There is no accuracy without trying and the failing should be challenges since the downfall of a man is not the end of the life. We are stronger than before if we allow experience to lead our ways. Failing once; earn hints for the preceding battle. Sometimes the success is delayed and only through the comeback that we can realize that it was the through time, effort, hardworking and dedication that shall swim us to the sea of victory. The old adage that goes by business before pleasure is real and the American dreams work for only those who are prepared for the pains, the challenges and the stumble blocks.

[1] Ege University, Izmir, Turkey
[2] Nusrat Senior School, Gambia
**Corresponding E-mail*: bajinkaousman@gmail.com

Key words: Fear of failure, Hardworking and dedication, Survival of the fittest.

Fear of Failure

By Maria Stenvinkel https://www.stevenaitchison.co.uk/drop-fear-failure/

When the 'things' are getting tough, the toughs are getting tougher however, the strongest ones will eat super against all odds. We fear to fail in our lives, we even fear to succeed because if we do, we fear that we would have more fights and fight and fear in failing.

The struggle of achieving the very best is real and not fictionalization. According the ***Bernard Mandeville***, man is selfish by nature and the hunting and gathering is still in progressive. We all live on our hopes and dreams[1]. These hopes and dreams are really true and will surely come to our way after far fetching a lot. The goodness and mercy we have for the other person might not only be our savior instead will be the key elements that retard our acceleration towards the achievement of those dreams. Forgive but don't forget is a principal of any good person. In our daily conversations, we try to make the best dialogue and keep the talk about however; the fight is deep inside us. We want to force out what we can't really do. We never want to be spontaneous due to the fear that our audience will discredit our capabilities. I remember when I first came to Turkey for master's degree program that will be instructed in Turkish Language. I have only 8 months to read and understand this highly cultural language. I struggled with all methods to fast track my ability of reading and understanding. With all those green energy and enormous effort, my supervisor told me that she helped me to pass with a marginal past. I kept the sadness in me, keeping on thinking about it and would never get the slightest opportunity to let it go off my mind especially when I had an academic argument with the said supervisor. While I get into the second semester, with little more experience and better understanding of the language, I deliberately choose one of her courses (this is what no other students would dare choose). Being the lone man in the class, I would only engage her by throwing questions, upon questions in order to make the lecture lively. During the exams, I persuaded her to translate the questions into English that will enable me understand since understanding a question is part of answering it. I thrilled with questions as excited as a young groom whose excitement was only shared by the bride. Afterward, she called and told that me she couldn't remember the date that any of the students score that kind of grade in this fearful exam. I smiled inside and presented an article for her to proofread before I would send for international journals to publish it. I learnt that the fight to win, to convince and hold that peace of mind has to go with time. Slowly but surely we will get there. The biggest winner in any fight is the one who proved something either wrong or correct.

In Gambia, a tiny West African nation, sometimes to sustain electricity for 24 hours is still a dream. One faithful summer night was awfully skin-boiling. The heat-laden and standing air was almost scorching indoors, perhaps not for all houses in the neighborhood, except those mansions with tight claddings as mine. Yet the inhabitants of those mansions could be saved if they, not like me, had any active standby generator.

Lounged in utter discomfort against the counter to my bamboo bed in my night cabinet, while my muscular thigh muscles stretched exhaustively pulling my relaxed lower feet that hanged down the right edge of the bed, rivers of waste water drained from every sweat pore in my skin triggering my resolution to open and draw away the curtains of all second floor windows. But even that was flimsy enough to arrest the burning heat that afflicted my mansion. My inability to sleep was justified. 'How long will it take NAWEC to damn settle this hell of a blackout?' I vented. 'Oh, did I just utter damn hell of a blackout', I rued for I couldn't let my clement soul get poisoned by my unfortunate situation. NAWEC is the power supplying company. Just then the notion of sleeping outside flicked through my mind but that was no ideal option. How could I have entertained such when I am allergic to dogs? After all there was a guard dog loitering somewhere within the confines of the fence that enclosed the mansion. As lucid as it was, I had no choice but to surrender my poor organs — both innate and superficial — to the tumultuous clutches of the seemingly magmatic heat.

The periodic bouncing of rather inadvertent skulking sounds on my tympanum interrupted my forced slumber. Whichever time of the night it was I couldn't specify. 'That echoes like human footsteps', I muttered in my breath. I craned my neck to fix my ear right in the line of the eerie sound. 'Indeed they are footsteps, a figure is walking down the staircase to the sitting room in the ground floor', I mumbled in preparedness. 'The sneaky burglar who escaped my resentful grip the other time has come once more, and this time around, he is so unlucky that there is a blackout and I am not snoring deafeningly', I hissed while making up for the challenge. I looked down the bed and caught sight of the baseball bat I had hidden there for such occasion. 'I am going to serve him a nasty bop on the skull', I resolved.

In classroom experiences, l will start by borrowing the words of the first black president of South Africa, Nelson Mandela, he pointed out that it always seems impossible until it's done. He further added that it's not where you start but how high you aim that matters for success. His statements have a lesson to drive home when it comes to the student and the classroom. There has always been some of element of failure buried deep inside the hearts of students. Students, of any level, are always sacred of failure. Society has always terrified their minds because we live in a generation where one's success is determined by the outcome of one's grades. Society measure the success or failure of students in the classroom based on their output. This has always put a psychological trauma in the minds of the students. They are sacred of failure. But I tell my students that anyone who has not failed has not tried anything new. To fail is not a shame but how one shake off from that failure to become one better determines his or her level of commitment towards achieving one's goals. The hope of winning is easy to cope with while the agony of defeat is the other side of the story.

Conflict of Interest

Conflict of interest by definition is when different interests come in the same time; the choice of chosen one would have to inhibit the other. This is a natural phenomenon. It happens in everywhere, all work places, and schools, among friends and even between lovers or among lovers in a situation of polygamy. In biology, we understood that human are not living all alone. In a lay man point of view, we call ourselves individuals however, are we really ourselves? The gut microbiologists would have a solid question to this 'we live with the microbes', they constitute more than half of DNA presents in our body and our gut micro biome weight up to 2kg of our body. 90% of these microbes are our cousins in a family; we live with them happily and in a mutual relationship. This great harmony persists until one or other factors come in. Then at this stage, a disease is caused and they stand at the conflict of interest with man. While our immune system is weaken, these faithful microbes due to their number are pathogenic and hence and enemy to man[2,3]. The real war begins..... relationships is sweet! A very sad but a real love exists between our two eyes; they see together, sleep together and even cry together yet they couldn't have the ability to visit or see each other. Despite the bilateral relationship between our tongue and teeth, the occasionally fight spontaneously, that's when the teeth bite the mixer tongue who is always busy mixing.

All of the above biological drama has taught us a great lesson. We fight with our friends, family, community and even with other nation all because of conflict of interests. Let the fight continues until we win! With fear, we fail, with courage, we cross and with hope, we hail! Why won't fight for what we want? We all want that American Dream, not sure it is really a dream (Still bunch of Americans are struggling to find a place to sleep). WE ALL WANT TO EXCEL! And the only way to live on our dreams is to know and understand that there will be conflict of interests in any point of our lives.

We should be very much alerted as when to face those challenges, how to combat the fear and conflict against the other party.

With my in encounter with him; I pulled the baseball bat gently from underneath the bed, still sweating profusely, and tiptoed to the balcony overlooking the sitting room. 'This isn't going to be easy for him', I thought with contempt. I proceeded downstairs counting my steps discreetly — preventing to be perceived and noticed. There he was, clad in a tight overall the color of which I couldn't discern owing to the gloomy darkness around. Moonlight poured down through widely opened overhead windows onto his figure which reflected a dazzling silhouette onto my eyes. After all I was the sole caretaker of the mansion. The owner had hired me to look after it until he gets ready to move in. He had already brought in some valuable furniture and household equipment and once a burglar had stolen a television set and two loud speakers for which my boss had reprimanded me emphasizing that if such should happen again, he would straightaway dismiss me. 'I can't let this burglar be the reason for losing my job', I pondered while fixing my poise. I vividly knew that in order to give him a fierce bop on target, I needed to hide in ambush which I swiftly did. I laid behind some curtain waiting for him to turn around in his ardent search for what to pick. I watched his silhouette keenly as he turned around and strode cautiously towards where I was hiding. He came nearer and nearer, and there he was — right in front of me, there was nothing left but to slap away the curtain beneath which I was stationed and force a ferocious bop into his skull. I poised the baseball bat in both my hands with a rigid grip. Then I removed the curtain from in front of me and while I raised my hands to land the bop on his skull. He turned in my direction. The end was just horrible.

In teaching professional and in classroom, among students, conflict of interests aroused and at certain occasions will go out of hand. Society homed people of different backgrounds, ambitions and personal interest and the discipline which studies society is sociology. From the sociological point of view, a conflict of interest arises when personal interest prevents an individual from performing his/her professional or public obligations in an unbiased manner. The consequences of these conflicts can be the loss of objectivity, the potential for decreased effectiveness as a professional, and the possibility of harm and/or exploitation of another party. Because objectivity is the essence of science, professional and scientific judgments that may be impaired by conflicts of interest are of concern.

Although financial interests have often been considered as the source of conflict of interest, bias can stem from other sources—personal interests and intellectual leanings (Korenman and Shipp, 1994; p. 131). Financial interests are tangible and therefore easier to detect. For example, a researcher may have a financial interest in a company and be asked to determine the effectiveness of a new service provided by the company. The results of this evaluation may determine the viability and profitability of the new service and therefore affect the financial gain of the researcher. However, the extent to which financial interests introduce bias is not always as clear cut as this example, particularly if these interests are disclosed and monitored closely by others to guarantee the integrity of the research or professional service.

Personal interests (such as situations where, as a professional, one is asked to provide services to a friend or relative) can result in potentially troublesome dual relationships. Faculty in a university may have the spouse of a close friend or colleague in class. The ability of the faculty to remain objective in evaluating the performance of the colleague's spouse can be compromised because of its potential for damaging the friendship with a colleague.

Social workers who become angry with a client must be careful not to respond impulsively and vindictively because doing so can easily generate a conflict of interest. For example, Mr. A.'s relationship with his client became more negative over time; eventually, Mr. A. collaborated with his client's ex-spouse and his attorney, thus creating a conflict of interest.

The Downfall of a Man is the End of His Life

I heard this from Les Brown, one of the motivational speakers that I look up to saying 'that; there is no enemy outside, the only enemy is inside'. And of course what didn't kill you makes you strong[4]. Life itself is a try; we are giving exams to pass. This exams comes to us in different ways; some in a form of eradicating poverty, some in a form of waking from the sick bed, some rescuing peoples life while some to merely pass and score good grades to earn better job for a decent life. All these boil to one thing that we had in common, that is to keep going. The fear of not coming back is always the inhibitory agents to our self-developments. We usually give a blind eye to those opened doors. These doors on the west might be closed, but not everyone who has been to US made that dream. In fact, there are very powerful and successful individuals who are contented with what they got. These are probably who were once denied a visa to US and today dancing to the tune of their achievements. My father once told me that the no matter how long a journey can take, it must come to an end. When we were young (I and my favorite bro; Lamin Bajinka), our Father has a big cashew plantation or orchard depending on how we see it. This farm contains more than 1000 cashew trees and cashew nuts in those days' worth fortunes. On weekends, he will lead a way for us to go see the harvest. As we were small boys, the journey was rather seemingly far and on occasions, I would express my feelings that the journey is tiring and disturbing. He (Daddy) will keep on saying that the journey to success is not an easy one and it only a patients to keep track of the unfinished journey in order to make a comeback. We try and try and try and fail but we should relent on not trying even harder with fresh energy.

With sheer prowess burning in my bosom, I went for the strike. I gave it my all. I couldn't have missed. Though he saw me by then, it was too late for him to duck from the baseball bat's line of strike. Upon hearing the sharp hissing sound that the bat had made while cutting through the air, heavenly hope bubbled up in my heart promising that the task had almost been done. Alas! The sound wasn't interrupted; the bat didn't fall on his skull. It fell on my feet instead. What could have happened? Where was he? 'How did he do it?' 'Oh! Perhaps I have a diabolic devil or ghost in company' I thought with overly fright. I found myself in a forward bent lean, the bat had already slipped off my grip and stroke my feet. I couldn't halt the strike, the Herculean force I gave it made it so uncontrollable that it had to hit my leg which I nearly broke. Instantly, I was plunged in a pit of frantic reverie. A terrific wave of failure travelled down my spine rendering my nerves numb. My heart pressed tight against itself and relaxed like a half-inflated ball that had been trod upon. In a split second, I pulled the only torch I had from my pocket and with trembling hands; I hastened to light it up. First, I oriented the dazzling beam on the settee in front of me, then on the lounge beside it, then on the refrigerator that stood beside the temporally stationed vanity near the main entrance. I looked around and around but there was no sign of anyone. And for a moment, I wished it were all a dream. 'I am deluded all the way into thinking that there is a burglarious figure in the house' I muttered with a sigh. The terrible atmosphere around me began to cool down. Oh! No! The torch in my hand was snatched away by a nasty blow that fell on my arm. Alas! I was trapped. I could hardly see anything. And there I lay, writhing, flat on the ground. He had struck me.

The old adage that the downfall of a man is not the end of his life has a very fundamental lesson to share. The downfall of a man does not in any way translate into the end of his life. Life is a transit and everyone has a story to narrate. Life is a story. Many successful people today in the world have a bitter story to narrate. They were once down but that was never the end of their lives. They continued the struggle and today they are harvesting the fruit of their struggles. Bear Grills said a man's pride can be his downfall, and he needs to learn when to turn to others for support and guidance. And Judy Smith added that the ambition and focus that propel you to success can also be your downfall. This shows that the road to success is not easy and is full of obstacles and stumbling blocks. I will take myself as an example. l have faced numerous challenges and failures before l reached where l am today i see myself in Richard C. Armitage quotation that he has a bit of pride, which is always his downfall. In life, one must faces downfalls but that should not determine the end of his life. The wise African man will say it is not right to ask a man with elephantiasis of the scrotum to take on small pox as well, when thousands of other people have not had even their share of small diseases. The simple truth is- no great success was ever achieved without failure. It is just that failure tends to be more public than success, or at least that's what we perceive it to be. We fret it, we try to avoid it, and we question ourselves every time we have unconventional ideas. But life is all about falling and getting up again. As John Wooden put it, failure isn't fatal, but failure to change might be in life, everything you want is on the other side of fear. And Coco Chanel has rightly said that success is most often achieved by those who don't know that failure is inevitable. Robert F. Kennedy concluded that only those who dare to fail greatly can ever achieve greatly.

The Comeback

While I wreathed in pain with my back pressed against the tiled floor, another callous punch dug harshly into my groin. Instantly, in response to the lethal punch, an involuntary bubble of air forced its way out through my mouth in a loud echoing voice. I had missed a breath. My back bounced wholly against the tile. The pain was unbearable. I could conspicuously hear my heart huffing and puffing with intense fright. Though, I couldn't see an inch away from my eyes, I knew I had to fight back to save myself. And then for almost two minutes, there was absolute stillness. 'He is waiting for me to hoist myself up' I conjectured. In no time had I got on my feet, staggering backwards to rest my almost gory body on whatever was behind. Alas! There came another smash which banged on my skull. He had hit me with my own baseball bat. I tumbled smoothly like a falling tree onto the floor. I laid there partly unconscious with my eyes bloodshot. Even though I had forced to retain my tears, a lone drop crept across the bridge of my nose.

Suddenly, I sensed his near presence. He probably knelt over me thinking that I had fainted. My vindictive forebrain fumed with contempt. It was time to punch back. I threw a clenched fist, with my utmost strength, upward through the air. Wow! I did it. Though, my knuckles nearly went off their hinges, they didn't return in shame. Just then the house got lit up. NAWEC had brought the electricity. Huh! 'Is he really a burglar', I asked inwardly after peering at the stagnant body that lay beside me. He wore a face mask and a night goggle. In a flash of lightning, I crept towards him. I had struck him on the neck which justifies why he got unconscious. I removed his mask cautiously in case he was feigning. 'What?' my instincts asked. I blinked and blinked again. 'No, my eyes aren't blurred', I ascertained. 'It's him; yes it's him, my boss'.

Gena Showalter stated that giving up is the only sure way to fail but l will say coming back after failure is the path to success. Just as Richard Yates said, if you don't try at anything, you can't fail... it takes back bone to lead the life you want. When you take risks you learn that there will be times when you succeed and there will be times when you fail, and both are equally important. So failing is normal but coming back to struggle harder is equally important. l will say, failure without coming back is complete failure because it's failure that gives you the proper perspective on success. Coming back is so important. Coming back is regaining the necessary energy and determination to continue the task ahead. "Success is not final, failure is not fatal: it is the courage to continue that counts." - Winston Churchill.

And the great Chris Hardwick said that no human ever became interesting by not failing. The more you fail and recover and improve, the better you are as a person. Ever meet someone who's always had everything work out for them with zero struggle? They usually have the depth of a puddle. Or they don't exist. l see wisdom in his statement. The coming back after failure is what makes failure a worth course to remember. When we give ourselves permission to fail, we, at the same time, give ourselves permission to excel.

The Victory

I was lost within myself. I found it very queer to believe that the person who employed me to watch over his belongings would in the least attempt to afflict me. Just then a faint vibration that travelled through the tiled floor caressed my nerves. I leaped swiftly in awe, merely feeling the visceral pain that lurked within my head, belly and left arm. The vibration seemed to be emanating from beneath his apparel. 'Should I pick the vibrating material?' I speculated momentarily. A terrific current circulated in my torso thus seizing my volition. However, the intense wave of curiosity that fumed within me led me to pick it up anyway. I sneaked my numb wrist deep into his left thigh pocket and collected a vibrating NOKIA cellphone. I threw a gaze onto the screen only to grimace in sheer wonder. A plain text slightly above the incoming call logo on the screen wrote 'Inspector of Police'. Consequently, in the blink of an eye, I knew all I needed to know. A governmental conspiracy triggered my presence in that mansion by that time.

I was one of those unemployed bachelor's degree holders famous of criticizing the government on social media — the only means to showcase our dissatisfaction with our malfeasant and recalcitrant dictator. And for 'this', they had schemed to silent me at my ultimate peril.

For fear of leaving any traceable evidence, I discerned, the assassin hadn't come with a pistol, instead he came for a death strangle. And roughly after a minute, the caller called again. This time around, a burning courage in my heart led me to press the green button. 'Is it done?' a heavy voice from the other end of the line asked innocently. 'Done', I uttered in a hoarse. My voice went, as planned, without a speck of feeling. I didn't wait for any more word from him. I terminated the call immediately and switched off the phone. Without wasting much time, I lamely dashed to the door that led to the backyard, sneaked thorough the darkness, jumped over the fence and galloped away.

The rise of the sun on the next day found me in intensive care. The bop on my cranium had caused me a serious depressed skull fracture. But thank God, after all I survived.

It is hard to define the term victory. People see victory in different perspectives. Does victory mean to be successful, or to win a game or defeat an opponent? If you had to choose between being successful or victorious, which would you pick? You probably think, "What's the difference? Either one would be great!" But there is a big difference between success and victory, even though most people don't know it. Success is something you receive, make, or achieve. For example, if you make a great sale, or receive a promotion at work, or achieve fame or a fat bank account balance, you could think of yourself as a successful person. Success can be measured by external things, whether it's your worldly possessions, popularity or fancy titles. Victory is something deeper. You are victorious when you overcome an internal challenge. For example, if you overcome a fear of expressing your feelings and dare to be yourself, if you overcome an addiction and take back control of your life, if you learn to forgive and let go of resentment, then you can consider yourself a victorious person. The payoff from a victory is priceless and enduring, while the payoff from success can be fleeting. That's why many people who do achieve success may start to feel unsatisfied and empty after a while, and need to obtain more and more.

Racking up successes is great, it can make you feel powerful, but you shouldn't base your self-worth as a human on them. People who achieve success aren't necessarily victorious. You could earn a lot of money and think, "I'm successful!" But if you still feel insecure on the inside, that's no victory! Real victory gives you true satisfaction over the long-term. Think about what happened over the last year. Did you experience success, or victory? Maybe you fell into debt, or lost your job, or went through a painful breakup, and now you think: "I had a year full of failure!" But if you dared to face something you were afraid of, if you demanded the respect you deserve, if you were more patient, if you didn't let criticism get to you, if you got out of a situation that wasn't good for you, or if you loved more and were at peace in your life, be proud of yourself, because it was a victorious year. Always go after victory, because success will automatically follow.

REFERENCES

[1] Mandeville, Geoffrey de. *The* 1911 *Encyclopedia Britannica*. An excellent short presentation of Mandeville's thought, 17: 564.

[2] Gorbach, Sherwood L. Chapter 95 Microbiology of the Gastrointestinal Tract Medical Microbiology. 4th edition.

[3] Goldin, B.R., Lichtenstein, A.H. and Gorbach, S.L. (1994). The role of the intestinal flora. *In:* Shils, M.E. and Young, V.R. (*eds.*), Modern Nutrition in Health and Disease. Lea and Febriger, Philadelphia, p. 500.

[4] Ousman, B. and Drammeh, P.M. (2017). The misery behind the flashlight. *J. Pol. Sci. Pub. Aff.,* 5: 286. DOI: 10.4172/2332-0761.1000286 Bottom of F

Subject Index